CW00622125

Journalist *Adrian Tame* was born in England in 1944. Before coming to Australia in 1972 he lived and worked in Canada and Mexico. Since his arrival he has been involved in the researching and scripting of several television documentaries, including 'Thunderground', the story of a Hell's Angels motorcycle club. In recent years he has spent considerable time researching the effects of radiation and other toxic chemicals. At present he lives with his family in Melbourne.

Rob Robotham was born in England in 1935. In 1957 he began work on radiation protection with the UK Atomic Energy Research Establishment at Harwell. He taught health physics in Teheran between 1962–63 and came to Australia to work for the Atomic Energy Commission in 1966. Since 1968 he has been Radiation Protection Officer at Melbourne University. His previous publications include *Uranium: Metal Of Menace* (Australian Conservation Foundation booklet 1975), *Ground For Concern* (contributor, Penguin 1977) and *Uranium: Energy Source Of The Future?* (co-author with Sir Ernest Titterton, Nelson, 1979).

MARALINGA

British A-Bomb
Australian Legacy

Adrian Tame
& F. P. J. Robotham

Fontana /Collins

The authors would like to thank
Mr Frank Smith of Mt Gravatt,
Queensland for his kind permission
to use the photographs appearing in
this book. During the atomic tests
Mr Smith was a Staff Sergeant in
the Royal Australian Signals Corps.
He worked as a member of The Australian
Health Physics Team.

First published in Fontana Books 1982
© Adrian Tame and F. P. J. Robotham 1982
Typeset, printed and bound in Australia by
The Dominion Press, Melbourne

National Library of Australia
Cataloguing-in-publication data:

Tame, A. S. (Adrian Sanigear), 1944–.
    Maralinga.

    Includes index.
ISBN 0 00 636391 1

    1. Veterans—Diseases—Australia.   2. Atomic bomb—
Physiological effects.   3. Radiation—Toxicology.
4. Atomic weapons—testing.   5. Radioactive
fallout—South Australia—Maralinga.
I. Robotham, F. P. J. (Francis Patrick Joseph), 1935–.
II. Title.

355.1'2

Preface

One of us (F.P.J.R.) is a physicist who, because of his professional interest in radiation hazards, has long been concerned with the threat posed by nuclear warfare. He was a member of a small team that went to Tahiti in 1972 to protest directly to the French authorities about their continuing atmospheric nuclear test programme.

The other (A.S.T.) is a journalist who spent some considerable time researching the effects of Agent Orange. This led to research into the cases of people exposed to radiation during nuclear weapons tests and the publication of a magazine article on the subject. Harold Crosbie of the Australian Nuclear Veterans' Association (ANVA), who knew us both, suggested a meeting to discuss the scientific content of the article before publication. From that meeting in mid-1980, evolved the idea of this book.

We have had one principal aim and several subsidiary ones. The main object has been to gather together as much information as possible about what happened at Maralinga, both at the time of the tests and during the subsequent clean up. We hope that this will help enlighten the Australian (and British) public and encourage them to support the ANVA in its fight for some recompense.

Our subsidiary aims include showing the evasive nature of governments in nuclear matters, the unthinking and complaisant nature of some sections of the press, and the futility of the continuing arms race—a race in which Maralinga (plus Monte Bello and Emu) played an important role.

To these ends we have both made what amount to personal statements in the Prologue (A.S.T.) and Epilogue (F.P.J.R.).

The views expressed herein are our own, as are the interpretation of events, although, as always with a book of this nature, there are many people who directly and indirectly contributed ideas, suggestions and the occasional healthy dash of scepticism. It is not feasible to mention all who have helped (sometimes unwittingly) but one who must be thanked is Harold Crosbie, not because he brought us together, but because of his tireless help in tracking down obscure references, obtaining (goodness knows how) rare and long-forgotten papers, and his continued support and encouragement. It is to him and, through him, the members of the Australian Nuclear Veterans' Association that we would like to dedicate this book.

A. S. Tame
F. P. J. Robotham
Melbourne, 1981

Contents

Prologue

A compulsive reader, flipping idly through copies of old news-papers, could be forgiven the odd shudder of disbelief if he chanced across coverage of the British A-bomb tests in Australia during the 1950s. Three Mile Island may have been years away, and the hazards of nuclear science a virtually closed book, but the phraseology used by the Australian and British media had about it a carnival air of celebration and self-congratulation. None of the trained observers present seemed to look beyond the fireworks display of blinding flashes and rolling fallout clouds. There was no thought for the hideous nature of the destructive power being unleashed before their eyes, no consideration of the inevitable aftermath of such wilful sport with the forces of nature. Strangely, it was left to the untutored descriptive powers of the servicemen present to capture the sickening violence and menace of the history being made by scientists in the desert. One soldier spoke of the bowel-churning fear of the moment of explosion, of the realization that many of his colleagues were running for dear life away from the fury that had suddenly erupted on the horizon, and then the secondary realization that his own feet were rooted to the ground, paralysed by a combination of awe and terror. The vision of scores of blind rabbits, their sight taken by the flash, skidding and careening in unco-ordinated flight, could have done little for that particular soldier's self-control.

Somehow the journalists present contrived to miss all that. Writing for the November 1980 edition of Australian *Penthouse*, I noted that the description of events provided by the professional journalists present at the tests would have been more appropriate had they been detailing the crowning of Queen Elizabeth II in the dustbowl at Maralinga, and not the unveiling of the most destructive agent known to man. Either way, it is doubtful that a more mindlessly self-deluding reaction has been evoked from the Australian media before or since.

The Melbourne *Argus* of 27 September 1956 captured the mood best with its coverage of the Maralinga test of the same date. 'Bombs Away!' trumpeted the paper's front-page headline, followed by the immortal first paragraph: 'Maralinga, Thursday: The atom bomb's gone up at last.' Worse was to follow. 'Minutes after the explosion, Government members cheered and Labor MPs shouted: "Thank goodness," and "At last, at last," as Mr Beale, Supply Minister, announced in the House of Representatives the test had been successful.' Still later in the story the euphoria and hysteria increased: 'As the cloud [radioactive] faded, convoys of trucks and jeeps brought back the servicemen who'd faced the blast at close range. AND EVERY FACE WORE A SMILE. [Their capitals, not ours.] They could have been coming back from a picnic.'

Featured on the menu at that picnic was the equivalent of 20 000 tonnes of TNT, slightly more than was required for the slaughter of 100 000 people at Hiroshima a decade earlier. The radioactive indigestion that was to follow the feast was even more frightening to contemplate. But who at the time would ever have believed it? Helping to cloud the issue were journalists of the calibre of Chapman Pincher, then the celebrated science correspondent for the British *Daily Express*. Pincher had composed the words for a song entitled: 'Pining for the Mushroom Cloud', which, he claimed in his dispatches home, the servicemen were chanting in throaty unison. No blind rabbits or animal fear for Chapman Pincher and his readers. The Australian newspaper-buying public was faring little better. The blithe assurances of Supply Minister Beale that 'the test had gone completely to plan, and there would be no radiation hazard to anyone in Australia', were dutifully trotted out by papers such as the Melbourne *Sun* of 28 September 1956.

Nobody seemed to notice the ease with which the scientists of the day made their glib assurances of total safety while wielding their aimless scalpels at Nature's arteries. There were seemingly no politicians, no journalists, no 'long-haired, sandal-footed, do-gooders'* to question the authorized version of events.

The picture today, of course, is very different. Federal and State parliaments have become familiar with the arguments of politicians such as Tom Uren, men determined to probe behind the curtain that the current Government has attempted to draw across Britain's mushroom-shaped legacy. The deserts of the interior have been crossed and re-crossed by teams of doctors and anthropologists, investigating the extent of the harm done by the tests to Australia's Aboriginal population. The law courts have begun preparation for the avalanche of compensation actions expected to follow the successful lobbying of Australia's 2000 nuclear veterans. Even the media have awoken from slumber. Much column space was devoted, initially, to the clean-up operation at Maralinga, when Britain was dragged, protesting, to retrieve her nuclear litter from the desert. Later, when the health of those connected directly and indirectly with the tests became a major consideration, even fashionable television current affairs programmes began to take notice.

The intention of this book is to trace, in its first section, the history of the bomb and the inevitability of Australia's

---

* Sir Ernest Titterton's description of those opposed to nuclear power.

becoming Britain's testing ground. The second section is devoted to an explanation of how reaction in Australia evolved, from blindly patriotic enthusiasm to angry demands for explanations and compensation for Britain's ill-conceived rehearsal for Armageddon.

1

Atomic Theory to Atomic Bombs

'It was the best of times, it was the worst of times, it was the age of wisdom, it was the age of foolishness . . .' Thus Dickens described the situation following the great social revolution of the eighteenth century. His was a tale of two cities: Paris and London. This book tells a tale of two countries, Australia and Britain, following the great scientific revolution of the early twentieth century. That revolution was the unlocking of the secrets of the atom and the release of atomic energy. It could be described as 'it was the best of scientific times, it was the worst of scientific times, it was the age of scientific wisdom, it was the age of scientific foolishness'. 'The best of scientific times' because the concentrated theoretical and practical work that went into the development of the atom bomb was an outstanding example of scientific and technological achievement. Within four years of the detection of the process of nuclear fission, a controlled chain reaction had been produced, and less than three years later the first atomic bombs had been made. It was also an 'age of scientific foolishness' because this inspired outpouring of some of the world's greatest scientific brains was devoted to one desperately sad end—the more efficient killing of people.

EARLY EXPERIMENTS IN RADIATION

To understand how and why this massive effort took place, it is necessary to go back to the end of the last century. The era of the lone gentleman-scientist pottering around his laboratory, making fortuitous discoveries, was coming to an end. The days of government funding and government controlled 'big science' were approaching very rapidly. However, in 1896 the style of scientific research as we now know it, with large, expensive, scientific hot-houses, had not quite arrived. In that year a serendipitous discovery by a sole worker in Paris led to the biggest scientific/military hot-house of them all.

Shortly after Roentgen announced his discovery of X-rays, the French physicist, Antoine Henri Becquerel, attended a lecture on the subject at the Academy of Sciences in Paris. In answer to a question, the lecturer, Henri Poincaré, stated that the X-rays appeared to originate in the brightly glowing luminescent spot produced where the cathode rays hit the discharge tube. This particularly interested Becquerel, as his father, Edmond Becquerel, also a physicist, had made a particular study of luminescence, that is the emission of visible light. Becquerel junior, who was forty-four at the time, had in his possession some potassium uranyl sulphate that his father had used in his work. In an attempt to discover some connection between X-rays and the luminescence exhibited by the uranium salt, Becquerel wrapped a photographic plate in black paper, laid a thin crystal of the uranium salt on the paper, and exposed the whole lot to sunlight. He did this because it was the sunlight falling on to the salt crystal that caused the luminescence. When the photographic plate was developed, it was found to be darkened, showing that the uranium salt had emitted some form of radiation that had indeed penetrated the paper, that is it had emitted some form of invisible radiation. Becquerel went on quite quickly to show that the rays could pass through thin sheets of both aluminium and copper and still darken the photographic plates.

At the time, his opinion was that the uranium salt had

emitted the invisible rays as a result of exposure to sunlight. However, while doing those experiments he made a chance discovery that turned out to be totally revolutionary and led to a whole new branch of science—nuclear physics.

If scientific genius is the ability to recognize and understand the unexpected, then a scientific genius Antoine Henri Becquerel certainly was. In describing his work with uranium salts that led to his momentous discovery, it is appropriate to use his own words.

> Some had been prepared on Wednesday, February 26th and Thursday, February 27th, 1896 but as on these days the sun shone only intermittently I kept the experiments that had been prepared and returned the plates to the darkness of a drawer . . . leaving the crystals of the uranium salt in place. The sun not showing itself again the following days, I developed the photographic plates on March 1st, expecting to find very faint images. On the contrary the silhouettes appeared with great intensity . . . A hypothesis which occurs . . . to the mind will be to suppose that these radiations (emitted by the uranium salt) . . . are similar to invisible rays emitted by (luminescent) substances, except that the time of persistence is infinitely greater than that of the visible radiations emitted by such bodies.

Thus Becquerel showed that the uranium salt emitted rays, even without being exposed to sunlight, and that the emission of these rays persisted for a very long time. From the mere chance of the sun not shining, Becquerel immortalized himself by discovering the remarkable phenomenon that two years later Marie Curie was to name radioactivity. It was soon shown that it was the uranium atoms present in the potassium uranyl sulphate that produced the curious rays. Becquerel's discovery was followed quickly by the identification of other active elements, namely, thorium, radium, actinium and polonium. Nowadays a large number of radioactive substances are known, some of which occur in nature and some of which are made artificially in atomic bombs, nuclear reactors or particle accelerators.

Maralinga

Pierre Curie and his wife, Marie Sklodowska Curie, were particularly energetic in separating out the new radioactive substances. The Curies' work was not given a high priority and they were given a bleak draughty laboratory in the Chemistry School of the Sorbonne University. Marie persuaded the owners of the Joachimstal silver mine in Bohemia (now Czechoslovakia) to send her several tonnes of pitchblende, a waste product from the mine. She separated first polonium (which she named after her native Poland), then radium. In one way it was a blessing that their laboratory was so bad. Pitchblende, like all uranium ores, gives off a radioactive gas called radon. When breathed in, the radon (or more precisely its radioactive daughters)* can cause lung cancer. This was not realized at the time, although it was known that the Bohemian miners died relatively young of a strange disease they called mountain sickness, now known to be lung cancer. Fortunately, the Curies' draughty laboratory did not allow the radon concentrations to build up. Pierre Curie however, was among the first to realize that these new mysterious rays could affect living tissue. After carrying a small phial of radium salt in his pocket for a few days, he noticed that a patch of his skin had become very red. Pierre himself was knocked down and killed by a dray in 1906, whereas Marie lived till 1934 when she died of leukaemia contracted as a result of her work with radiation.

The early twentieth century saw intense scientific effort as an understanding of the riddle of radioactivity was sought. Just what were these mysterious rays? Why did some atoms emit them whereas most elements did not? What could radioactivity tell us about the inner workings of the atom? Answers to these questions and many more were to be found in the next four decades. Some of the answers have been of great benefit to mankind; some could lead to its ultimate extinction.

One of the main centres of research into the mystery of radioactivity was McGill University in Canada where the New Zealander Ernest Rutherford was doing some quite brilliant

*Physics is still somewhat sexist. The product of decay of a radioactive nucleus is called its daughter product.

16

work. It was soon found that uranium and some of the other newly discovered radioactive substances gave off three different types of radiation. These were named (the first two by Rutherford) alpha, beta and gamma rays, after the first three letters of the Greek alphabet. Later research showed that the alpha and beta rays consist of parts of atoms; alpha particles are actually the nuclei of the element helium; beta particles are electrons; gamma rays are actually electromagnetic radiations similar to light and radio waves.

The behaviour of these radiations is discussed more fully in Chapter 3, however it is important to note here that each has the ability to produce ionization (see p. 262). It is this property that can make these rays dangerous to life. If ionization takes place in the atoms making up human cells, the effects can be quite serious and the biological effects of ionizing radiation are also discussed in some detail in Chapter 3.

From here on the more general term *radiation* will be used and unless indicated otherwise the reader is to assume that ionizing radiation is being referred to. (There are many, many non-ionizing radiations, e.g. visible light, radiowaves, microwaves, ultra-violet light.) Similarly the terms *atomic* and *nuclear*, although strictly not interchangeable, are in common parlance often used one for the other. What we are talking about in this book is the destructive release of energy from the atomic nucleus. If we compare the atom with the solar system, the nucleus occupies the position of the sun, and it is the nuclear energy that is our concern. However, the phrases 'atomic bomb' and 'atomic energy' are so well established they will be used throughout this book.

To summarize the properties of the three types of rays, it may be said the *alpha particles* have a very weak penetrating power, being completely absorbed by a sheet or two of paper. They are, however, able to produce intense ionization of materials through which they pass. *Beta particles* are much more penetrating than alphas, some millimetres of aluminium being needed to absorb them, and their ionizing power is considerably less. *Gamma rays* are highly penetrating, several centimetres of lead or over a metre of concrete being required to stop them. However, they produce relatively little ionization per unit distance in their path through air. (X-rays, although different in origin, are very similar to gamma rays.) All three types of radiation can affect photographic film.

The work of the Curies, Rutherford and others showed radioactivity to be the spontaneous disintegration of an atomic nucleus with the emission of some form of ionizing radiation. A radioactive nucleus is said to be an excited state and it changes (decays is the word usually used) into a stable or unexcited state by emitting radiation. In other words, the excited atom gets rid of its energy by spitting it out in the form of radiation.

Most naturally occurring radioactive elements radiate either alpha or beta particles, although in a few exceptional instances both are emitted. In many cases gamma rays accompany the alpha or beta particles.

In recent years a large number of 'artificial' radioactive elements have been produced. 'Radioactive fallout' from nuclear bombs consists of 'artificially' produced radioactive substances. The essential nature of the rays is the same irrespective of their origin, natural or artificial. Some radioactive substances undergo just one decay before they reach a stable non-radioactive state, others can decay through many stages. Uranium for instance can go through fourteen different states before it ends up as stable non-radioactive lead.

There are two properties that become important when considering the hazards associated with ionizing radiation. One is the *energy* of the radiation (see p. 77), the other is the *half-life* of the radioactive substance emitting the radiation (see p. 77).

DEVELOPMENT OF ATOMIC THEORY

To understand the development of atomic theory, we need to move on to 1908 and catch up with the peripatetic Ernest Rutherford, then in Manchester, England. Rutherford was one of the first to realize that because of their sub-atomic size, these new radiations could be used as powerful tools to probe inside atoms. With his assistants, Hans Geiger (who later won fame as co-inventor of the Geiger-Müller tube) and Ernest Marsden, he investigated what happened when alpha particles passed through very thin sheets of metal. The sheets had to be thin as alphas have very little penetration. What the experimenters found was that some of the alpha particles were deflected from their course or scattered, presumably as a result of some interaction with the atoms of the material through which they had passed. The fact that excited the observers most was that a few of the alpha particles, about one in 20 000, were scattered through large angles, some even emerging on the side of incidence. In his lectures, 'The Background to Modern Science', given in 1936, Rutherford described the totally unexpected nature of this result in the following words: 'It was about as credible as if you had fired a 15-inch [38 cm] shell at a piece of tissue paper and it came back and hit you.'

Until this stage, the general view of the atom was of something rather like a Christmas pudding, with the electric charges scattered about within it like currants and raisins. Rutherford, working in collaboration with the equally brilliant Danish theoretical physicist, Niels Bohr, changed all that and produced the concept of the atom as a miniature solar system. The atomic *nucleus* occupies the place of the sun and the *electrons* whirl around like the planets in their everlasting orbits. The nucleus contains the atom's positive charges, the electrons carry the negative charge. The positive charges in the nucleus are carried by separate particles called *protons*, each balanced by an orbiting electron so that the complete atom is electrically neutral. The simplest atom, that of hydrogen, consists of one proton in the nucleus and one circling electron.

While all this exciting experimental work was taking place, a young mathematician working in the patents office in Berne, Switzerland, was thinking about some of the fundamental problems of physics. In just one year, 1905, he published four scientific papers, each of which introduced important new concepts and ideas. The two best known are the special theory of relativity and, of greater importance to our story, the equivalence of mass and energy, of which more anon. The Swiss patent clerk was of course Albert Einstein. It has been said that 'Nature and Nature's mysteries were all hidden in night, God said let Newton be, then there was light', to which was subsequently added, 'The devil seeing this saith Ho! let Einstein be and restore the status quo!'—reference to the difficulties experienced by many people, including physics students, in understanding Einstein's theory of relativity.

Fortunately that theory does not concern us here, but what seemed an abstract concept—that energy and mass are two sides of the same coin—came together with the developing understanding of the atom in the 1930s, when it was found that the atomic nucleus could be 'split' with a loss of a small amount of mass from the nucleus. Einstein had shown that mass and energy correspond to each other and if mass can be converted to energy the relationship between the two is given by the formula $E = mc^2$. What this says is that E is the amount of energy produced when an amount of mass m is converted. The symbol c stands for the speed of light, i.e. 300 000 km per second, so c squared (i.e. multiplied by itself) is a very large number indeed. This indicated to the physicists of the time that, if a small amount of matter could be changed into energy, a very large amount of energy would be produced. An interesting thought, but considered at the time to have little practical application.

To see how wrong this view was we need to continue our story. At the start of the 1930s, Rutherford had moved yet again and was now head of the Cavendish laboratory in Cambridge. Along with many others, he had been working away at trying to understand the structure of this newly discovered nucleus.

Work had stopped during the First World War, when Rutherford's team in particular had been involved in developing undersea listening devices to help combat the threat of the German U-boats. Some served in the armed forces, and Harry Moseley, who had carried out the experiments that confirmed

Bohr's atomic picture, was killed at Gallipoli.

In 1920, during a lecture to the Royal Society in London, Rutherford suggested:

> Under some conditions . . . it may be possible for an electron to combine much more closely with the hydrogen nucleus [i.e. the proton] forming a kind of neutral doublet. Such an atom would have novel properties. Its external field would be practically zero . . . and consequently it should be able to move freely through matter. Its presence would probably be difficult to detect.

It took until 1932 for James Chadwick to demonstrate clearly that such a particle, already dubbed *neutron,* did exist. This fundamental particle was to play, and still plays, a major role not only in atomic science but in the fate of nations. It had actually been discovered, but not recognized, a few years earlier by Irène Joliot-Curie, Marie's daughter, and her husband, Frédéric Joliot. They had found that, when beryllium is bombarded with alpha particles, some penetrating radiation is emitted, but they thought it was a form of gamma radiation. When Rutherford met Joliot some time after Chadwick's work, Rutherford asked the Frenchman, 'Did you not realize that you had those neutrons which I discussed in my Bakerian (Royal Society) lecture in 1920?' Joliot replied, 'I never read your lecture, I thought it would be the usual display of oratory, not of new ideas!' How wrong he was. However the Joliots got their own back within two years, when they discovered artificial radioactivity, which Rutherford had missed (as he admitted) by looking in the wrong direction.

The neutron completes the simple picture of the atom and explains why there can be different isotopes of the same element. It is worth pausing here to consider this new concept, as isotopes become extremely important when we start to talk about bombs.

The word *isotope* was coined by Frederick Soddy in 1913, from the Greek words 'isos' (equal) and 'topos' (place), to indicate substances occupying the same place in the periodic table of elements, that is having the same chemical properties but distinguishable from each other by some other property, such as the way they decay radioactively. The position an element occupies in the periodic table is determined by the number of protons in the nucleus, called the *atomic number*. Hydrogen has one proton, while helium has two protons, lithium three, and so on. If a nucleus of hydrogen contained one proton and one neutron, it would still be hydrogen but with a different mass. Such an isotope of hydrogen does exist; it is called deuterium, and natural hydrogen consists of 0.014 per cent deuterium and 99.986 per cent 'light' hydrogen. Deuterium can be separated from natural hydrogen and, if it combines with oxygen, it produces 'heavy' water, usually written as D_2O, not the more usual H_2O.

There is even a third isotope of hydrogen, consisting of one proton and two neutrons—called tritium. It is radioactive and emits a low energy beta particle with a half-life of 12.4 years. Tritium occurs in nature, in minute traces, but is made in relatively large quantities in nuclear reactors. It is actually a very useful isotope or, to be precise, radioisotope. It has been used to replace the much more hazardous radium in a wide range of applications, from luminous wrist watches to cinema exit signs.

Of particular interest to us are the two main isotopes of uranium. The atomic number of uranium is 92 and its principal isotopes are uranium-235 (containing 143 neutrons) and uranium-238 (containing 146 neutrons). To behave chemically as uranium, the nucleus of each isotope must contain 92 protons, so that they are written as U-235 or U-238.

It was soon found that because neutrons carried no electric charge, they were particularly effective bullets for firing into the nuclei of atoms. Alpha particles had been used extensively but because they carry a double charge, they were generally repelled by positively charged nuclei. Some reactions took place and the alpha bombardment of nitrogen and beryllium had lead to the discovery of the proton and neutron respectively. Alpha particle irradiation had one last surprise in store, however. In 1934, reporting on their current work, Joliot-Curie and Joliot wrote:

> Our latest experiments have a very striking fact, when an aluminium foil is irradiated . . . (with alpha particles) the emission of positrons (positively charged beta particles) does not cease immediately when . . . (the source of alpha particles) is removed. The foil remains radioactive and the emission of radiation decays exponentially as for an ordinary (naturally occurring) radioelement.

The Joliots had made an artificially radioactive isotope of phosphorus.

Later in 1934, the Italian Enrico Fermi showed that nearly every element in the periodic table can undergo nuclear transformation when bombarded by neutrons. Thus had come true the ancient dream of the alchemists, the transmutation of elements. Unfortunately, even nuclear reactors cannot turn base metal into gold. The starting point has to be platinum, so the 'philosopher's stone' remains as elusive as ever.

The business of banging neutrons into anything and everything continued merrily, until in 1938 came the biggest surprise of all. Fermi had fired neutrons into uranium (the heaviest element known) and thought he had made some transuranic elements, that is elements beyond uranium in the periodic table. In Berlin meanwhile, Lise Meitner and Otto Hahn had been doing the same thing but had a different interpretation of the results. Meitner saw how difficult it was to account for the large number of new elements, some apparently *lighter* than uranium. Hahn, an outstanding chemist, confirmed that three of the new substances behaved like radium—four places below uranium in the periodic table. Lise Meitner had by this time left for Sweden, Germany being a very uncomfortable place for Jews, and she wrote to Hahn asking him not to publish such an incomprehensible result. Along with Fritz Strassmann, Hahn repeated the experiment even more carefully and what they found were isotopes of barium, very much lighter than uranium. It seemed something very strange and unexpected had happened. Somehow a large clump of protons and neutrons had been gouged out of the uranium nucleus. The uranium atom had been split.

Late in 1938, Meitner's nephew, Otto Frisch, visited her in the small Swedish town of Kungälv (near Gothenburg) where Lise had gone to spend the Christmas holidays. Frisch himself had left Germany in 1933 and after a short spell in London had spent the period from 1934 working with Niels Bohr in Copenhagen. His aunt had just received the letter from Hahn confirming that isotopes of barium had definitely been produced by bombarding uranium with neutrons. Frisch asked if it could be a mistake; but Hahn was too good a chemist for that. Up to this time, nothing larger than protons or neutrons had been chipped away from nuclei, and to remove a big bit containing over 130 protons and neutrons seemed to require too much energy. Bohr, in his early classic description of the atom, had suggested that the nucleus was not a solid block but more like a drop of liquid. Perhaps, argued Frisch, a drop could divide itself into two smaller drops by splitting rather than having bits chopped off. According to Frisch this discussion took place during a walk in the snow. They sat down on a tree trunk and started to do the calculations on a scrap of paper (not the first nor the last 'back of envelope' calculation but surely one of the most far reaching).

The electric charge on the uranium nucleus was large enough to overcome the surface tension forces that tends to stop an ordinary liquid drop dividing into two. The uranium nucleus could indeed be thought of as a large wobbly unstable drop, ready to divide itself at the slightest provocation, such as a single neutron being fired into it. After separation the two drops would be driven apart by their mutual electric repulsion, both being positively charged. They would acquire high speed and this would require a lot of energy; about 200 MeV* altogether. Meitner remembered the formula for computing the masses of nuclei and worked out that the two new nuclei would

---

* An electron volt (eV) is the energy of an electron being acted on by an electrical potential of 1 volt.   MeV = mega electron volt = 1eV × 10⁶.

be lighter than the original uranium by about one-fifth of the mass of a proton. Einstein, you remember said mass and energy were equivalent and $E = mc^2$ gives about 200 MeV of energy for the conversion of 0.2 of a proton. As Frisch put it '. . . here was the source of that energy: it all fitted'.

He went back to Copenhagen, discussed his and Meitner's speculations with Bohr who agreed with their views. Biologists use the term fission to describe the process where single cells divide into two, so Frisch sent off a paper to the British scientific magazine, *Nature*, describing the process of 'nuclear fission'—a term to become much more widely known six years later.

It had been an exciting journey from Becquerel's lucky discovery to the splitting of the atom. It had involved an informal network covering many nationalities on both sides of the Atlantic. Most work had been done in Europe, but Fermi's experiments had been repeated in the United States and, more importantly, American physics had come of age with Ernest Lawrence's invention and development of the particular type of charged particle accelerator called the cyclotron. (This device was to play a major role in the study of the various forces at work within the atomic nucleus.)

THE ADVENT OF THE SECOND WORLD WAR

While exciting things were happening in the apparently remote world of physics, events in the world outside the laboratory were starting to have an impact. And this is where the story really starts.

Hitler's troops had already occupied Austria and, Neville Chamberlain's claims of 'peace in our time' notwithstanding, it was obvious to many people that once again the dogs of war were about to be let slip. Many of the scientists involved in our story were either totally or partly Jewish. Hitler's misguided concepts of racial purity treated all non-Aryans alike and, by the mid-1930s, the exodus of those Jews who could manage it had started.

It is one of the great ironies of modern history that Hitler's obsessive antipathy to Jews cost him victory in the Second World War. If the brain power of people like Meitner, Frisch, Teller, Rotblat, Einstein and even Bohr (who had a Jewish mother) had been used to develop the bomb for Germany, coupled with German developments in rocketry, the war would have had a totally different outcome. One of the great fears and spurs to greater effort during the American/British atomic bomb project was the thought that such work was continuing in Germany, and many of the scientists involved in the Allied side saw it as a race against their erstwhile scientific colleagues. We now know that even by 1945 nuclear weapons research in Fascist-controlled Europe had not progressed very far, but all through the early 1940s such a hideous prospect was all too real to those few who knew the terrifying potential that a nuclear bomb represented.

Early in 1939, shortly after his talk with Frisch, Bohr left on a visit to the United States. He reported Frisch's conjectures about nuclear fission at a theoretical physics conference in Washington DC on 26 January. Almost immediately, physicists in various laboratories devised experiments to detect the products formed by the splitting of the uranium nucleus. By the middle of February, when Frisch's paper was published, confirmation of nuclear fission had been obtained in four laboratories in the United States alone.

Apart from barium which had provided the original clue, groups in France, England, Germany, Holland as well as in the United States had detected a wide range of fission products (as they are now known) including strontium and caesium. Most of the work had been completed within three months of the original announcement of the theory of nuclear fission. So within a very short space of time, a revolutionary new concept had become widely accepted.

One other very important point was very soon realized. The fission fragments contained sufficient surplus energy to eject a neutron or two each. Under the right circumstances, each of these might cause another fission and generate more neutrons, which in turn would cause more fission and more neutrons, and so on, and so on. By such a 'chain reaction', the neutrons would multiply in uranium like 'rabbits in a meadow', to use Frisch's apt analogy.

Surprisingly, the concept of the chain reaction had already been patented in 1934 by Leo Szilard, a Hungarian then living in London. Szilard's university life was spent in Germany, but by 1933 he was certain Hitler would come to power and that war was inevitable. He packed his bags and left for England. In September of that year, Lord Rutherford (as he now was), addressing a meeting of the British Association for the Advancement of Science, remarked that atomic energy would never become real. (He died in 1937 so never saw his prophecy so devastatingly refuted.) The word 'never' provoked Szilard and while walking to work at Bart's Hospital he deduced that if you hit an atom with a neutron and it releases two then you could have a chain reaction. He wrote a specification for a patent which contains the words 'chain reaction'.

Szilard in fact was one of the first to see and worry about the way nuclear science could be heading and was one of the first to express those worries. He wanted to keep the patent secret to stop science being misused. (He assigned the patent to the British Admiralty and it was not published until after the war.) Early in 1939, Szilard wrote to Joliot asking him if a prohibition on publication of work on fission could be established and tried again in vain to get Fermi not to publish. But the feeling of openness and desire to communicate was too long an established part of science. The excitement of the concept of fission and the rush to get into print with the latest findings continued unabated. Finally, in August 1939, Szilard prepared a letter which Einstein signed. Einstein was no longer a patent clerk but an American resident and an internationally respected scientist and humanitarian. In view of subsequent developments it is worth reading the Szilard/Einstein letter*:

---

*Quoted in *Ascent of Man*, J. Bronowski, BBC and Angus and Robertson.

Albert Einstein,
Old Grove Rd,
Nassau Point,
Peconic, Long Island.

August 2nd 1939.

F. D. Roosevelt,
President of the United States,
White House,
Washington, D.C.

Sir:

Some recent work by E. Fermi and L. Szilard, which has been communicated to me in manuscript, leads me to expect that the element uranium may be turned into a new and important source of energy in the immediate future. Certain aspects of the situation which has arisen seem to call for watchfulness and, if necessary, quick action on the part of the Administration. I believe that it is my duty to bring to your attention the following facts and recommendations:

In the course of the last four months it has been made probable — through the work of Joliot in France as well as Fermi and Szilard in America — that it may become possible to set up a nuclear chain reaction in a large mass of uranium, by which vast amounts of power and large quantities of new radium-like elements would be generated. Now it appears almost certain that this could be achieved in the immediate future.

This new phenomenon would also lead to the construction of bombs, and it is conceivable — though much less certain — that extremely powerful bombs of a new type may thus be constructed. A single bomb of this type, carried by boat and exploded in a port, might very well destroy the whole port together with some of the surrounding territory. However, such bombs might very well prove to be too heavy for transportation by air.

The United States has only very poor ores of uranium in moderate quantities. There is some good ore in Canada and the former Czechoslovakia, while the most important source of uranium is Belgian Congo.

In view of this situation you may think it desirable to have some permanent contact maintained between the Administration and the group of physicists working on chain reactions in America. One possible way of achieving this might be for you to entrust with this task a person who has your confidence and who could perhaps serve in an inofficial capacity. His task might comprise the following:

(a) to approach Government Departments, keep them informed of the further development, and put forward recommendations for Government action, giving particular attention to the problem of securing a supply of uranium ore for the United States;

(b) to speed up the experimental work, which is at present being carried on within the budgets of University Laboratories, by providing funds, if such funds be required, through his contacts with private persons who are willing to make contributions for this cause, and perhaps also by obtaining the co-operation of industrial laboratories which have the necessary equipment.

I understand that Germany has actually stopped the sale of uranium from the Czechoslovakian mines which she has taken over. That she has taken such early action might perhaps be understood on the ground that the son of the German Under-Secretary of State, von Weizsäcker, is attached to the Kaiser-Wilhelm-Institut in Berlin where some of the American work on uranium is now being repeated.

Yours very truly,

Albert Einstein.

One month after the Einstein letter, Szilard got his wish regarding secrecy. Hitler invaded Poland and once again the lights went out all over Europe. Research on fission continued apace but the interchange of ideas and results between Germany and the Western Allies ceased abruptly.

One of the last ideas to be bandied about before the darkness descended was Bohr's view that a violent explosion from nuclear energy was not possible. It was based on the isotopic composition of uranium. Natural uranium consists of two isotopes 99.3 per cent U-238 and 0.7 per cent U-235. Bohr argued that the neutrons which are sent out from the uranium in the fission process would have too little energy, only about one fortieth of an eV, to cause fission in the main isotope U-238 (they are called thermal or slow neutrons even though they are travelling at around 2.2 kilometres per second). They would simply get swallowed up by the nucleus, forming a transuranic element. Only a small fraction of the neutrons would be caught by the lighter, rarer, U-235 isotope which would then undergo fission, producing a few more neutrons but not enough to sustain a chain reaction. Fast neutrons with energies of a few MeV are also released during fission and it was thought that slowing them down by some process would increase the number of fissions. Even if that were possible, Bohr pointed out it takes a significant time (on the nuclear scale) to slow down the neutrons and therefore such a chain reaction could only grow at a moderate rate. It might be a source of making energy, as indeed it is, but not an effective bomb, as indeed it isn't. The process of slowing down neutrons is known as moderating them. Experiments were proceeding in France using heavy water as a possible moderator, whereas in the United States graphite was being tried.

WORK IN THE UNITED KINGDOM

After the war started, Frisch, working in Birmingham under (Sir) Mark Oliphant, realized that, if the uranium-235 could somehow be separated from the uranium-238, only a few kilograms would be needed to sustain an explosive chain reaction based on fast neutron fission. He, along with Rudolph Peierls, another German scientific refugee, calculated the quantities of uranium-235 required. They also worked out a way of separating the isotopes by first converting the uranium into a gas, then using a technique that had been used for separating isotopes of neon. (Frisch's idea didn't work and in the event another process was used.) To put it as simply as possible: natural uranium appeared to be useless for bomb production but, if the rarer uranium-235 could be used, nuclear weapons were feasible. It was a big IF. Isotopes cannot be separated chemically so some other techniques had to be found. Frisch's assistant at that time was Ernest Titterton, now Sir Ernest and Professor of Physics at the Australian National University, Canberra. While studying the effect of neutrons on uranium, Titterton and Frisch noted that the ionization chamber produced an occasional pulse when there were no neutrons present. Thus they were the first to observe the process of spontaneous nuclear fission, a discovery kept secret till after the war.

At Oliphant's suggestion, Peierls and Frisch wrote to Sir Henry Tizard, one of the British Government's major scientific panjandrums, outlining their views that nuclear bombs were possible. The great fear was that the Germans had come to the same conclusions and were developing such a bomb. A committee was established to review the data and consider possible lines of development. It was given the code name 'Maud Committee'. The name came from a telegram sent by Niels Bohr around the time of the German occupation of Denmark. The telegram ended with the enigmatic phrase: TELL MAUD RAY KENT. This was taken to be an anagram meaning either 'Radium taken', presumably by the Nazis, or 'U and D may react' indicating a chain reaction could be produced by mixing uranium and deuterium. Only after the war was it found that Maud Ray used to be a governess in Bohr's house and lived in Kent!

Many of the people who worked on the British bomb project, now code-named 'Tube Alloys', were refugees from Hitler's Europe and therefore technically aliens. Most British physicists, including Oliphant's group, were hard at work on radar which appeared to be one of the most promising ways of defending the country against enemy aircraft. It was work that was to pay handsome dividends a few months later in the Battle of Britain. The leading physicists of the day had gone from peering into the seas like Rutherford in the First World War to scanning the skies in the Second World War.

On literally the last boat to leave France before the German occupation was completed, the French stock of heavy water was smuggled out in an event worthy of the Scarlet Pimpernel. The Earl of Suffolk had been appointed Attaché at the British Embassy in Paris with the express purpose of salvaging what he could during the collapse of France. He had drawn up a list of about 150 influential scientists and engineers who, he considered, should be rescued along with some rare machine tools, about £2.5 million in industrial diamonds, and the heavy water—about 130 litres of it. Only forty people made it to the collier *Broompark* tied up at Bordeaux, but the diamonds and heavy water contained in twelve sealed aluminium cans were safely embarked. The buccaneering Earl made a raft, lashed the cans and diamonds to it and made the crew solemnly promise that if the ship was sunk they would make every effort to get the precious cargo to Britain.

Some of those on Suffolk's list, including Joliot, felt it their duty to stay in France. When the ship moored next to the *Broompark* in the Gironde estuary was blown up by a magnetic mine, Joliot was able to convince the Germans it was actually the ship they wanted. The *Broompark* arrived safely in Falmouth four days later containing most of the world's supply of heavy water. With this moderator, work continued on the possibility of fission based on slow neutrons, which was soon found to be inappropriate for bomb production just as Niels Bohr had predicted. However, the Allies assumed that the German scientists were still pursuing this line of research. During the war British intelligence forces mounted a series of complicated plots and operations to mislead the Nazis into believing that heavy water was vital to bomb production. A series of air, sabotage and commando raids were carried out against both the heavy water factory at Trondheim in Norway and the transportation of the material to Germany. The sole object of the raids, which cost about 100 Allied lives all told, was to convince the Germans that their research was running along the right lines and that the Allies were prepared to do whatever they could to foil any experiments with heavy water.

In the event, the nuclear physicists who remained in

Germany, led mainly by Werner Heisenberg, director of the Kaiser Wilhelm Institute for Physics in Berlin, didn't get very far in the creation of a Nazi-controlled nuclear weapon. They experimented with cubes of uranium metal suspended in a tank of heavy water. The 1.5 tonnes of uranium used were insufficient to sustain a chain reaction and, before more uranium could be obtained, the village where the experiments were being conducted was occupied by US troops in April 1945.

WORK IN THE UNITED STATES

Meantime in the United States, a Uranium Committee had been formed as a result of Einstein's letter to President Roosevelt. It did not proceed very energetically—its budget for 1939–40 was only $6000. As in Britain, some of the cleverest consultants employed by the Uranium Committee were refugees from Fascist Europe. They included Fermi, Teller and Szilard.

However, other research was getting results. Using Ernest Lawrence's cyclotron to pump beams of neutrons into uranium, Ed McMillan discovered two new elements beyond uranium. Element number 93 he named neptunium after the planet beyond Uranus in the solar system. Neptunium decayed too fast to be much use as a source of fission, but it changed into a longer lived radioisotope element 94. This one McMillan named plutonium, after the planet beyond Neptune. He could not tell much about it except that it seemed long lived and that it fissioned violently. For its discovery, McMillan subsequently received the Nobel prize.

What McMillan had found was of fundamental importance, as it opened up another way to the production of a fission bomb. Instead of separating uranium-235, it might now be possible to use uranium-238, by converting it into plutonium using some source of neutrons. It is now known that plutonium is a particularly toxic substance—it emits alpha particles with a half-life of 24 400 years. Given its relatively easy fabrication into nuclear weapons, its high toxicity and long half-life, it is very appropriate that it was named, however indirectly, after the Greek God of the infernal regions, Pluto.

McMillan published a note of his findings in the *Physics Review*. He soon received a visit from a British Embassy attaché asking him not to give away secrets to the Germans. The British had already discovered the new elements, even used the same names, but were keeping it all very secret. The National Academy of Science established a committee to censor scientific journals; so secrecy descended on America even though it was not at war. During 1940, however, American physics moved slowly into research areas related to the European war.

Following Britain's lead, most effort was initially directed into radar research, and McMillan moved into this field. Once again the British attaché got busy and called on Lawrence asking him to make sure the work on plutonium continued, and by March 1941 the first pure sample of plutonium had been isolated and analysed.

By mid–1941, the Uranium Committee had two projects going, both at Columbia University, New York. One was Enrico Fermi's work towards a self-sustaining chain reaction, using uranium blocks piled on top of each other, surrounded by other piles of graphite to both moderate the neutrons and reflect some of them back into the mass of uranium, where, it was hoped, they would produce additional fissions. The Uranium Committee looked upon Fermi's work as an interesting project but did not appear to realize its potential as a source of plutonium-239. The other project was John Dunning's attempts to separate uranium-235 from uranium-238. The only stable gaseous compound of uranium is uranium hexafluoride, a corrosive, poisonous gas. By diffusing it through a series of porous walls, Dunning found the lighter U-235 would go through a little faster and become a little concentrated.

By April 1940, Dunning had decided gaseous diffusion was the way to enrich the percentage of uranium-235. He calculated that, to get up to the estimated 93 per cent required for a bomb, at least five thousand successive separations would be needed. To achieve this would require a plant costing three or four million dollars—difficult to extract from the Uranium Committee's $6000 budget.

In Britain, the war was proving to be a tremendous drain on scientific and industrial resources. In August 1941, Mark Oliphant gathered together all the accumulated British bomb data, crossed the Atlantic to see both the Uranium Committee and Ernest Lawrence. He turned over the British information, which was ahead of the Americans and emphasized the need for nuclear weapons research. Lawrence by now one of America's most influential physicists, saw the logic of Oliphant's argument that the outcome of the war depended on whether Germany or Britain/America got the bomb first. (Mark Oliphant was engaged in radar research but he was chosen to be the British scientific emissary because of his forceful personality and ability as a speaker—qualities that were to stand him in great stead when he became Governor of South Australia over thirty years later.) Lawrence proceeded to devote his energies to stimulating the laggardly Uranium Committee.

UNITED STATES' ENTRY INTO THE WAR

The events of 7 December 1941, when without warning the Japanese bombed Pearl Harbour, gave the necessary additional impetus to the American programme. The next four years saw tremendous efforts as some of the world's best scientific brains turned theory into practice.

By early 1942, calculations had shown that considerably less than 40 kilograms of either uranium-235 or plutonium-239 could be used to produce a bomb equivalent to about 20 000 tonnes of TNT. However, the total stock of each material was less than one milligram, and the processes required for mass production were a long way from realization. The engineering, chemical, physical and mathematical challenges were tackled with all the ingenuity and effort that had marked the development of the United States as the world's leading technical innovator.

Maralinga

In the summer of 1942, Robert Oppenheimer, that strange and ill-used man, became actively involved by being put in charge of the bomb development programme. He called together a group of theoretical physicists to thrash out the problems. There were three clear areas of effort:

1. In ordnance—to design a piece of flyable hardware for an available plane
2. In chemistry—to determine the required purity of materials and how to get them
3. In physics—to work out a method of assembly detonation and to measure more exactly the behaviour of fission neutrons.

The importance of these tasks and the answers found will become apparent in Chapter 2 when the mechanics of bombs are discussed.

Things were going well when Edward Teller dropped a bombshell (if you'll pardon the expression). He explained that a few weeks before, he and Fermi had discussed the heat that would be generated inside a fission bomb. It would be sufficient to fuse deuterium atoms into helium. Each pair of fused deuterium bombs would release five times as much energy as a fissioning uranium atom. Deuterium (heavy hydrogen) was cheap and it was possible to wrap as much as desired around a fission bomb to produce a superweapon of unlimited power. (Teller's ideas worked. After the war the 'super' was developed and Teller has ever since enjoyed/suffered the title of Father of the hydrogen bomb.) By using Teller's calculation, it seemed the heat released was also sufficient to produce a further reaction involving atmospheric nitrogen. If this was true, the bomb could ignite the whole planet. There were some very worried scientists, until a week and much intense cogitation later, an error was found in Teller's maths. The deuterium reaction could (and did) work, the chance of the nitrogen reaction occurring was about three in a million. That was felt to be a low enough chance to take.

In the autumn of 1942, the US Army took over the industrial side of the work. The military leader was General Leslie Groves then forty-six. Groves was a blunt, shrewd soldier with a harsh aggressive manner. He didn't get on at all well with most of the physicists on the project nor they with him. He was never averse to pronouncing judgment on their work. Writing after the events he declared: 'They had lots of theories but they didn't know anything. We didn't know for example whether plutonium was a gas, solid or electric.' Groves was appointed director of the Manhattan District of the Corps of Engineers, and from then on the code name 'Manhattan Project' was used for the gigantic industrial/scientific/military complex that developed. Such was the universal penchant for code names, radiation monitors were called 'cutie-pies', a term still in use in the late 1950s.

Enrico Fermi's uranium-graphite-cadmium (the cadmium is used to control the neutron numbers) work transferred to what was code-named the Metallurgical Laboratory of the University of Chicago. There, in a squash court at Stagg Field, the first self-sustaining man-made chain reaction was achieved on 2 December 1942. The reactor behaved as predicted in what was a triumph of theory, deduction and experiment to which many scientists, engineers and technicians had contributed. (Because of the way the uranium and graphite blocks were first stacked on top of one another, nuclear reactors were long known as 'piles'.)

A medium-sized reactor was built at Oak Ridge as a preliminary to the construction of the giant (by those early standards) reactors at Hanford in the State of Washington. A whole new chemistry had to be developed to extract the plutonium from the irradiated uranium. It had to be learned under exceedingly difficult conditions, as the problems of radioactivity had to be coped with. Among the many new brands of science and technology that were developed, a group of physicists started to devote themselves to the health problems associated with radioactive materials. The profession of health physics (i.e. radiation protection) had started.

Parallel with the plutonium production and extraction work, the other possible route to a bomb was being followed.

At Oak Ridge two main techniques were tried—Dunning's diffusion, which was considered to be the least promising, and another technique developed by Lawrence. This latter involved ionizing the uranium gas and whirling it in a magnetic field where the uranium-235 atoms would follow a slightly different path to the uranium-238, thus allowing some separation. Strangely, the idea of centrifuging the gas, whirling it round at very high speed so that the heavier uranium-238 atoms would separate out at the end of the tube (like tea in a billy), was dropped at a very early stage. It is now considered to be perhaps the best separation method, but was not pursued by the Manhattan Project because of a clash of personalities at one of the early committee meetings looking at separation possibilities.

In 1943, Oppenheimer started up a new laboratory on top of an isolated mesa at Los Alamos in New Mexico. Its object was to develop methods to make the output of the production plants into pure metal and to fabricate the metal into the required shapes. Methods of initiating the chain reaction at the right moment, along with the actual construction of a deliverable weapon, had all to be worked out. Most of the problems had to be solved before any appreciable amount of fissionable material were available. The aim was to get the first adequate amounts into bombs and at the fighting front with the minimum delay. Based on their prewar collaboration, some of the refugee physicists believed the Germans could have developed a bomb by the end of 1944, but by the end of that year fears of a German nuclear threat had been dissipated by intelligence reports.

In 1943 and 1944, many of the British bomb physicists went over to the United States. Some, like Frisch, went to Los Alamos. Some, like Cockcroft, to Chalk River in Canada, where heavy water experiments were being conducted, leading eventually to the development of the natural uranium-fuelled heavy-water-moderated power reactors—but that is another story.

Niels Bohr had escaped from Denmark to Sweden in 1943;

from there he flew to England in a Mosquito bomber seated in the bomb bay. The headphones didn't fit his large head so he didn't hear the pilot's order to switch on the oxygen. He became unconscious but the worried pilot couldn't turn back. Once Norway was crossed, the pilot descended to a lower altitude and Bohr fortunately revived. He turned up at Los Alamos in 1944 and presumably explained his telegram.

By the spring of 1945, the intense effort was bearing fruit, and enough plutonium was available for a test explosion. The surrender of Germany had made no difference: the Manhattan Project started by the German threat now had a momentum of its own. A test explosion code-named 'Trinity' was set for 16 July. The spot chosen was at the Alamogordo Air Base. For three months, teams of physicists had been going through rehearsal after rehearsal. The complex and elaborate equipment that had been assembled had to work if a complete diagnosis of success or failure was to be obtained—there would be no second chance.

The test site was part of the forbidding desert of southern New Mexico, 145 kilometres of sand which had been called Jornada del Muerto by the early Spanish explorers. It translates as 'Journey of Death'. Did Oppenheimer, who chose the site and code name, have a macabre sense of humour?

As the test date got closer, bets were laid on the size of the explosion, ranging from zero to the equivalent of 18 000 tonnes of TNT (the bomb itself contained 5 kilograms of plutonium-239). Some of the team continued to worry about atmospheric ignition. Sunday, 15 July, was a day of considerable tension. Fermi invited bets against the contingencies, '. . . first the destruction of all human life and second just that of human life in New Mexico'. Some team members worried about the radioactive materials that would be produced by the bomb and another word entered the language—fallout.

General Groves had prepared a series of press releases to cover the various possibilities he could foresee. The most drastic was that Oppenheimer and other physicists in the forward station would be wiped out. This he planned to explain away by saying that they had accidentally touched off an Army ammunitions dump while holidaying at Oppenheimer's ranch.

In the event, the atmosphere didn't ignite, Oppenheimer wasn't killed and the bomb released energy equivalent to 20 000 tonnes of TNT. The cost had grown to $US2 000 000 000 and up to 200 000 people were employed overall.

The following graphic description of that fateful morning is taken from Frisch's memoirs.*

A steel tower, about a hundred feet [30 metres] tall, had been constructed to carry the explosive device (not really a bomb, without a streamlined case). When it finally arrived and was being hoisted to the top I was standing there with George Kistiakowsky (our top expert on explosives), at the bottom of the tower. 'How far away,' I asked him, 'would we have to be for safety in case it went off?' 'Oh,' he said, 'probably about ten miles [16 kilometres].' 'So in that case,' I said, 'we might as well stay and watch the fun.' Actually there was no real danger as the trigger mechanism was not yet armed, that was left to the last moment.

When finally the day came, the weather had changed; there were thunderstorms in the vicinity. We had reason to fear that lightning might set off the explosion prematurely, and many of the measurements would be ruined if the weather wasn't clear and quiet. So we had to wait. Some of the big shots went to a bunker only about ten miles away, but most of us were taken to a point in the open, twenty-five miles [40 kilometres] from the explosion site.

There we sat around through the night, waiting for the weather to clear up. For some hours I dozed in the car, waking up whenever the loudspeaker said something (in between it was playing dance music). Finally the announcement came that the count-down was beginning; now it was only minutes before the explosion took place. By that time the very first trace of the dawn was in the sky. I got out of the car and listened to the count-down and when the last minute arrived I looked for my dark goggles but couldn't find them. So I sat on the ground

*O. R. Frisch, *What Little I Remember*, Cambridge University Press, 1979.

in case the explosion blew me over, plugged my ears with my fingers, and looked in the direction away from the explosion as I listened to the end of the count . . . five, four, three, two, one . . .

And then, without a sound, the sun was shining, or so it looked. The sand hills at the edge of the desert were shimmering in a very bright light, almost colourless and shapeless. This light did not seem to change for a couple of seconds and then began to dim. I turned around but that object on the horizon which looked like a small sun was still too bright to look at. I kept blinking and trying to take looks, and after another ten seconds or so it had grown and dimmed into something more like a huge oil fire, with a structure that made it look a bit like a strawberry. It was slowly rising into the sky from the ground, with which it remained connected by a lengthening grey stem of swirling dust; incongruously, I thought of a red-hot elephant standing balanced on its trunk. Then, as the cloud of hot gas cooled and became less red, one could see a blue glow surrounding it, a glow of ionized air. The object, now clearly what has become so well known as the mushroom cloud, ceased to rise but a second mushroom started to grow out from its top; the inner layers of the gas were kept hot by their radioactivity and, being hotter than the rest, broke through the top and rose to even greater height. It was an awesome spectacle; anybody who has ever seen an atomic explosion will never forget it. And all in complete silence; the bang came minutes later, quite loud though I had plugged my ears, and followed by a long rumble like heavy traffic very far away. I can still hear it.

2

From Alamogordo
to Australia

> There floated through my mind a line from the Bhagavad Gita
> in which Krishna is trying to persuade the prince that he should
> do his duty: 'I am become death, the shatterer of worlds.'

Thus Oppenheimer described his feelings at the success (if
that's the right word) of the Trinity explosion. 'We felt the
world would never be the same again', was how Oppenheimer
summed up the reaction of most of the scientists. The military
on the other hand, in the person of General Groves, saw the
outcome in more limited terms: 'This is the end of traditional
warfare,' Groves is reported as saying while the awesome
mushroom cloud, that potent symbol of the twentieth century,
billowed skywards.

These diverse reactions reflected the differences in attitude
between the two groups. Many of the scientific personnel
involved had had early perceptions of what an atom bomb was
likely to do and did not believe it would ever be used in anger.
Early in 1943 for example, Lawrence had told one of his co-
workers: 'The bomb will never be dropped on people. As soon
as we get it, we'll use it only to dictate terms of peace.' But
history was against Lawrence and the others who thought like
him. The bomb project had grown out of pure physics

research. The realization of the military potential of that research had coincided with the start of the war against Germany. Early American developments had just preceded that country's precipitate entry into the war, so it became inevitable that military considerations became paramount during the Manhattan Project. The strong character of General Groves and the desire of many of the senior physicists to immerse themselves in problem solving and ignore the project's internal politics ensured the dominance of the Army. Thus, when the decision on how best to use this new weapon finally had to be made, the military view that it should be used directly on Japan was the one that prevailed.

Germany, the enemy most feared because of her advanced technological capability, was now defeated. It was accepted by the Western Allies that Japan did not have either the know-how or the infrastructure to develop an atom bomb of its own. So was there any real need to drop one on Japan? Many of the scientists thought not, but the weapon they had developed had become a political matter, not a purely technological one. From now on, events outside the great laboratories would more often than not determine the lines of research to be followed, as well as the use (or abuse) of their output.

It is difficult now to realize what a great change had taken place in such a short time. Even in the late 1930s, scientific research was in the main carried out in the universities, some industrial laboratories and a few government institutes. A really large project, like Lawrence's planned 150-centimetre cyclotron was estimated to cost less than $200 000 and Lawrence himself was involved in fund raising from largely private sources when the war intervened. After the Manhattan Project, big, very expensive, government funded laboratories became the order of the day. Military spending on research and development has reached (literally) astronomical heights. As well as the big ticket items like Apollo, all sorts of obscure research projects are funded, presumably with the hope that another super/secret weapon will emerge. On the civilian side, government spending is also very large. Every nation seems to

43

require an Atomic Energy Commission as well as an international airline as a symbol of its prestige.

So the bomb emerged into an already changed world. The military/industrial alliance, that Eisenhower was to warn against fifteen years later, was already firmly established. It is not without symbolic significance that the Los Alamos staff got a receipt for the bomb from the Army before the Alamogordo explosion. The Trinity test was technically a US Army venture.

THE DECISION

Truman had replaced Roosevelt as President in April and had been told about the atomic bomb at his first cabinet meeting on the day Roosevelt died. There was something of a vacuum in Washington concerning bomb policy following Roosevelt's death and Groves moved in to fill it. He and Henry Stimson, Roosevelt's and now Truman's Secretary of War, set up an interim committee to consider the use of the bomb as well as other atomic matters. Many of them had not heard of the bomb's development until the committee started meeting. A six-hour meeting on 31 May spent about an hour considering the dropping of a bomb on Japan. The committee had summoned Oppenheimer and three other very senior physicists to give as much scientific information as possible about the state of bomb development. Stimson opened the meeting in grandiloquent fashion:

> Gentlemen [he said, according to the recollections of Arthur Compton, one of the four] it is our responsibility to recommend action that may turn the course of civilization. In our hands we expect soon to have a weapon of wholly unprecedented destructive power. Today's prime fact is war. Our great task is to bring this war to a prompt and successful conclusion.

This seemed not to leave much room for any other opinion. Oppenheimer was spokesman for the group of scientists. He had two clear points to make. Uranium-235 was being delivered too slowly to allow a bomb test but the physics were by this stage fairly well understood and it would almost certainly work. The plutonium bomb was more complex being an implosion device (see p. 61) and could well be a dud. It would have to be tested and even if that worked the explosive force of the next one could not be guaranteed.

So in May the situation looked like this. The uranium bomb would probably work but couldn't be tested; the plutonium bomb could be tested fairly soon (within two months) but might well fizzle. So a test to demonstrate to the Japanese just what they were up against had no guarantee of success. On the other hand, estimates of US casualties in an invasion of the Japanese islands ranged from 40 000 (General George Marshall) to 1 000 000 (Secretary of War Stimson). The official minutes of the 31 May meeting spell out the decision quite clearly.

> After much discussion, the Secretary [Stimson] expressed the conclusion, on which there was general agreement, that we could not give the Japanese any warning; that we could not concentrate on a civilian area; but that we should make a profound psychological impression on as many of the inhabitants as possible. At the suggestion of Dr Conant [one of the scientific gang of four], the Secretary agreed that the most desirable target would be a vital war plant employing a large number of workers and surrounded by workers' houses.

This was the recommendation that went to Truman who, as Commander-in-Chief, had to make the final decision. Thus was the fate of Hiroshima sealed.

Leo Szilard in one area and James Franck in another organized petitions requesting that the bomb be used only as a demonstration warning. But, because of the Fermi/Oppenheimer view that the bomb could not be relied on, the petitions did not get very far. After the successful Trinity test, Oppenheimer telegraphed Groves asking that the decision to bomb Japan be reconsidered, part of his argument being that technical improvements could produce more and better bombs. Groves replied that it was too late: 'Factors beyond our control prevent us from considering any decision, other than to proceed according to the existing schedule for the time being.' Those all important 'factors' have never been explained.

Given the military thinking at the time, the dropping of the bomb on Hiroshima can be understood but not condoned. The destruction of Nagasaki, however, is totally inexplicable. After 6 August, the Japanese were faced with a completely un-expected situation. One aeroplane had dropped a bomb that had devastated a city and killed around 70 000 people. The inhabitants had been killed by the effects of blast and the effects of burns—just as in the Tokyo fire storms. But some showed strange, extra symptoms: nausea, lassitude, diarrhoea, loss of hair. Before the effects had even begun to be evaluated, before rescue and medical teams had barely started to move into the ruins, the same happened at Nagasaki, with 35 000 deaths. The Japanese surrendered on 15 August, nine days after Hiroshima and six days after Nagasaki.

One of the scientists involved, Victor Weisskopf, later said, 'Hiroshima was a blunder, and Nagasaki a crime.' It is always tempting to try and explain the inexplicable and like Oscar Wilde we can resist everything but temptation. We wonder was Nagasaki destroyed to see if the plutonium implosion bomb would work a second time? Hiroshima had been victim of the uranium-235 bomb, code-named 'Little Boy'. Untested, it had worked first time. Did the designers of the other type, code-named 'Fat Boy', want to show that theirs was as good over cities as over the New Mexico desert? Or was it the US Army wishing to make absolutely sure of their share in the victory over Japan? Ever since its beginning, the Pacific War had been principally a Naval affair. Island hopping Marines had borne the brunt of particularly bloody fighting and the Navy had been involved in some costly sea battles, not the least of them being the Battle of the Coral Sea that effectively saved Australia from Japanese invasion. The Army had organized the Manhattan Project. Did it want to demonstrate to the Navy it was not only a case of one bang and finish? Was it to show that the $US2 000 000 000 that could have bought many more ships or assault craft or aeroplanes had been well spent?

Or was the reason somewhat more subtle? Was it to impress the Russians who entered the war against Japan the very day the bomb was dropped on Nagasaki? It had finally dawned on the Americans that the major postwar problems would be with the USSR, not with Britain and France. At the various 'Big Three' (Churchill, Roosevelt and Stalin) Conferences, Roosevelt was often more concerned with curbing what he saw as Churchill's old-fashioned imperialistic aims than with trying to control Stalin's predatory plans for Eastern Europe. Were 35 000 Japanese sacrificed in an attempt to demonstrate to the Russians that Hiroshima was not a fluke? Was it done to show that America had sufficient material for at least three bombs (if the Trinity test is included), probably more, and was prepared to use them? If that was the aim, it was singularly unsuccessful as the current state of the world demonstrates all too clearly. Maybe it is not given for mere mortals to understand the workings of statesmanship and we will never know. This book refers to many ironies, one is that the victims of Hiroshima are remembered each 6 August, whereas the victims of Nagasaki are virtually forgotten and Nagasaki was undoubtedly the greater evil.

Certainly military intelligence and presumably Groves, who played an active role in the security work surrounding Los Alamos and the other plants, knew about Russian work on a Soviet atom bomb. In 1943, with invading German armies still deep inside Russia, a research institute was set up in Moscow under the directorship of Igor Kurchatov with the express purpose of developing an atomic bomb. Scientists were drafted from other war work, and exceedingly scarce resources were devoted to the project, which indicates how seriously it was taken. The Russians were aware of German and British/American work in the field, information that had almost certainly been supplied by some of the scientists working on the Manhattan Project.

That the Americans were aware of at least some of the Russian developments is demonstrated by the raid on Oranienburg, just north of Berlin. In the last few weeks of the war it was discovered that a plant in the town was producing uranium from ore. About 1500 tonnes of high explosives were dropped on the plant, not to destroy the last remains of the potential German nuclear bomb but to ensure that the advancing Russian Army, then getting close to the town, did not capture the uranium-making facilities. So before the hot war had even finished, the cold war had started.

POSTWAR DEVELOPMENTS

After the Japanese surrender, the Americans were faced with the dilemma of what to do with their two thousand million dollar investment. A Senate Special Commission on Atomic Energy started hearings and was relieved to find that General Groves estimated it would take Russia twenty years to develop its own atom bomb. If the United States kept their own project going, they could probably stay well ahead. Some of the scientists who fronted up to the Senators were less sanguine. Harold Urey, for instance, said the aim should be for some international agreement, leading to the eradication of the whole nuclear fission business. Unhappily for Urey, the genie was already out of the bottle. The vacillating Oppenheimer, as always, was the star witness but, as always, answered questions without necessarily making any firm recommendations. He could not guess how long the Russians would take, but the British could develop a bomb in about two years. He agreed with Urey that international controls were desirable and would warrant destroying the existing stockpile, consisting of one bomb with another on the way.

The upshot of all this soul searching was an idealistic plan and a misguided piece of legislation, the consequences of which eventually affected Australia.

The plan was the disarmament proposal put by the United States to the newly established United Nations, which became known as the Baruch Plan, after Bernard Baruch the man chosen to present it. If it was genuine, it was exceedingly idealistic. It proposed an international agency to control all sources and handling of uranium, to direct all nuclear research, and to be the sole owner of nuclear weapons technology. The pre-conditions demanded for the implementation of the plan were anathema to the Russians. Baruch wanted the international agency to have full authority for regulation and inspection. Stalin's paranoia interpreted this merely as an attempt to spy on Russia. Andrei Gromyko put forward an alternative proposal calling for the outlawing of nuclear weapons and destruction of stockpiles before inspection and control procedures were established. As the only country with a stockpile, albeit very small, this plan was clearly unacceptable to the Americans. So the melancholy pattern of negotiations on nuclear disarmament was begun — set too many pre-conditions known to be virtually unacceptable to the other side, thus guaranteeing failure for which the opponents could be blamed.

The legislation was the *Atomic Energy Act* of 1946, known more popularly as the *McMahon Act* after its principal sponsor, Senator Brian McMahon, a Democrat from Connecticut. Its aim was to bring some order to post-Nagasaki nuclear research in the United States. By setting up a civilian Atomic Energy Commission, it wrested nuclear weapons research from military control. It was welcomed by those physicists who had stayed within the bomb programme as it gave a freer hand for research into nuclear energy. The age-old dream of turning swords into ploughshares had led to optimistic forecasts that electricity produced from nuclear power reactors would be so cheap that it would not be worth installing consumption meters in users' houses. But the *McMahon Act* contained one unfortunate clause. It forbade American scientists sharing their nuclear secrets with anybody else. This clause led to bitter resentment on the part of the British, Canadian and French scientists who had led the way in the early days and who had made valuable contributions all through the bomb programme.

Whether McMahon wanted only to control nuclear weapons or to keep the potential benefits of nuclear energy reserved for sole American use is academic; the result was the same. The British, then later the French, took strong exception to the American decision. The British in particular felt they had a right to the bomb. Britain still considered itself a great world power. Of the Big Five victors of the Second World War, Britain alone had fought all the way through. China and France had both been occupied by enemy soldiers then liberated by, among others, British troops. Russia and America had both been pitchforked into the war by attacks against them, whereas Britain had entered the war voluntarily in support of its ally, Poland. All through the war Britain had considered itself at the very least an equal in nuclear weapons research. The British had started the first developmental programme and it was not until Oliphant visited the United States that the American programme had gained any impetus. The work had gone to the United States mainly to get away from German bombing and to take advantage of America's industrial resources. Britain was slowly becoming a gigantic aircraft carrier and the wide open spaces of the United States were obviously much more suited to the bomb project. Some of the angriest verbal exchanges of the war took place towards its end as British scientists became increasingly frustrated by the refusal of the Americans to share their information.

Unfortunately, the Americans had the 1943 Quebec Agreement to point to. In one of his more regrettably expansive gestures, Churchill had agreed that postwar exchange of information on nuclear bombs and nuclear power would be left to the discretion of the President of the United States. The basis for this agreement was the by now massive financial contribution of the Americans. Given the relationship between Churchill and Roosevelt, the agreement was probably not thought to be very significant. The relationship between Truman and Attlee was a very different matter and the *McMahon Act* rankled for a very long time.

Thus as far as Britain was concerned, development of an atomic bomb was merely a continuation of the work started in 1940. If the Americans would not continue joint projects, then Britain would go it alone, even if it meant finding their own test sites. Enter Australia, stage right!

Even in a nation noted for its penchant for understatement,

the British announcement of its bomb programme takes some beating. George Jeger, a backbencher in the governing Labour Party, rose at question time on 12 May 1948 to ask the Minister of Defence, A. W. Alexander, whether he felt adequate progress was being made in the development of the most modern types of weapons. The Minister replied in the affirmative.

As was made clear in the Statement Relating to Defence, 1948, research and development continues to receive the highest priority in the defence field. All types of weapons, including atomic weapons, are being developed.

In a supplementary question, Jeger asked: 'Can the Minister give any further information on the development of atomic weapons?' 'No', replied Alexander, 'I do not think it would be in the public interest to do that.' As Norman Moss wrote in *Men Who Play God,* 'That phrase, "including atomic weapons" must be one of the great throwaway lines of British history.'

It is worth noting this decision was taken by a Labour Government which, because of its socialist outlook, might well have been expected to resist the temptation. In May 1945, the wartime all-party coalition was disbanded and a general election was held. The Conservatives pinned their faith in the great wartime leader, Winston Churchill. But the British electorate gave Churchill a metaphorical reverse version of his famous V-for-Victory sign and Labour swept into power with a massive majority. It was a government of both vast energy and great reforming zeal. At home, certain key industries such as coal and transport, were nationalized; Aneurin Bevan's great dream of a universal, free health service was implemented; public housing and education underwent great improvements. Abroad, starting with the Indian subcontinent, the process of returning the colonies to their rightful owners got under way. To understand why such an apparently enlightened government took such an apparently unenlightened decision as to continue to develop atomic weapons, it is necessary to see how the world looked at the time. (It is perhaps fairer to state that the decision was made not by the full government but by the Prime Minister, Clement Attlee, in conjunction with a small Cabinet defence subcommittee.)

THE WORLD AFTER 1945

Even though the great struggle against the Axis powers had ended successfully, the world still looked a very dangerous place. The Russian Government soon made its expansionist aims very clear. The Tsarist dreams of warm water ports in Europe had been taken over lock, stock and barrel by the Bolsheviks. The disruptions in Europe following the collapse of Germany gave Stalin his chance for expansion. Puppet Communist governments were installed in the countries liberated by the Red Army. A Communist revolt was fomented in north-west Iran (Azerbaijan) and a supposedly independent state set up. In Greece, fighting continued in the north as a Communist army, supported from Yugoslavia, fought the Athens Government, supported directly by Britain.

By early 1947, Britain decided its commitment to Greece was proving too costly and notified the United States it was withdrawing its support. That crisis led to a very important development in American policy. President Truman put US resources behind a general effort to check any further expansion of Soviet power. He promulgated what became known as the Truman Doctrine. In a message to Congress he stated,

> . . . it must be the policy of the United States to support free peoples who are resisting attempted subjugation by armed minorities or by outside pressures.

Such a statement merely intensified the growing division of the world into two camps, loosely defined as East and West. Countries such as Britain and France, once among the dominant powers of the world, wished to maintain their independence and saw nuclear weapons as a way of staying in the big league. On several occasions during the war, the British Army had deceived Germany about its true fighting strength by using dummy tanks and guns. But there was no way a cardboard cut-out atom bomb would fool anybody. British Foreign Secretary, Ernest Bevin, said that without nuclear weapons to support his arguments it would be like going naked into the negotiating chamber.

It was in Europe, very close to home for Britain, that the US/USSR standoff became most intense. In June 1947, the US Government offered massive credits to the countries of the war-ravaged continent to enable them to increase their rate of economic recovery. Known as the Marshall Plan, it was extended to the USSR and Eastern Europe. Stalin feared a capitalist trap: US money would only enslave the borrowers. He declined to take part and forbade the countries under his control to accept any American money. The Marshall Plan was very successful in putting Western Europe back on its feet.

In Eastern Europe events took another turn for the worse. The Czechoslovak Government tried desperately to act as a bridge between East and West. When it hesitated about withdrawing from the Marshall Plan, the Soviets decided that only a Communist government would stand proof against the American blandishments. A nasty coup took place in March 1948 and a pro-Soviet government was installed. Yet another of these ironies. Czechoslovakia, which had been sacrificed by Chamberlain in 1938 in return for 'peace in our time', was sacrificed again as the Western Allies were powerless to prevent the Soviet takeover. The Foreign Minister, Jan Masaryk, son of the State's first President and a strong anti-communist, was assassinated by defenestration and, after a certain amount of manoeuvring, a 'People's Democracy' was declared on 9 May. The last chink in the Iron Curtain had been closed.

After the war, Germany had been divided into four occupation zones: British, French, American and Russian. In March 1948, the Western Powers decided to unite their zones of Germany into what is now colloquially known as West Germany. Berlin, as befits a capital city, had been treated as a separate case. Although set deep in the Soviet occupation zone, it too was divided into four areas, each under the control of one of the victorious nations. As a retaliation to the Western decision to re-unify western Germany, the Russians set up a road, rail and waterway blockade of Berlin. The blockade started on 24 June 1948. By 26 June, the British and Americans had started to airlift vital supplies into Berlin. The airlift continued until September 1949, by which time more than 2 300 000 tonnes of fuel, food and machinery had been flown into Berlin at a cost of \$US224 000 000.

Further afield, China became a communist power when Mao Tse-tung finally achieved victory over Chiang Kai-shek in October 1949. Then in June 1950, North Korea invaded the South. After the Japanese surrender, Korea which had been annexed by Japan in 1910, was divided into two. The northern half was occupied by Russia (one of the spoils of its intensive war effort against Japan!) and the southern half by the United States. Both countries installed governments to their own liking, then withdrew. Each of the new governments claimed all Korea as theirs by right. The North attempted to assert the claim by force and very nearly succeeded. A hastily assembled United Nations force, principally American, but supported with varying degrees of enthusiasm by fifteen other countries, including Australia and Britain, held on. They eventually pushed the North Koreans back over the boundary, and General MacArthur set out to unite the country from the South just as the North Koreans had intended to unite it from the North. This brought the Chinese into the war and the fighting dragged on until a provisional armistice agreement was reached in July 1953. Twenty-nine years later, the Korean peace negotiations still bicker on.

BRITISH DECISIONS

It was against this sombre background that British decisions about the bomb were made. No evidence is available about how much weight the Cold War shenanigans carried or whether they were even an element in whatever debate took place. One factor may have weighed heavily with the decision makers. In September 1945, Igor Gousenko, an NKVD (later KGB) agent in Ottawa, defected. Although ostensibly a cipher clerk at the Russian Embassy, Gousenko told the Canadians that his main job had been to obtain data on the atomic bomb. His principal contacts had been Allan Nun May, a British physicist, and Bruno Pontecorvo, an Italian. So the Russians were presumably well on the way to exploding their own bomb. This was confirmed on September 1949, when high-flying aircraft fitted with fallout monitoring equipment detected traces of a Russian atomic explosion. 'Joe One' as it was nicknamed had arrived earlier than most Western leaders had expected or wanted.

The Americans decided to press ahead with the development of the 'super'. Teller's idea of using an atomic bomb to fuse together hydrogen atoms was now capable of realization. Russia was certainly developing a hydrogen weapon (in fact they beat the Americans in the race for a truly droppable bomb). In late 1949, Klaus Fuchs, then Deputy Scientific Director of Britain's Atomic Energy Research establishment, confessed to the Establishment's Security Officer that for many years he had been passing information to the Russians. The German-born Fuchs had worked at Los Alamos and had not only passed information concerning the plutonium bomb but had also been privy to much of the early work on the 'super'. Fuchs had spied for ideological reasons and, after serving his prison sentence, left Britain to teach physics in East Germany.

The defection of two British diplomats, Burgess and Maclean, who had been spying for the Soviets for some considerable time, again for ideological reasons, all added to the Cold War hysteria and the demand for a nuclear shield.

The spy scandals had some terrible effects in the United States, culminating in the unhappy period known as McCarthyism, when the Republican Senator from Wisconsin purportedly discovered 'Reds' everywhere—especially in the State Department. Among others, Linus Pauling had his passport taken away, but the shabbiest episode of all came in 1954 when Oppenheimer's security clearance was suspended. At the subsequent hearings demanded by a stunned Oppenheimer, many of the old Los Alamos team turned out, most supporting their erstwhile Director. The charges against Oppenheimer boiled down to the fact that, before 1940, he had been associated with several left-wing organizations and had given part of his income to a fund for the relief of Spanish War victims—Spain of course was the *cause célèbre* of the left-wing groups in the late 1930s.

The other charge was that he had opposed the building of the 'super'. He had spoken against that project in several committees, but so had other scientists using, like Oppenheimer, essentially moral arguments. Long before it became the fashion with pop stars, Oppenheimer had studied Eastern religions and was much influenced by the concept of ahimsa, love or gentleness. How he reconciled this view with the activities at Los Alamos is not clear, unless he saw the atom bomb as imposing gentleness on Germany as his Jewish heritage revolted against the inhumanity of the Nazis. Even so, one of the most quoted remarks of Oppenheimer's came in a talk he gave in 1948 when he said, 'We [the physicists] have known sin.' But when it came to the 'super', Oppenheimer found it impossible to put his support behind a device a thousand times more destructive than the bombs that had destroyed Hiroshima and Nagasaki.

Teller's testimony at the security hearing was ambiguous, to say the least. When asked directly by the lawyer representing the Atomic Energy Commission if he believed Oppenheimer was a security risk, Teller replied:

> In a great number of cases, I have seen Dr Oppenheimer act—I understood Dr Oppenheimer acted—in a way which for me was exceedingly hard to understand. I thoroughly disagreed with him in numerous issues, and his actions frankly appeared to me confused and complicated. To this extent I feel I would like to see the vital issues of this country in hands which I understand better, and therefore trust more. In this very limited sense I

would like to express a feeling that I would feel personally more secure if public matters could rest in other hands.

Although others including Hans Bethe, one of America's most respected physicists, testified on Oppenheimer's behalf, the Review Board chose to place most weight on Teller's evidence and Oppenheimer's security clearance was not renewed. In fact it never was, but at least he was not placed under house arrest and banished to Siberia, the fate that befell Andrei Sakharov, father of the Russian nuclear bomb. Still more irony—ex-Nazis were building rockets for America, while the man who had directed the making of the first nuclear bomb no longer had access to the laboratories he had built.

Although the hearings were secret, word soon got around the scientific community and for a long time Edward Teller was cut dead at scientific meetings and conferences. (A Teller-Oppenheimer *rapprochement* finally took place in 1963 when the Atomic Energy Commission awarded its Enrico Fermi Gold Medal to Oppenheimer. A change of government had brought about a more sympathetic view, President Johnson travelled to Princeton to present the medal personally. After the ceremony, Teller approached Oppenheimer to congratulate him on his speech. The two shook hands and one of the most serious rifts in American science more or less ended.)

Thus the British bomb policy was developed, albeit secretly, in a confused and confusing world. A weapon like the atomic bomb, and its potential successor the hydrogen bomb, had another possible appeal to the British Government. It had never been British policy to maintain a large standing army in peacetime. A large navy? Yes. Forces for policing the colonies? Yes. Large numbers of drunken and licentious soldiers in Britain? No! For one thing it prevented any prospect of a military coup. So although National Service continued after the war, with most young men serving an 18- to 24-month period in one of the armed forces, it was never very popular and was finally stopped in 1960. Nuclear weapons, deliverable by the V bombers also being developed, offered a way of countering the massive standing armies being maintained by Russia. Our all-too-recent ally was now our all-too-possible enemy.

Throughout the autumn of 1945, the British scientists and many of the refugees trickled back from the United States and Canada carrying little more than their notebooks and memories. The two leading British scientists by this time were John Cockcroft and William Penney (both subsequently knighted). Cockcroft had been director of the joint Canadian-US-British plant at Chalk River, some 200 kilometres north of Ottawa. During the Manhattan days it had been chosen as the site for the first reactor outside the United States, and work on a heavy-water-moderated, natural-uranium-fuelled reactor system had progressed steadily. Interestingly, Canada became the first nation to consciously reject the atom bomb. They turned the Chalk River facilities into a nuclear energy research establishment and ignored weapons.

In Britain, a nuclear division was established within the Department of Supply, so that right from the start the whole enterprise was Government controlled. (The United Kingdom Atomic Energy Authority, UKAEA, known fondly as the UKELELE to its ex-employees, was set up later.) Cockcroft became director of the Atomic Energy Research Establishment set up on a wartime airfield about 20 kilometres south of Oxford. It took its name from the nearby village of Harwell, known locally more for the quality of its cherries than for nuclear research. The first two reactors were ZEEP (Zero Energy Experimental Pile) a very small unit, and BEPO (British Experimental Pile Oh). Even the British are not so illogical as to call their first true reactor number zero and it seems that the 'O' was added for the sake of euphony. The man in charge of BEPO was the Australian, (Sir) Charles Watson-Munro, now Professor of Physics at Sydney University.

Other plants were set up at Springfields, to manufacture reactor fuel; at Capenhurst, to develop uranium-235 enrichment facilities; at Windscale to develop reactors and to reprocess the uranium rods coming out of the reactor to extract the plutonium; and at Aldermaston to make nuclear weapons. Penney became Britain's nuclear bomb chief when he was appointed Director of the Atomic Weapons Research Establishment.

As the fifties approached and the bomb programme developed, Britain's need for a test site became acute. The bitterness between Britain and the United States over the *McMahon Act*, exacerbated by the spy scandals, obviously precluded the use of any American facilities even though Britain had wanted to use them. So bad had relations between the two countries become in the nuclear field, that the wartime agreement that neither would use the bomb without the other's consent was terminated in 1948.

STATE OF NUCLEAR KNOWLEDGE

Before considering the radiation hazards involved with bombs and the long-term health threats their testing causes, we need to backtrack a little to see what problems had been solved and what Britain in particular still had to do before she could call herself a nuclear power.

The first and vital question was: how many neutrons are produced each time a uranium or plutonium atom fissions? It had to be greater than one if a chain reaction was to be sustained. The figures are, surprisingly, an average of 2.43 neutrons produced for each U-235 fission and 2.89 neutrons per Pu-239 fission. Obviously it is not possible to get 0.43 of a neutron; the figure is an average for a very large number of fissions.

When a uranium or plutonium atom fissions, it breaks into two separate new elements, called fission products. They, in turn, eject one, or more, neutrons. But interestingly, fissioning atoms do not all behave the same way. One will break into two particular elements, its neighbour into two quite different elements, a third into even more different elements. Fission products are overwhelmingly radioactive with a wide range of half-lives*. In the fission of U-235, something like 210 different

---

* The half-life of a radioactive substance is the time required for it to lose 50 per cent of its activity by radioactive decay. See p. 77 for further details.

radioisotopes, including both fission fragments and their radioactive decay products, have been detected. About 97 per cent of U-235 nuclei yield fission products falling into two broad groups—a 'light' group of products with mass number between 85 and 104, and a 'heavy' group with mass numbers of between 130 and 149. Only 0.01 per cent break up into the symmetrical division of two equal fragments of mass numbers 117 and 118. Because of the wide range of fission products, the numbers of neutrons ejected per fission varies, so the average number is not a whole one. Importantly, however, it is substantially greater than one.

The next question was rather more difficult: how to get the critical mass together at just the right place and long enough for an explosion to occur. Because of the permanent presence of stray neutrons from the occasional spontaneous fission, the critical mass can only be assembled at the very instant it is required. It has to be done remotely with no margin for error.

The process used by Fermi to build his pile was no use; it was too slow and anyway the object was entirely different. Fermi's aim was to get a just self-sustaining chain reaction. Bomb builders want an explosive chain reaction. Fermi's work, however, gave the most important clue to the answer. Below a certain mass, a chain reaction will not take place as too many neutrons escape from the surface. This is called a *subcritical mass*. Bring two or more subcritical masses of the right shape together, under the right geometrical conditions, and a *supercritical mass* can be formed. The first theoretical design at Los Alamos, nicknamed the Thin Man, consisted of a spherical mass of U-235 with a deep hole or groove running through it. Then, from a gun of some sort, the remaining lump of critical mass was fired into the hole. The trick was to get the speed right. If it went in too slowly, the bomb would fizzle by pre-detonation. The interacting neutrons would produce a small chain reaction as the two masses approached one another, releasing a small amount of energy, enough to blow the approaching lumps apart but not a whopping great explosion.

Plutonium-239 presented a more complex problem. For one

thing, it emitted alpha particles which were in turn capable of producing additional stray neutrons—after all that was how neutrons were first discovered. The effect would vary widely with the amount of impurity in the plutonium. Consequently, by comparison with U-235, the plutonium bomb was subject to more variables. It was expected that, as the two subcritical masses of plutonium neared each other, they would grow more violently and unpredictably unstable. The gun would therefore have to be considerably faster. In the event, the problem was overcome by using implosion—the opposite of explosion. This was a very clever trick worked out by Seth Neddermayer, a former student of Oppenheimer. If a large number of TNT charges are placed around the outside of a spherical subcritical mass and detonated, they will produce a converging shock-wave. This will then very rapidly squeeze together the fissile material into a critical mass. With this idea it would be possible to produce better bombs from both plutonium and uranium.

Work on both these ideas, gun barrel and implosion, proceeded in parallel at Los Alamos. It was the relatively complex nature of the implosion bomb that made Oppenheimer seek the Trinity test and also made him reluctant to guarantee a test explosion before a group of watching Japanese. The idea of course worked at Alamogordo, Nagasaki, Maralinga, and in hundreds of other tests. The gun barrel type worked, without testing, at Hiroshima. Because of their shapes the bombs were nicknamed 'Fat Boy' (the implosion device dropped on Nagasaki) and 'Little Boy' (the successor of the theoretical 'Thin Man', gun barrel bomb).

The other thing that had been learned from the first three bombs was that the initial explosion not only releases heat, blast and radiation but also produces vast quantities of radioactive substances. Apart from the fission products formed during the actual explosion, what are called *activation products* are also important. During the brief life of the chain reaction, vast numbers of neutrons are produced. Only some of them are needed to produce fission. The others escape and many of them interact with the nuclei of any nearby atoms to produce a whole range of radioactive species. In effect this is a repeat of Fermi's 1934 experiments on a truly massive scale. So there is a huge additional source of radioactivity—activation products which have been made radioactive by the bomb's surplus neutrons. Anything the fireball touches is vaporized, so if it touches earth, as happened with the first three tests, a vast amount of additional radioactivity is caught up in the mushroom cloud. Some of it comes back to earth quite quickly, fairly close to the test site, but a lot of it stays aloft for quite some while, coming to earth at sites quite remote from the bomb blast. The problems posed by this fallout will be discussed in more detail in Chapter 3.

BIOLOGICAL IMPLICATIONS

Even the early work on fission showed that some of the fission products were going to be biologically more important than others. In the 'light' group of fission products, *strontium-90* is most important. It has a half-life of 28 years, behaves like calcium when taken into the body and gets incorporated in bone. It emits beta particles and can damage blood-forming bone marrow. It can get into people either by being breathed in directly or, more insiduously, by settling on to grass and getting into milk via grazing cows.

In the heavy group, *caesium-137* has a half-life of 30 years and emits both beta and gamma radiation. It was not realized at first that *iodine-131* is also very dangerous. Although it only has an eight-day half-life, it concentrates in the thyroid gland. Children are particularly at risk from iodine fallout (as they are from strontium) because iodine also gets into people via the grass-cow-milk route. Children with relatively large milk intakes and small thyroids take in bigger radiation doses than adults. They also have growing bones, so the radioactive strontium is more easily incorporated into their systems. The radioisotopes can concentrate at each of the various stages of the food chain, so the hazard from them can actually increase with the passage of time. When the USAEC first started measuring fallout levels, they measured strontium in 'sunshine units'. When questioned by Congressmen about its meaning, the terminology was dropped.

The activation products produced can obviously vary depending on which materials the neutrons hit, so bomb designers set out to make the most of them. One early idea was to make a cobalt bomb. The radioactive form of cobalt, mass number 60, emits a very penetrating pair of gamma rays. Their energies are 1.17 MeV and 1.33 MeV. So if some non-radioactive cobalt-59 is added to the bomb casing, a rather nasty extra addition can be made to the bomb's delayed effects. The half-life of cobalt-60 is 5.3 years, so it affects the bombed area long after the explosion is over, and, if injected into the atmosphere, adversely affects people in the fallout zone for many years. This concept is known as an *enhanced radiation weapon* and its development was only part of the work that went on in the research into nuclear bombs.

POSTWAR BOMBS

The first new postwar programme tackled by the Americans was the *super* or *hydrogen bomb*. A device was exploded in November 1952 in the Pacific—it was a complex piece of equipment, and could not be classed as a true bomb. Work also went forward into making small bombs for use on battlefields, and enhanced radiation weapons of various sorts.

Another nasty one was the so-called *dirty bomb*. Here is the approximate recipe: First take your plutonium atom bomb, surround it with a blanket of lithium to make a hydrogen bomb, then add some uranium-238 which will undergo fission when bombarded with the surplus high speed neutrons from the hydrogen explosion. You have now made a *fission-fusion-fission bomb* designed to produce maximum fallout. (Hydrogen bombs as such don't produce fallout in the present sense—the radioactivity from them comes primarily from the fission bomb trigger and activation products.)

A newer trick is to make a bomb that produces as little blast

63

as possible but great showers of neutrons. The neutrons are very effective in killing people. So buildings and other structures can be left standing while the people are killed. The neutrons will produce some activation in the buildings and so on, but the areas involved could soon be occupied by forces whose commanders were prepared to let them accept some radiation exposure.

There is now a whole range of nuclear weapons—relatively small 'tactical weapons', around 1 kilotonne or so for battlefield use, up to massive 'strategic weapons' of 20 megatonnes or more, straightforward fission bombs, 'clean' fission-fusion bombs, 'dirty' fission-fusion-fission bombs, neutron bombs, bombs fired by field mortars, bombs delivered by massive missile systems. The *cobalt bomb* has not been developed, although the residual contamination at Maralinga indicates that Britain certainly carried out experiments on such a device. The residual radiation affects potential occupying troops just as much as the inhabitants and is therefore less attractive than a neutron bomb. (The current state of nuclear weaponry is discussed in the Epilogue, see p. 251.)

BRITAIN'S TESTS

So the British bomb designers had some answers. The basic ordnance problem had been solved. Subcritical masses could be kept apart and brought together at the right moment. Production methods for uranium-235 and plutonium-239 were well in hand. This is not to underestimate the problems the British scientists faced. No Briton had ever been allowed inside the Oak Ridge diffusion plant and no non-American had ever seen the Hanford plutonium-producing piles. Techniques for separating plutonium from irradiated uranium had to be re-invented; hard decisions on which type of power reactor research to pursue had to be made—all in a country trying to recover from six years of physically and economically debilitating war.

The effects of the bomb in terms of blast, heat and initial

radiation were known at least as far as their effects on cities was concerned. (The problems of fallout and delayed radiation were not considered to be too serious at this stage.) But Britain is a maritime nation and most of her major cities are on or near the coast. Would a bomb exploded on a coastal area produce different effects? One of the first aims was obviously to test a bomb under those conditions.

Civil Defence authorities needed as much information as possible about atomic explosions. So the decision was made that the first British device should be exploded in a ship moored near land thus simulating a nuclear attack on a port. What was needed was a piece of water that resembled the estuary of a typical British port like the Mersey or the Thames. Navy personnel, familiar with the western coast of Australia, suggested that a group of islands known as the Monte Bellos would be suitable. They are a group of some 100 small uninhabited islands surrounded by shallow water about 160 kilometres north of Onslow.

The Australian Government apparently saw no objections and sent HMAS *Karangi* to make a preliminary survey of the area. The survey showed that the islands were suitable for the test and the Australian Government gave permission for the test to be held there. This took place in 1950, and it is interesting because the agreement must have been reached between the Attlee Labour Government, which had just been returned by a very narrow margin, and the Menzies Liberal Government that had won the 'ration card' election the previous year.

The question of Britain's using Australia as a nuclear arena had first arisen in Federal Parliament as far back as 1946 but had been denied by Ben Chifley's Defence Minister, J. J. Dedman. It was the same Dedman who had made his reputation as the arch exponent of austerity during the Second World War by banning pink icing sugar and Father Christmas, both being too frivolous for wartime.

By 1949 there were strong rumours that the central desert was going to be used for the testing of atomic devices, following

Maralinga

Australia's agreement to let Britain use the Woomera area for its rocket programme. Britain's original hopes to use American facilities for its first atom bomb test had failed with the deteriorating relations between those two countries. Prime Minister Attlee finally wrote to Prime Minister Menzies, in March 1951, that it had been decided not to wait any longer for the Americans and the British Government would be grateful for the Australian Government's agreement to the use of the site for a weapons test in October 1952, and for help in preparing and carrying out the test.

On 18 February 1952, Menzies made the following brief announcement:

> In the course of this year, the United Kingdom Government intends to test an atomic weapon produced in the United Kingdom. In close co-operation with the Government of the Commonwealth of Australia, the test will take place at a site in Australia. It will be conducted in conditions which will ensure that there will be no danger whatever from radioactivity to the health of the people or animals in the Commonwealth.

It has never been made clear why Britain chose Australia rather than Canada. Suitable estuarine sites would certainly have been available there, but perhaps the Canadian Government wanted to concentrate on nuclear energy and not be distracted by the preparations required for bomb tests. Maybe the scientists wanted a bit of sun on their backs. Whatever the reason, Australia it came to be. The Federal Government bent over backwards to help. On 4 June 1952, Minister for Defence, P.A.M. McBride, introduced into the House of Representatives the Defence (Special Undertakings) Bill 1952, which was subsequently passed by both Houses.

McBride stressed that executive control of the project rested with the UK and any Australian forces involved were only concerned with logistic support and security of the area. In the meantime, HMAS *Warrego* had made a more detailed survey of the rather treacherous waters and all was set for the (southern) spring of 1952.

66

The device (it was not at this stage a droppable bomb) was brought out from Britain in the frigate HMS *Plym* which was also to be the ship blown up by the bomb. It arrived off Monte Bello on 8 August 1952, accompanied by a small armada carrying marines, navy personnel and an assortment of scientists and engineers. Extreme security precautions were taken. A watch was kept on all newcomers to Onslow, planes were prohibited from flying over the islands and the area was declared a danger to shipping. The weapon was based on an improved implosion technique developed by William Penney. It was detonated on 3 October 1952.

Three Australian scientists (including Ernest Titterton) were present as observers only, the Australian Government having agreed to the use of the Monte Bello site without having struck any hard bargain over technical collaboration. Its success was announced publicly on 23 October by Sir Winston Churchill who had replaced Clement Attlee as Prime Minister. Changes of government have never had any significant effect on the atomic juggernaut.

The need for a land test site had been realized back in 1950 and a place had already been picked out. A long-range reconnaissance party from the rocket range at Woomera found a section of desert scarred with clay pans, covered in red bush, spinifex, mulga and she-oak. The terrain contained large expanses of sand dune and drift, but in places was quite hard enough to allow landings of large transport planes. It was called Emu Field and, on his way to the Monte Bello test, the British supremo, William Penney, visited the site and declared it to be just what he needed. Thus nuclear tests came to mainland Australia.

The man who chose the Emu and later the Maralinga site, Sir William Penney (he was knighted after the success of the Monte Bello test) had made his scientific reputation at Alamogordo. That test was so successful that many of the instruments set up to measure the effects of the bomb failed to stand up to the unexpected intensity of the blast. Penney thought up a very simple way of measuring blast effects and it proved brilliantly successful. The 'instrument' was the tin can. Whenever a petrol or other can is subject to an excess pressure, it is partially squashed. Penney showed that the amount of crushing in a can exposed to the pressure wave from an atomic bomb is proportional to the size of that pressure wave. An overpressure of several kilopascals might reduce the can's volume by 10 per cent. A higher pressure might reduce it by 50 per cent and so on. The decrease in the can's volume is measured simply by filling it with water and comparing its weight with that of an uncrushed one filled with water. Cans are cheap and hundreds can be used to get an average measure of the blast which in turn is a good indicator of the size of the explosion. Penney was among the first members of the Manhattan team to enter Hiroshima and Nagasaki. He went around collecting squashed petrol cans and bent tubes to make his own estimates of the size of the bombs. He had to pay £450 excess baggage on his way home and customs officials found it hard to believe it was for a collection of old cans and battered concrete.

However it was not only the dropping of bombs that killed people, the experimenters also yielded victims. One of the more dangerous experiments performed at Los Alamos had been called 'tickling the Dragon's tail'. It was basically to verify theoretical calculations of critical assembly masses. The chief experimenter was Louis Slotin, the man who had received the Army's receipt for the Trinity bomb. Slotin sat in his laboratory between geiger counters and neutron monitors and slowly pushed the subcritical hemispheres together using a pair of screwdrivers. The increasing neutron counts gave him the information he needed about approaching criticality. He performed this experiment on both the Alamogordo and Nagasaki bombs as part of their preparation.

Sulking somewhat because he had not been allowed to go to Japan to see the bombs' effects at first hand, Slotin took a holiday. His chief assistant, Harry Daghlian, carried on experimenting with the material for what would be the first of the Bikini tests. The Dragon rules said that no-one should work alone or hold material in such a way that if dropped it could become critical. Daghlian broke both rules and on 21 August 1945 dropped a huge chunk of the heavy plutonium metal on to an almost completed assembly. The massive release of neutrons and gamma rays was accompanied by the characteristic blue glow and ozone smell of highly ionized air. At first he felt nothing, but became sick on the way to hospital (he had reported the accident by phone). Gradually, Daghlian lost sensation in his fingers, he complained of internal pains and eventually became delirious. He died three weeks later of a trivial infection his body could no longer fight, his blood count being way down.

Nine months later Slotin himself died. He was using the plutonium hemispheres to show some colleagues the way the neutron count increased as his screwdrivers pushed them together, when one of the screwdrivers slipped. He pushed the segments apart with his bare hands, thereby sealing his own fate but probably saving the lives of his fellow workers. The one standing with his hand on Slotin's shoulder survived but did develop cataracts. Slotin died on 30 May 1946, nine days after making his heroic but fatal gesture. Further similar Dragon experiments were stopped until entirely different and safer procedures were devised.

So the effects of high doses of radiation had been demonstrated all too clearly. What was not clear was the damaging effects of exposure to low levels of radiation and the significance of that is still being debated. The biological effects of ionizing radiation and their relationship to atomic bombs and fallout are discussed in Chapter 3.

3

Biology,
Bombs and Bans

> The relationship between the dose received by an individual
> and any particular biological effect induced by irradiation is a
> complex matter on which much further work is needed. For
> radiation protection purposes it is necessary to make certain
> simplifying assumptions. One such basic assumption under-
> lying the Commission's recommendations is that regarding
> stochastic effects, there is, within the range of exposure
> conditions usually encountered in radiation work, a linear
> relationship without threshold between dose and the proba-
> bility of an effect.

So wrote the members of the International Commission on
Radiological Protection (ICRP) in their latest set of
recommendations published in 1977. However that has not
always been the view. Certainly up until the 1950s, the
assumption was that there was a dose of radiation below which
no biological effects would occur—the so-called threshold
dose. Some schools of thought even considered a little bit of
radiation might do you good. For instance, in all the study that
went on after the discovery of radioactivity it was found that
some of the famous spa waters of Europe were slightly
radioactive. Here, it was claimed, was the secret of their

success. So why not add a little bit of radium salt to ordinary water, bottle it and make a fortune? Now, in the eighties, a much more responsible view is taken of radiation exposure. ICRP make it clear that their recommendations relate to **MAXIMUM** permissible levels and all radiation protection work must conform to the concept of 'alara', that is all radiation exposure must be kept 'as low as reasonably achievable'. Of course, endless argument can revolve around what is and what is not 'reasonably achievable'.

Knowledge of the damaging effects of ionizing radiation goes back almost to 1895 when Roentgen announced the discovery of X-rays. In January 1896, Grubbe, a manufacturer of vacuum tubes, contracted hand dermatitis. Thomas Edison, who was experimenting with fluoroscopes, reported soreness of the eyes in March 1896, and a case of epilation of the scalp was reported in April. By 1897, twenty-three cases of X-ray dermatitis had been reported and constitutional symptoms such as sickness and diarrhoea were known. In 1898, spasmodic muscular contraction was reported in two patients, indicating some effect on the central nervous system.

In 1901, a guinea pig was killed by X-rays without the burn effect which had been associated with former exposures. A case of cancer development in a chronic X-ray ulcer was reported in 1902. An experiment on bone growth inhibition was reported in 1903, when the ends of bones of young animals were irradiated. Experiments on the sterilization of rabbits and guinea pigs were also reported at this time. Blood changes were reported in 1904, and the following year the lymphocyte was demonstrated to be the most sensitive blood cell. By 1911, ninety-four cases of X-ray induced tumours in humans had been reported.

The first known death from X-rays occurred in 1914. A radiologist in Bergamo, Italy, who had worked for 14 years with X-rays, suffered in later years from dermatitis of the left hand and the side of the face. In the last three years of his life, he gradually lost strength and the cause of death was aplastic anaemia. By 1922, it was estimated that 100 known deaths had occurred among radiologists as a direct result of their work.

Not long after the separation of radium, it was found that exposure to the radiations emanating from it could lead to painful skin burns. Marie Curie described in her biography how her husband Pierre

> voluntarily exposed his arm to the action of radium during several hours. This resulted in a lesion resembling a burn that developed progressively and required several months to heal.

Pierre Curie started research into the possible beneficial uses of radium. He reasoned correctly that, if the radiations can damage healthy tissue, they could also damage unhealthy tissue.

A report appeared in 1920 indicating that half of the employees of the London Radium Institute had low white cell counts. However, the most significant effects were those resulting from the ingestion of radium, especially in industry. Luminous watches had become very popular, using a paint consisting of zinc sulphide mixed with a radium salt. Women working in the luminous dial factories used the age-old painter's habit of rolling the paint brush tip on their lips to get a fine point. In doing so, they continually 'ate' small quantities of radium. In due course, most of the girls became sick with bleeding gums and anaemia, and eventually many developed bone sarcoma—cancer of the bone. A particularly detailed study of the industry in New Jersey showed that one plant alone produced more than forty cancer cases from staff employed between 1915 and 1926. The deaths had occurred, on average, 23 years after the cessation of exposure.

There was evidence from other areas. It had long been known that many miners from the Joachimstal silver mines (the source of Madame Curie's pitchblende) died young from Berkranheit—mountain sickness. By 1930, this had been diagnosed as lung cancer, caused by breathing in the radioactive gas, radon. Patients in the 1930s and 1940s who were treated with X-rays for ankolysing spondylitis (rheumatoid inflammation of the vertebrae), or with thorium X for tuberculosis, developed leukaemia or bone cancers. American uranium miners of the 1940s and onwards developed, and are still developing, lung cancer as a result of exposure to radon in the mines. Israeli migrants who were treated with X-rays for ringworm developed thyroid cancer. Some people who happened to be in the vicinity of Hiroshima or Nagasaki when the first nuclear bombs fell, and who survived the holocaust, later developed leukaemia or some other form of cancer. Cancer observed in the first ten years of a child's life can in many cases be related to the fact that the mothers were X-rayed during pregnancy.

The list above is concerned solely with radiation induction of cancer in humans, or what are termed the somatic effects of radiation exposure and it is by no means exhaustive. (Radiation injuries can be divided into two groups: *somatic effects* in which the damage appears in the irradiated person, and *hereditary* or *genetic effects* which arise in the offspring of irradiated persons as a result of damage to germ cells in the reproductive system—the gonads.) It does, however, show quite clearly that from the earliest days of man's attempts to use ionizing radiations or radioactive materials for some real or imagined benefits (as in the case of radium injections for quite trivial illnesses) the possible risks have not been appreciated at all or have been grossly underestimated. This is true also for what are called the genetic effects of radiation—effects that are passed on to future generations and therefore of important long-term consequence for the well-being of mankind as a whole.

In the 1920s, steps were taken to introduce controls on levels of radiation exposure. It was not a burning issue. The public was not really involved; those at risk were mostly radiologists and research workers. It was not until the start of the Manhattan Project that large numbers of non-radiation specialists started to work with radioactive materials and thus became exposed to the radiations they emitted. The development of nuclear energy has further expanded the number of exposed people and increased the need for controls.

But it was the extensive testing of atom and hydrogen bombs, throwing vast quantities of radioactive materials into the atmosphere, that has led to worldwide radiation exposure as the radioactive debris filters back to earth.

The word that first worried some of the younger physicists before the Trinity test—fallout—was a word that worried the whole world by the end of the 1950s. It was the problem of fallout that eventually led to a voluntary ban, by the major nuclear powers, on the atmospheric testing of nuclear devices—a ban that only France and China have consistently ignored.

EFFECTS OF RADIATION

Before getting to the question of bombs and fallout we must first understand how radiation affects humans, and look at the maximum permissible levels of radiation exposure and the way control procedures work. Even before that, we need to tackle the rather awkward business of units for the measurement of radioactivity and radiation. Briefly, radioactivity is measured in either curies (C) or becquerels (Bq). Radiation is measured in either roentgens (r), rads, rems, coulomb/kilograms (C/kg), grays (Gy) or sieverts (Sv).

The list is so long because there are currently two sets in use, the historical ones that have been developed over the last 80 years or so, and the mks units or Système Internationale that are now replacing them. It is just the same as inches, pounds, and miles being replaced by centimetres, kilograms and kilometres, but unfortunately rather more complicated.

A full treatment of units including their historical development is given in Appendix 1, see p. 261.

In summary

Quantity measured	SI unit	Previous unit
Radioactivity	becquerel	curie
Exposure dose	coulomb/kilogram	roentgen
Absorbed dose	gray	rad
Dose equivalent	sievert	rem

The various reports and papers relating to the events at Maralinga use, of course, the older units and for that reason they will be used throughout the rest of this book. Thus, radioactivity will be quoted in curies and radiation doses in rems.

HAZARDS

Apart from having the common ability to produce ionization, the five types of radiation—alpha particles, beta particles, gamma rays, X-rays and neutrons—all have different properties and produce differing hazards. Only the first three are important when considering the long-term problems of fallout. Gamma and neutron irradiation are of greatest concern at the time of a nuclear explosion.

The different types of radiation give rise to two quite distinct hazards. The problems caused by beams of radiation outside the body are called *external radiation hazards*. Radioactive material that is inhaled or ingested and gets lodged inside the body is called, not surprisingly, an *internal hazard*.

Alpha particles are, in effect, the nuclei of the gas helium with the two electrons stripped off. They consist of a very tightly bound unit, made up of two protons and two neutrons. (The proton, you will remember, is a constituent of the atomic nucleus carrying one unit of positive electrical charge. The neutron is also part of the atomic nucleus but it is electrically neutral—hence the name.) By atomic particle standards, alphas are quite heavy. Their range in air is only a few millimetres and they are stopped by a sheet of paper.

We are all covered by a layer of dead skin which is just as effective as paper at stopping alphas. So a lump of radioactive material emitting alpha particles does not represent a hazard as long as it is kept out of the body. However, as we said earlier, on a nuclear scale, alpha particles are very heavy and produce a lot of ionization in the short distance they travel. When taken into the body, where no sheet of paper intervenes, alpha active materials are exceedingly hazardous.

Beta particles are high speed electrons, moving about nine-tenths the speed of light. They carry a single unit of negative charge. (There are positively charged beta particles called positrons but they need not concern us in this story.) They are about 100 times more penetrating than alpha particles, but are fairly easily stopped by thin sheets of aluminium or perspex.

From outside the body, betas can penetrate a few millimetres of tissue and cause a burn or eye damage. Once inside the body, beta particles are quite hazardous, although, because they give up their energy in a bigger volume, they are not as bad as alphas. (The beta radiation from tritium and carbon-14 is of very low energy and does not represent an external hazard.)

Gamma rays are electromagnetic rays of very short wavelength. They are part of the broad spectrum of electromagnetic radiation, from the long wavelength radio waves through light, to ultra-violet, to gamma rays. They are very penetrating with a range of up to one and a half kilometres in the air and represent a high external radiation hazard.

When inside the body, some gamma radiation can escape from the surface and no longer be a problem to the person containing the radioactive material. (Although what it might be doing to somebody in very close proximity is another matter.) Thus on a relative scale, gamma active materials represent a low internal hazard.

X-rays are also electromagnetic radiations, but usually of longer wavelengths, therefore less penetrating than gamma rays. X-rays are produced in an atom when an electron jumps from one orbit to another. If the energy required to keep the electron in that orbit is less than in the orginal orbit, the excess is emitted in the form of radiation that we now call X-rays. It requires some external stimulus to make electrons change their orbit. An X-ray tube is designed to produce what are called cathode rays to provide this stimulus. When the electric current supplied to the tube is switched off, the X-ray beam stops. Gamma rays on the other hand originate in the nucleus — they cannot be switched off.

X-rays in general represent a high external hazard,

exceptions being the low energies used in dental radiography where a skin burn is the major risk. It is impossible to imagine anyone swallowing an X-ray set, so that is definitely not a hazard.

Neutrons, those world-shattering particles, are uncharged constituents of the nucleus and, because of their penetrating power and ability to make whatever they interact with radioactive, are a major external hazard. As neutron sources are quite large, i.e. nuclear reactors, accelerators, neutrons are not an internal hazard.

The energy of the radiations is usually measured in thousands or millions of electronvolts—abbreviated to keV and MeV respectively. Suffice it to say that the greater the energy, the more penetrating the radiation, especially with beta, gamma and X-radiation.

A summary of the hazards is given in Table 3.1, the degree of hazard depending very much on the quantities of activity involved and the energy of the particular radiation.

TABLE 3.1
Hazards associated with ionizing radiation

Type of radiation	Degree of hazard	
	Internal	*External*
α alpha	high	nil
β beta	medium	medium
γ gamma	low	high
X neutron	nil	high

One other important property in determining the degree of hazard associated with a particular radioactive material is the length of time it takes to decay to a stable non-radioactive state. Obviously materials that lose their radioactivity in say minutes or hours will in general be less hazardous than those that remain radioactive for years or centuries.

One way of measuring this property is by a concept called *half-life*. This was introduced by Rutherford in 1904, and the half-life is formally defined as the time required for a radioactive substance to lose 50 per cent of its activity by radioactive decay. Suppose, for the sake of illustration, that a particular radioelement has a half-life of one hour. Starting with one gram of the element, one half, i.e. 0.5 gram, will have disintegrated by the end of one hour, so that 0.5 gram remains. During the next hour, one half of this amount, i.e. 0.25 gram, will disintegrate, leaving 0.25 gram. By the end of the third hour, another 0.125 gram will have decayed, and so on. In each successive hour the actual amount which disintegrates is less than in the preceding hour, although it is always the same fraction of the amount present at the beginning of that particular hour.

Figure 3.1 shows the pattern of radioactive decay. It is called an exponential curve.

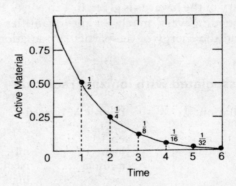

Fig. 3.1   Radioactive decay, illustrating the principle of half-life.

In general it takes ten half-lives for a substance to decay to one-thousandth of its original activity, and twenty half-lives to drop to one millionth.

Each radioactive substance has its own unique half-life, which ranges from millionths of a second (radon-215) to billions of years (uranium-238). One way of determining the nature of a particular unknown radioelement is to measure its radioactive decay rate, so finding its half-life. This can be compared with tables of known half-lives to ascertain the unknown substance.

EFFECTS OF RADIATION ON PEOPLE

We can finally get round to discussing what happens when ionizing radiation interacts with people.

The basis of all biological material, including humans, is the cell, consisting essentially of a cell wall, cytoplasm and nucleus. In man, the average diameter of the cell is between 0.01 and 0.05 millimetre. The cell nucleus contains the chromosomes, which in turn contain the genetic code in the form of deoxyribonucleic acid (DNA). It is the genetic code, in the form of the double helix made famous by the work of Crick and Watson, that contains the information that governs the cell's behaviour. There are 46 chromosomes in the human cell, normally visible only at cell division. The information contained in sex cells determines the make-up of parents' offspring, i.e. tall parents are more likely to have tall children because of the genetic coding of the parents' cells.

Experiments with microbeams of radiation have shown that it is the nucleus which is most easily damaged by radiation, and the cell is much more radiosensitive during the process of cell division known as mitosis, rather than in the so-called resting state. Cell reproduction occurs in two ways, known as *mitosis* and *meiosis*. The mitotic cells are the ordinary cells in the body, and in mitosis the chromosomes duplicate themselves by splitting lengthwise. The original cell divides into two new cells, each identical to the original.

Meiosis is the special kind of division which occurs in the formation of sexual reproduction cells, i.e. the sperm in males and the ovum in females.

For our purposes we can consider the cell as really just a bag of water. The ionizing radiation passing through the cell splits the water into H and OH (instead of H_2O). These H and OH radicals, as they are called, now act like chemical poisons within the cell. The effect upon a single cell can be:

1. Death of a cell due to either loss of respiratory ability or severe damage to the chromosomes.

2. Delay in the process of mitosis so that normal replacement of cells in the living organism is affected.

3. Chromosome damage which can be either:
   (a) loss of chromosomes
   (b) gene damage leading to an alteration of the genetic blueprint so that incorrect information is passed on to future generations of cells.

If this occurs in sex cells, the result can be mutations in the offspring of the irradiated parent. In Kerala, India, where the background radiation levels are much above the world average due to thorium in the soil, Down's syndrome, inappropriately named mongolism, is also above world average levels due to chromosome damage. If the genetic damage occurs in non-sex cells, the alteration to the blueprint can cause the cell to divide in an uncontrolled fashion, a characteristic of cancer. Herein lies one of the paradoxes of ionizing radiation. Judicious use of radiation can often stop a cancerous growth by inhibiting mitosis in the affected cells. On the other hand, radiation exposure of healthy cells can initiate tumour growth by damaging the genetic material in the cell nucleus.

When the whole body is irradiated, the situation is much more complicated. We know that cells undergoing mitosis are more easily damaged by radiation than resting cells. In general, we can say that, the more simple a cell is and the more frequently it divides, the more radiosensitive it is. This probably explains why certain tissues in the body are more prone to radiation damage than others. Thus, in the adult human, the most radiosensitive tissues are the blood-forming organs (red bone marrow), the gonads (sex organs) and the lymphatic glands. It is also the reason why children are more prone to radiation damage than adults and why the foetus is particularly radiosensitive—mitosis is taking place at a very rapid rate.

In considering the biological effects of radiation certain important distinctions are made. The *somatic* effects of radiation are those that appear in persons irradiated, and can include leukaemia, various forms of cancer and life shortening. The *genetic* effects are those that appear in the offspring of the person or persons irradiated. Experiments with animals and fruit flies have shown it can be several generations after the irradiation takes place before the effects show up.

The *acute* effects of radiation occur after a large single dose of radiation given in a short period of time. They can range from nausea to death within a short period of time or effects such as cancer that appear many years after the exposure occurred.

The effects of *chronic* irradiation are due to small incremental doses given over a long period of time. The effects range from life shortening to cancer of various types as well as genetic effects.

The actual effects produced depends on a number of factors including:

1. *Size of dose received*. If the dose of radiation is large ($\simeq 600$ rems) and is received by the whole body in the space of a few minutes, a severe and possibly fatal illness is likely to develop within a few hours and certainly within a few weeks. Some of those who survive this early illness may die several weeks later from one of the other effects of radiation such as anaemia. Exposure of the whole body to the same dose of radiation spread over a period of months or years will not cause the early illness, but there may still be an increased risk of death from the delayed effects.

2. *Extent of body irradiated*. If only a fraction of the body is irradiated, as in radiotherapy, immediate general effects are rare, although some patients may develop a mild form of the early illness known as 'radiation sickness'. It is often necessary to give a large dose locally and there may be local reaction in the irradiated area with temporary reddening of the skin or blistering, similar to that which occurs in sunburn.

3. *Part of body irradiated.* Experience has shown that there is a difference in the general effects of radiation according to the part of the body irradiated. Even quite a large dose ($\simeq 200$ rems) given to a portion of a limb will usually produce no general ill effects, whereas a similar dose directed to a similar volume of tissue in the upper abdomen, for example, may produce severe radiation sickness in a few hours.

4. *Type of radiation.* The severity of effects produced by radiation may also depend to some extent upon the type of radiation concerned, because radiations differ in their powers of penetration and in their biological effects. For example, fast neutrons are about thirty times more effective than X- or gamma rays in causing cataracts in the lens of the eye, although these three forms of radiation differ very little (dose for dose) in their capacity to cause the early acute form of radiation sickness after whole body irradiation.

Table 3.2 shows the somatic effects of acute whole body irradiation and the lesser effects experienced when only the skin is irradiated. (Explanatory notes for this table appear on p. 84.)

TABLE 3.2
Somatic effects of acute whole body and skin irradiation

Effect due to whole body irradiation	Dose equivalent (rems)	Effect due to skin irradiation
Reduction in lymphocyte count. [a]	25	
Temporary nausea. [b]	100	
Nausea, diarrhoea within a few hours. Reduction in certain blood cell counts. Loss of hair. A few people may die due to failure of blood-forming organs.	350	
Similar symptoms but more severe: up to half exposed group may die due to failure of blood-forming organs. $(LD_{50})_{30}$ dose. [c]	400	
	500	Loss of hair
Symptoms even more severe. Majority sick within half an hour. Death within 2-3 weeks due to loss of vital body fluids through damage to intestine wall.	600	Redness of the skin
	1000	
Death within a few days due to damage of central nervous system. [d]	1200	
	1600	Peeling of the skin. Radiation burns although similar in appearance to heat burns take longer to develop and are slower to heal.

Notes to Table 3.2:

[a]This is the lowest level at which biological effects can be detected by microscopic examination of blood samples.

[b]The lowest dose at which the irradiated person notices any effects, 'radiation sickness'.

[c]$(LD_{50})_{30}$ is short for 'Lethal dose for 50 per cent of the exposed population within a period of 30 days'.

[d]If the reader anticipates getting a dose of radiation this is the one recommended. You are unconscious within a short while and die within a few days, without a long period of illness harrowing to both the patient's relatives and attendants.

The course of sickness following a median dose is shown in Table 3.3.

TABLE 3.3
Symptoms observed at various times after exposure to a dose of 400-600 rems

Time after exposure	Symptoms observed
0-48 hours	Loss of appetite, nausea, vomiting, fatigue and prostration.
2 days to 2-3 weeks	The above symptoms disappear and the patient appears quite well.
2-3 weeks to 6-8 weeks	Purpura and haemorrhage, diarrhoea, loss of hair (epilation), fever and severe lethargy. It is during this period that fatalities occur.
6-8 weeks to several months	This is the recovery stage during which surviving patients begin to show a general improvement and the severe symptoms tend to disappear.

The long-term effects of irradiation of either the whole body or specific organs, such as eyes or thyroid, are shown in

Table 3.4. These effects can show up after either acute or chronic irradiation. Thus, after a bomb test, the effects shown could be expected in both those personnel who received a large dose at the time of the explosion and those who spent some days or weeks in areas of high fallout during post explosion clean up.

TABLE 3.4
Some long-term effects of radiation

Effect	Mean latent period	Evidence
Leukaemia	8-10 years	Atomic bomb casualties. Medical X-ray treatment.
Bone cancer	15 years	Radium luminous dial painters.
Thyroid cancer	15-30 years	Atomic bomb casualties. Medical treatment.
Lung cancer	10-20 years	Mine workers.
Life shortening		Experiments with mice.
Cataract formation	5-10 years	Atomic bomb casualties.

It is not possible to determine beforehand which people are most susceptible to damage from radiation. If one hundred people were each given a dose of 500 rems, there is no way of knowing which 50 or so would die and which 50 would survive. Nor is there any way of predicting which of the surviving 50 will eventually develop which disease. Coupled with the fact that cancer or leukaemia caused by radiation appears to the physician to be just the same as the cancer or leukaemia occurring in some other way, it makes the job of determining whether a particular case was caused by radiation or not rather difficult. The parallels with cigarette smoking are obvious. If a heavy smoker dies of lung cancer, the probability is that the smoking caused the cancer. Not certain, but probable. If somebody exposed to relatively high levels of radiation dies of cancer, it is probable the radiation caused the cancer. Probable, but not certain. The study of such cases has led to a whole new field of medical mathematics—called epidemiology. Because the study of such effects has to deal with probabilities not certainties, it provides loopholes for both cigarette manufacturers and nuclear power promoters— loopholes they are only too happy to exploit.

There are whole libraries of reports, books, articles, pamphlets on the biological effects of ionizing radiation. The two of highest repute are the reports of the United Nations Scientific Committee on the Effects of Atomic Radiation (UNSCEAR) and the Biological Effects of Ionizing Radiation (BEIR), reports prepared by a committee of the National Academy of Science in the United States.

The third BEIR report in 1978 gave these estimates of cancer risk based on a dose of one rem: between 192 and 756 cancers for every million males exposed and between 344 and 1306 cancers for every million females exposed, with between 70 and 353 cancer deaths per rem per million people exposed. The number would be the same if 100 000 people each received 10 rems or 10 000 000 people each received 0.1 rem. The population radiation burden, as it is called, is a product of the number of people exposed multiplied by the average dose they received.

The genetic effects (damage to the hereditary material of the cell) are not so easy to quantify. Offspring receive a complete set of genetic material from each parent. Thus a child receives two complementary sets of genes, one from each of its parents. In general, one gene is 'dominant' and the other 'recessive'. The dominant gene determines the particular characteristic with which it is associated, for example, eye colour.

Radiation can induce gene mutations which are indistinguishable from naturally occurring mutations, and which are generally recessive and so it is generally assumed that all mutations are harmful as the pool of recessive genetic damage can be carried on for several generations. Some radiobiologists now argue that many and perhaps most human diseases, including cancer, are related to a genetic factor. One of the first investigators into the mutagenic effects of radiation was H. J. Muller back in the 1920s. He suggested that there were 10 000 non-visible or small mutations that result from each observed mutation. Muller emphasised that in the long run these small mutations, which result in a lack of vigour, susceptibility to disease, a slight reduction in mentality and physique etc, may be a far greater burden to society than the easily identifiable dominant mutations. This is because the small mutations are eliminated so slowly from the gene pool.

During the early years of the atomic age, it was generally assumed that the genetic risk from low level radiation exposure far exceeded the risks of chronic somatic damage, such as cancer or life shortening. However, it has become increasingly clear that this assumption may be unwarranted and untenable. As the BEIR Committee pointed out:

> Until recently, it has been taken for granted that genetic risks from exposure of populations to ionizing radiation near background levels (about 100 millirems) per year were of much greater import than were somatic risks. However, this assumption can no longer be made if linear non-threshold relationships are accepted as a basis for estimating cancer risks.

The Committee then went on to supply many pages of data, most of which support the linear hypothesis. In 1971, the International Commission on Radiological Protection (ICRP) made a similar observation:

> It could be concluded that the ratio of somatic to genetic effects after a given exposure is sixty times greater than was thought 15 years ago.

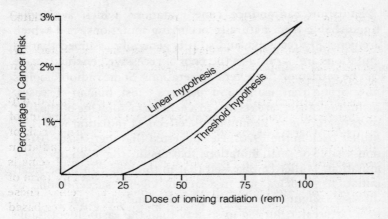

Fig. 3.2: The differences between the concept of threshold dose and linear dose-effect relationship.

This increasing evidence about the greater risk of cancer from exposure to low levels of ionizing radiation comes from many sources. One is the controversial study of the causes of death among workers at the spent nuclear reprocessing plant at Hanford on the west coast of the United States. The report, published in September 1977, is entitled 'Radiation Exposures of Hanford Workers Dying from Cancer and Other Causes'. The authors are Thomas Mancuso, Alice Stewart and George Kneale. In his foreword, Dr Mancuso made the point that the research contract was established in 1965 and the US Atomic Energy Commission kept pressing him to publish his findings, while they appeared to show no increase in cancer deaths among Hanford workers. (Hanford is the longest operating reprocessing plant, having started in 1944 to produce plutonium for the US nuclear weapons programme.) Mancuso refused premature publication, arguing that the latency period for cancer production required several decades of study. When his data began to show a positive correlation between radiation exposure and cancer production, his research grant was cut off and the project transferred to Oak Ridge Associated Universities.

Mancuso published nevertheless, in the respected international radiation protection journal *Health Physics* in November 1977.

In the Hanford study, a total of 3250 cases were studied, 670 of these died of cancer. Estimates were made of the amount of radiation that would be needed to double the normal risk of developing any of the cancers known to have definite radiation associations. According to Mancuso's estimates, 12.2 rems is sufficient to double the normal risk of dying from any form of cancer. For lung cancer it is even lower, 6.1 rems. These doubling doses are so much lower than those estimates based on the Hiroshima and Nagasaki survivors that they have not gone unchallenged.

Mancuso's work on Hanford is only part of the steadily accumulating evidence. Dr Thomas Najarian of Boston Veterans' Hospital (USA) found that 38.4 per cent of nuclear workers at the Portsmouth Naval Shipyard (USA) died of cancer. The comparable level for non-radiation workers was 21.7 per cent, while the US national average is 18 per cent.

The finding was based on a survey of 1722 death certificates and interviews with 592 next of kin. Najarian has been unable to review the radiation exposure records of the nuclear workers because the US Navy, which runs the Portsmouth Yard, has repeatedly refused to release the relevant documents.

Radiation work began at the Portsmouth Naval Shipyard in 1959 with the overhaul of the USS *Nautilus*, the first US nuclear submarine in operation. Since then, up to 5000 civilian employees have been exposed to radiation. In line with the 1966 exposure standard laid down by the International Commission on Radiological Protection (ICRP), the US Navy has limited the amount of radiation to which each employee is exposed at the shipyard to 5 rems for each year. The navy maintains that no shipyard worker has ever accumulated more than 40 rems.

Maralinga

The Portsmouth study showed not only that the shipyard's workers had a cancer mortality twice as high as the national average, but also that the rate of leukaemia was 450 per cent higher than that of the general population. Also, the incidence of lymph gland cancers was 125 per cent higher than the national rate. The most startling statistics concerned mortality among workers aged 60-69. In this age group, nearly 60 per cent of the nuclear employees had died of cancer, while the cancer death rate among non-nuclear workers was 26 per cent. Moreover, the high death rate for nuclear workers has remained relatively steady since 1959, ranging from 43 per cent in the 1960s to 37 per cent for 1976–77. This is perhaps surprising because radiation-induced cancers usually do not appear until many years after exposure.

In August 1957, the US Army arranged for 3153 soldiers to witness the explosion of a 48 kilotonne atomic bomb code-named 'Smoky'. The aim was to test the psychological and physiological reaction of the men involved. The men were shielded from the direct blast of the bomb and exposed to only about one to two rems of fallout. There is now evidence of a high incidence of leukaemia among the men exposed. To date, there have been eight deaths from the disease traced so far, when only two would have been expected in the members of the exposed group.

This data is of great relevance to what happened at Maralinga. The effects on the people who lived close to the Nevada testing site will be discussed later in this chapter (see p. 99).

The Australian experience, based on radiation exposures of underground miners at the Radium Hill uranium mine, although based on a small sample, is in line with overseas findings. An analysis of cause of death was carried out as a pilot study on a group of 600 people who had worked at Radium Hill. The information was obtained from the South Australian Register of Deaths.

TABLE 3.5
Preliminary findings of the Radium Hill study

	Total deaths	Cancer deaths				
		Lung	Respiratory	Digestive	Other	All
Above ground	20	1 (5.0%)	—	2	—	3 (15.0%)
Underground 1-12 months	16	1 (6.3%)	1	1	—	3 (18.8%)
Underground more than 12 months	22	6 (27.3%)	—	2	1	9 (40.9%)
Compared with:						
Australian miners (1968-75)		5.9%				17.8%

Details of the six cases of pulmonary cancer found among miners who had worked underground for more than 12 months are:

Usual job	Age at death	Latency years
Miner	45	16
Shift boss	69	20
Miner	50	18
Labourer	68	24
Storeman	41	9
Miner	60	21

In January 1980, figures released by the South Australian Health Commission showed that the incidence of lung cancer had risen threefold since the 1950s and is now claiming more deaths than all other types of cancer. The figures showed that the cancer rate in South Australia had risen faster than in any other State. Whether or not this increase is related to the testing of nuclear weapons in South Australia is hard to say, but while the Federal Government continues to reject calls for a comprehensive inquiry, such data can only add to the air of uncertainty that surrounds the whole question.

Other important data have come from people who were exposed to X-ray radiation in medical practice. Increased leukaemia has been found among men irradiated to relieve the pain of the spinal disease ankolysing spondylitis, and higher levels of cancer especially leukaemia have been found among children irradiated while still in their mothers' wombs.

The accumulating evidence of the effects of exposure to low levels of ionizing radiation has already led to calls for a reduction in the permissible levels of radiation exposure. At the February 1978 Congressional hearings on low level radiation, Chairman Edward Radford said that the BEIR Committee had erred in 1972 and, in certain cases, the permissible levels were set at least ten times too high. He went on:

> The absolute risk estimate for total cancer incidence is probably at least twice as great as was estimated in 1972.

In a carefully considered article on cancer and low level ionizing radiation, published in the September 1978 *Bulletin of the Atomic Scientist,* Karl Morgan, one of America's most senior and respected health physicists, suggested a halving of permissible doses with a reduction by a further factor of five to be considered at some later date.

The whole history of maximum permissible levels has been one of steady reductions. Table 3.6 shows how the figures have changed, from 1925 when the first limits were suggested, to the current figures recommended by the International Commission on Radiological Protection, the body that sets the figures.

TABLE 3.6

Changes in levels of permissible exposure to ionizing radiation

Recommended values		Date	Recommended by
For radiation workers			
0.1 erythema dose/yr	52 R/yr	1925	A. Mutscheller, R. M. Sievert
(1 R/wk for 200 kV X-ray)			
		1934	IRCP (used world-wide until 1950)
0.1 R/day (or 0.5 R/wk)	36 R/yr	1934	NCRP
0.3 rem/wk	15 rem/yr	1949	NCRP
		1950	ICRP (for total body exposure)
5 rem/yr	5 rem/yr	1956	ICRP
		1957	NCRP (for total body exposure)
For members of the public			
0.03 rem/wk	1.5 rem/yr	1952	NCRP (suggested, for any body organ)
0.5 rem/yr	0.5 rem/yr	1958	NCRP (suggested)
		1959	ICRP (suggested, for gonads or total body)
5 rem/30 yr	0.17 rem/yr	1958	ICRP (suggested for gonads or total body)
25 mrem/yr	0.025 rem/yr	1977	EPA (suggested for any body organ except thyroid)[a]
5 mrem/yr	0.005 rem/yr	1974	ERDA (suggested for persons living near a nuclear power plant)[b]

Note to table 3.6

R	=	roentgen (1R = 0.88 rem)
rem	=	roentgen equivalent man
mrem	=	millirem
NCRP	=	National Council on Radiation Protection and Measurements
ICRP	=	International Commission of Radiological Protection

[a]The limit set by the Environmental Protection Agency for the thyroid was 0.075 rem per year.

[b]Present radiation protection guide of the Nuclear Regulatory Commission (US successor to the US Atomic Energy Commission)

So it was about the time of maximum weapons testing in the atmosphere, the late 1950s, that major reductions of acceptable levels for radiation workers took place. Overall, the permissible level for workers has fallen by a factor of 10, and for members of the public by a factor of 300.

The long-term problem with atmospheric bomb tests arises from the fact that they throw radioactive materials into the atmosphere. These sink slowly back to earth. They get into food and water, and then into people. In other words, they give rise to an internal radiation hazard.

When radioactive elements are taken into the body, they behave just as their non-radioactive siblings and each element has a preference for a particular part of the body. Iodine concentrates in the thyroid gland, uranium in the kidneys, strontium and radium in bone, and so on. In its recommendations on maximum permissible levels for internal exposure, ICRP gives a list of what are called permissible body or organ burdens, the maximum amount of radioactive material allowed in a particular organ. They are based on the concept of a particular amount of radioactive material in an organ giving a particular dose of radiation to it. Some typical body burdens of important radioisotopes are given in Table 3.7, taken from ICRP Publication 2, 1959.

Top: Erecting a warning sign in the desert north of Maralinga in March 1957.

f Abo izines photographed in October 1956 at Giles

Staff Sgt Smith steam cleans gerry cans contaminated during tests.

TABLE 3.7
Selected maximum permissible body burdens

Radioisotope and type of decay	Critical organ	mpbb in μCi
Tritium	Body tissue	1000
Carbon-14	Fat	300
Strontium-90	Bone	22
Iodine-131	Thyroid	0.7
Caesium-137	Total body	30
Radium-226	Bone	0.1
Natural uranium	Kidney	0.005
Plutonium-239	Bone	0.04

The Commission does not give figures for internal irradiation of members of the public but it is generally assumed that levels one tenth of those given above would apply.

In its 1977 recommendations, the International Commission (ICRP 26) allows for joint consideration of the effects of internal and external doses. It moved the basis for calculating maximum exposure levels away from consideration of 'critical organ' doses—based on maximum acceptable doses to organs most susceptible to a particular radioisotope—to a method which calculates a general level of risk by integrating the risks posed to various parts of the body. The integrated risks are weighted to allow for the radiosensitivity of the various organs and their biological importance. This is a major advance in the thinking about radiation hazards and shows that concepts and ideas in this field are constantly being reviewed and often changed. The historical treatment of internal and external levels has been discussed because that was the thinking among health physicists at the time of the Maralinga tests.

It is important to remember that there have been three major changes since the mid-1950s. They are:

1. The concept of a dose of radiation below which no effects

occur, the so-called 'threshold dose', is no longer valid. Some diehards will doubtless still argue that there is such a dose, but then again it is still possible to find people who believe Bishop Ussher's claim that the world started in 4004 B.C.

2. A much greater emphasis on the need to keep all exposures 'as low as reasonably achievable'. The ICRP's recommendations are for MAXIMUM permissible exposures. Twenty years ago, such figures were often called 'tolerance doses'—the idea being that the body could 'tolerate' such levels.

3. The integration of internal and external exposure risk estimates.

These changes have lead to a greater awareness of the need for radiation protection for both occupationally exposed personnel and members of the public.

We quite rightly regard the practices of the past to be somewhat loose. No responsible health physicist would recommend that pilots fly directly into clouds of fallout to take samples, or allow servicemen to hose down contaminated aeroplanes wearing only shorts and singlets. This prompts a question about our present practices, which we now smugly consider to be quite acceptable as people in the 1950s thought their procedures acceptable. Will the next generation of health physicists look with disdain at the things we do now and the levels of radiation we let people receive?

No matter what future generations may think of us, we are most certainly entitled to look back in anger at the criminal way the nuclear arms race was conducted in the 1950s. For a time it seemed as if the Americans and the Russians, followed swiftly by the British, French and Chinese, were trying to institute an international birth control programme based on fallout. Bomb after bomb, bigger and bigger, on they went, contaminating mainly the northern hemisphere, but Britain used Australia to ensure the southern hemisphere didn't feel left out. What was good enough for Britain, became good enough for France. After they could no longer use the Algerian

desert, the French used Polynesia for their new nuclear playground—yet another paradise lost.

Each explosion injected more and more radioactive material into the atmosphere (it was not until 1958 that any significant number of underground or underwater explosions took place). In 1957, a total of 40 atmospheric explosions took place, rising to 84 in 1958. There was a lull in 1959. France got into the act in 1960 with three tests, and in 1962 another 79 nuclear bombs were let off in the atmosphere. The Russians exploded 41 and the Americans 38. In that year, the Americans exploded 88 nuclear bombs of one sort or another, and altogether the world rocked to a total of 133 nuclear explosions let off by four different countries. That year, 1962, was also the year Kennedy threatened the Russians with nuclear annihilation if they insisted on installing nuclear armed missiles in Cuba. Khrushchev, to his credit, recalled the fleet carrying the missiles westward, and the world survived another crisis in brinkmanship. What is certain is that, if nuclear war had started, the generals on both sides had had plenty of practice at getting bigger and better bangs for their money.

Table 3.8 on page 98 shows the total atmospheric tests up until 1980. Only China continues to flout the atmospheric test ban treaty.

Weapons testing finally brought public involvement into the area of nuclear policy. After tests in the Pacific, in 1946 and 1948, the United States Atomic Energy Commission established a testing site in the Nevada desert where atmospheric tests continued until 1963. Even the first series of tests in 1951 caused problems. Radioactive fallout contaminated straw used for packing photographic film. The radiation fogged the film, much to the annoyance of Eastman Kodak. The USAEC agreed to notify Kodak of fallout patterns that could affect their film, but astonishingly little attention appears to have been paid to the effects of fallout on people. In its thirteenth report in 1953 the AEC noted:

> Fallout radioactivity is far below the level which could cause a detectable increase in mutations or inheritable variations.

TABLE 3.8
Atmospheric explosions

Date	USA	USSR	UK	France	China
1945	3				
1946	1				
1947					
1948	3				
1949		1			
1950					
1951	15	2			
1952	10		1		
1953	11	2	2		
1954	6	2			
1955	31	4			
1956	14	7	6		
1957	26	13	7		
1958	53	26	5		
1959					
1960				3	
1961		30		1	
1962	38	41			
1963					
1964					1
1965					1
1966				5	3
1967				3	2
1968				5	1
1969					1
1970				8	1
1971				5	1
1972				3	2
1973				5	1
1974				7	1
1975					
1976					3
1977					1
1978					2
1979					
1980					1

It suggested that the only possible hazard to humans who ate animals that had been grazing on grass contaminated by strontium-90 would arise from

> the ingestion of bone splinters which might be intermingled with muscle tissue during butchering and cutting of the meat.

This overlooked completely the fact that strontium, which is chemically similar to calcium, can be transferred from grass to people via the milk of grazing cows.

The body cannot distinguish between calcium and strontium, so the latter gets readily incorporated into bone where it can irradiate the particularly radiosensitive bone marrow.

The significance of fallout really hit home in 1953. On 25 April, the USAEC let off a 43 kilotonne blast at Yucca Flats in Nevada. The test, which was code-named 'Simon', was an atmospheric test, detonated at a height of 100 metres above the ground. The radioactive mushroom cloud rose to a height of about ten kilometres, then proceeded to drift north-east. Two days later, over northern New York State, it met a violent thunderstorm which washed much of the radioactivity down to earth. Some radiochemistry students in Troy (NY) found their geiger counters giving much higher readings than normal. Outdoor readings were even higher, especially near rainwater. The students' teacher, Professor Clark, called a colleague in the USAEC Health and Safety Laboratory in New York City and a major survey was started.

The report was classified, presumably with the erroneous idea that what the people do not know will not hurt them. All the public was told was that from 35 to 70 curies of fallout had been deposited per square kilometre around Albany and Troy.

Nearer to the test site, the citizens of St George in Utah and Las Vegas in Nevada were getting far more than their fair share of fallout, but in the main accepted the bland reassurances of their elected officials and their tame scientists that all was well. They had no reason to believe otherwise — this was well before the days of Watergate and the widespread development of public cynicism about the statements, motives and intentions of the governing to the governed.

However, the lid could not be kept on the simmering pot for ever and, in 1954, the question of nuclear weapons fallout became an international issue. The Americans had first exploded a hydrogen device—it could not be called a bomb as it consisted of over 60 tonnes of delicate equipment—on 1 November 1952. On 12 August 1953, the Russians let off a truly portable, droppable H-bomb. The American reply was the Castle Bravo test, a fission-fusion-fission bomb. It was expected to produce the equivalent of about seven million tonnes of TNT (seven megatonnes). In the event it yielded 15 megatonnes. It was exploded at Bikini (from which the miniscule swimsuit gets its name) on 1 March 1954. The three inhabited islands of Utirik, Rongerik and Rongelap are about 140 kilometres east of Bikini. Wind, blowing in a direction not anticipated by the bomb testers, carried the fallout all the way to the islands. On 11 March, the USAEC issued one of their all too familiar, soothing, reassuring press statements.

> During the course of a routine atomic test in the Marshall Islands, twenty-eight United States personnel and 236 residents were transported from neighbouring atolls to Kwajalein Island according to plan as a precautionary measure. These individuals were unexpectedly exposed to some radioactivity. There were no burns. All were reported well. After the completion of the atomic tests, the natives will be returned to their homes.

The 'plan', of course, was only developed after the explosion, and an 'atomic test' which was twice as big as expected could hardly be classed as routine.

The victims sustained beta burns, spotty epilations of the head, skin lesions, pigment changes and scarring. And many of the natives did not feel well at all. They suffered from anorexia (appetite depression), nausea, vomiting and transient reduction in some blood cell counts. Over the next 16 years, twenty-one of the natives on Rongelap Island would develop thyroid abnormalities and thyroidectomies would be conducted on eighteen of them. All but two of the nineteen children who were less than ten years old when the accident happened developed thyroid abnormalities; and two of them were dwarfed for life. The first of the islanders to die was Lekoj Anjain, who contracted leukaemia and died in 1972 at the age of 19. Rongelap was uninhabitable for over three years after the Castle Bravo test; such was the level of contamination from the 'routine atomic test'.

The attempt to play down the significance of the drastic miscalculation came unstuck within a month when the name Lucky Dragon echoed around the world. The *Fukurya Maru*, to give it its Japanese name, was a small trawler that had been fishing for tuna just outside the test exclusion zone to the east of Bikini. The fishermen thought the sun had risen in the west that morning. This disconcerting omen was followed a few hours later by a strange white ash that settled over the boat and crew. By evening, two of the crew were vomiting, and three days later most of the others shared similar symptoms, along with itching skin and aching eyes. The captain ordered the boat home to port in Yaizu. When it arrived a fortnight later, all the crew were suffering from what was then diagnosed as radiation sickness. The boat was still contaminated from what was now found to be radioactive fallout.The radio-operator, who because his shack was above deck had received the highest radiation dose, died on 23 September 1954, so the Japanese yielded the first hydrogen bomb victim as well as the first A-bomb victims. But Aiticki Kuboyama did not die entirely in vain. The voyage of the ironically named *Lucky Dragon* alerted world opinion to the problems of radioactive fallout. It took another eight years, but eventually a ban on atmospheric tests was accepted by the major powers.

In 1955, the United Nations established a Scientific Committee to study the Effects of Atomic Radiation (UNSCEAR). They reviewed among other information some of the now partially declassified US data on fallout. Three important points emerged.

1. Fallout is deposited principally in the hemisphere of origin and not distributed world wide.

2. Much of it comes down within a few months, not remaining safely aloft while short half-life isotopes decay.
3. Most importantly, the fallout comes to earth in temperate middle latitudes where the bulk of the earth's population lives.

Two days before his death in 1955, Albert Einstein co-signed a manifesto drafted by Bertrand Russell calling on scientists of all nations to stop the nuclear madness. About the same time, Joseph Rotblat, now involved in the beneficial medical applications of nuclear science, organized a non-government scientific conference to seek a way off the nuclear treadmill. The meeting was held at Pugwash in Canada, and what came to be known as the Pugwash movement has been ever since a major contact area for scientists from both Eastern and Western blocs. Linus Pauling, he of the two Nobel Prizes and one withdrawn passport, drew up a petition—eventually signed by over 11 000 scientists in 48 countries—demanding a ban on nuclear tests. Protest was gradually building up.

In 1957, the USAEC finally got round to admitting fallout might be somewhat damaging. A report by the Biological and Medical Advisory Committee concluded that the fallout from the bomb tests up to the end of 1956 could produce between 2500 and 13 000 major genetic effects per year in the world's population. Critics were quick to point out that this was almost certainly a serious underestimate of the biological damage fallout was causing. Pauling showed that the USAEC had ignored carbon-14, and iodine-131 was often overlooked in monitoring surveys because of its relatively short eight-day half-life.

In its triennial reports UNSCEAR produced graphs showing global inventories of fallout going up and up. At Harwell the Health Physics Division Conference Room had a wall chart with strontium-90 levels indicated. Certain far-sighted members of the staff were already expressing concern about the steadily increasing levels. These feelings were lost on a young trainee health physicist (F. P. J. R.) as well as most of the public, but a fire at the Windscale plutonium-producing reactor awakened many more people to the hazards of radioactive contamination.

In May 1957, a British hydrogen bomb was exploded at Christmas Island in the Pacific Ocean. Maralinga had served its purpose; an atomic trigger had obviously been devised in the mainland tests and Britain joined the 'super' league. A few months later, J. B. Priestley wrote an article in the *New Statesman* arguing that Britain should give up its nuclear weapons as a positive contribution to ending the insane rush to a nuclear apocalypse. This was the first major call for what became known as Unilateral Disarmament. Priestley's article, although couched in rather extreme terms—he talked about 'three glasses too many of vodka or of bourbon on the rocks, and the wrong button may be pushed'—produced over 1000 supporting letters to the editor, Kingsley Martin. Using these letters as a base of interested and concerned people, a public meeting was called at Central Hall, Westminster. The Canon of St Paul's Cathedral, Rev John Collins, chaired the meeting. Over 2000 people attended and the Campaign for Nuclear Disarmament was off and running.

Another group of pacifists was already planning direct action. One member of the group, Harold Steele, flew to Christmas Island with the announced intention of sailing a boat into the test area. He arrived too late but his idea has certainly been used with varying success by others, ranging from anti-nuclear to anti-whaling groups. The group also planned a four-day march during the 1958 Easter holidays from London to Aldermaston, the weapons research centre. The response overwhelmed the organizers—5000 set out from Trafalgar Square and 10 000 assembled outside the Aldermaston wire to listen to speeches from Canon Collins, left-wing MP Michael Foot and Pastor Martin Niemoller from Germany.

'Ban the Bomb' was the theme and the CND symbol soon became internationally famous. It was formed from the semaphore signals for N and D, Nuclear and Disarmament. One of the marchers was an American negro civil rights leader Bayard Rustin. He was enormously impressed with the power of the demonstration and the opportunity it gave to people to show directly their concern about a particular issue. He took the message to the US and the Aldermaston march became the inspiration for the American Civil Rights marches. By 1960 there were CND marches in 20 other countries.

On the political front, the 1960 British Labour Party Annual Conference voted for unilateral disarmament. The party was in the middle of its thirteen-year spell in opposition, so the vote had no real effect except to cause massive internal dissension within the Party. The vote was reversed at the 1961 conference, after the Party leader, Hugh Gaitskell, had fought and fought to change the 1960 vote. Just twenty years later, at its 1980 Conference, the British Labour Party again voted to renounce nuclear weapons. Whether it can carry its unilateral policy into government remains to be seen.

Michael Foot, who addressed the first Aldermaston rally, was then leader of the Party (once again in opposition) and on 26 October 1980 over 80 000 people assembled in Trafalgar Square for a disarmament rally. It is encouraging to see that the British pacifist conscience is at least still alive and well. The second half of 1981 has seen an enormous revival of anti-nuclear feeling. Most European capital cities have been the scene of massive marches and rallies, protesting against the continuing insane build-up of nuclear armaments.

The moral questions surrounding nuclear weapons, their production and, therefore, potential use, are too great to be left undebated. In Australia, the anti-nuclear weapons movement had nothing like the force or strength of its British counterpart, which is surprising because it was here that the early bombs had been tested. In a 1957 parliamentary debate, Doctor Evatt called for a complete ban on nuclear weapons testing, mainly as a result of increasing concern over hydrogen bomb tests and, by association, all nuclear weapons, but it was a call that fell on deaf Liberal-Country Party ears. There were some anti-Maralinga protests, and one bluestone wall in Batman Avenue, Melbourne, still bears the slogan 'Stop Maralinga—build homes not A-bombs'.

The British movement changed course and focus several times. Demonstrations were held at US nuclear submarine bases such as Holy Loch in Scotland. In London, Bertrand Russell led a large column of marchers to the Admiralty in Whitehall. There he solemnly stuck a petition on the door protesting against Britain being used as a base for American Polaris submarines.

The marches gradually faded away to be replaced by other causes—in the United States, civil rights and anti-Vietnam and, more recently, anti-nuclear power. The protest techniques used by the ban the bomb movement—marches, sitdowns, peaceful and not so peaceful demonstrations—have been copied by many subsequent pressure and would-be pressure groups. That movement was against a 'thing'; not against a war or a political party but against a device for causing mass destruction. It was a great exercise of conscience. It went largely unheeded by the politicians, with the brief exception of the Labour Party, and, in the sense that the world is still bound by the balance of terror, it failed. Not one country has renounced nuclear weapons once it has made them, and many countries still strive to get them. The major nuclear powers keep getting 'better' bombs and better delivery systems and the number of minor nuclear powers steadily creeps up.

The movement succeeded in two ways, however. The force of public opinion, allied to growing scientific concern, stopped most atmospheric tests. The movement also stirred many people into playing an active political role. The activist movements of the '60s and '70s owe more than they imagine to the Campaign for Nuclear Disarmament.

But here in Australia, an acquiescent government and a largely unconcerned population applauded each bomb test. Throughout the test period, newspapers carried glowing reports of the British activities in South Australia. They quoted unquestioningly the reassurances of the government and their scientific advisers that all was well. No problems from fallout, nobody at risk and really Australia was privileged to play host to bomb testers. How wrong they were will become apparent in later chapters as we discuss just what went on in the actual testing programme, the subsequent clean up and the mistakes that were made.

4

Maralinga:
Field of Thunder

> If atomic bombs are to be added to the arsenals of a warring
> world or to the arsenals of nations preparing for war, then the
> time will come when mankind will curse the names of Los
> Alamos and Hiroshima.

Thus spoke the prescient Oppenheimer at a ceremony marking
the presentation of an Army certificate of commendation to the
Los Alamos Laboratory. The presentation took place on 16
October 1945, two months after the Japanese surrender. If he
had been making the same speech today, Oppenheimer could
have quoted a longer list of accursed places: Novaya Zemlya,
Bikini, Lop Nor, Mururoa and Maralinga.

The Field of Thunder, which is a translation of the
Aboriginal word Maralinga, was not the first test site on
mainland Australia. That doubtful honour goes to Emu Field.
During the preparations for the Monte Bello test, arrangements
were already being made for the development of the Emu site.
A long-range reconnaissance party from the Woomera rocket
range, led by Len Beadell, had located some claypans in an
uninhabited (apart from nomadic Aborigines) area of the Great
Victoria Desert. The location was about some 250 km west of
the opal mining town of Coober Pedy in South Australia. One

claypan was about one and a half kilometres long, iron hard, and smooth as a billiard table, so aeroplanes could land on it easily. The area was also reasonably free of sandhills, so it was an ideal site (as such things go). This desolate bush became the scene of much frenzied activity during 1952 and 1953, with eventually a township of over 400 people living and working to the one end—as Beadell titled his book describing his discovery of the Emu and Maralinga sites—to 'blast the bush'. But what a blast—the effects of the radiation and radioactivity produced are still being felt by some of those who took part.

There were two tests at the Emu site on 15 and 27 October 1953. Even before the first of these tests, it had been decided that the inhospitality of the region and the high logistical costs involved made the location unsuitable as a permanent site. Somewhere nearer the trans-Australian railway line which arrowed its way westward across the Nullarbor desert was thought to be more suitable. Beadell was dispatched south to find another, perhaps more permanent site.

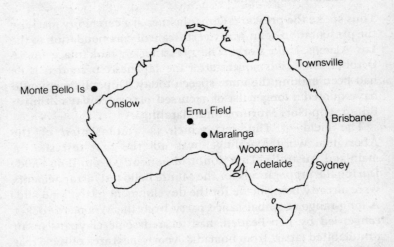

Fig. 4.1 ● = Major test sites used in Australia from 1953 to 1957.

While this site was being developed, two further tests were conducted in the Monte Bello Islands in 1956, one in May, the second in June. By September, Maralinga was ready, and four nuclear explosions occurred in quick succession, giving a total of six explosions in or close to Australia during that internationally troubled year. (It was the year of the brutal Russian intervention in Hungary and the 'Suez Crisis' when British and French forces invaded the Suez Canal Zone during one of the various rounds of the Israeli-Egyptian war.)

The site that became known to the world as Maralinga is on Tietkins Plains, about 240 kilometres east of the WA border and about 80 kilometres north of Watson, a siding and fettlers' base on the Transcontinental Railway. Tietkin and Giles had explored the area in the 1880s and 1890s. On the road from the present Maralinga police post in the old test camp hospital, to the firing range, one of Tietkin's wells is passed. Digging it must have been hard and unrewarding. It goes down over twelve metres and the shoring used is still in excellent condition, the well being dry. When one of the authors visited the site he was saddened to note it contained that ubiquitous symbol of modern civilization—a Coca-Cola can.

The plain is almost flat and is virtually free of scrub cover, which meant the visibility for the tests would be good. A barrier of sandhills separates Tietkins Plain from the Nullarbor Plain—this fact was used to provide security to the site. But this choice of a site relatively close to the coast, but north of the railway line, was to have some unfortunate consequences.

The layout of the Maralinga site is shown in Figure 4.2 (see p. 110). It became quite a thriving community. The maximum population was about 1000, over 90 kilometres of bitumen road were constructed, and an airfield with a 2500 metre bitumen runway was carved out of the bush. All that remains today is the airfield, the rather bare airport building, the base hospital used as the police headquarters and a few storage buildings. Those who knew Maralinga will be pleased to know that the 'Bridge of Sighs' is still intact. This is a small bridge over what was an ornamental pool at the front of the airfield reception centre. British National Servicemen sighed with agony as they crossed it before entering the building and starting their stint in the alien Australian bush. They sighed again with relief as they recrossed it twelve months or so later to fly back to Britain.

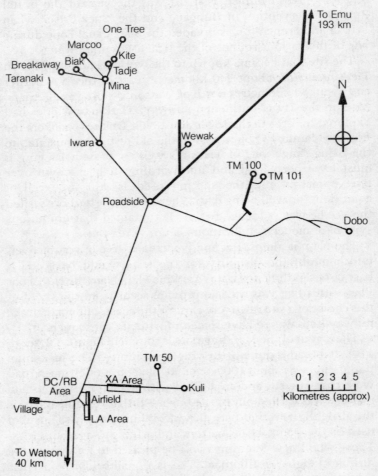

Fig. 4.2   Layout of the Maralinga site.

The major tests carried out during the nuclear weapons tests in 1956 and 1957 are listed in Table 4.1.

TABLE 4.1
Major trials conducted at Maralinga

Code name	Date	Platform	Yield
Buffalo series 1956			
One Tree	27 Sept.	tower	kilotonne range
Marcoo	4 Oct.	ground surface	low yield
Kite	11 Oct.	air drop	low yield
Breakaway	22 Oct.	tower	kilotonne range
Antler series 1957			
Tadje	14 Sept.	tower	low yield
Biak	25 Sept.	tower	kilotonne range
Taranaki	9 Oct.	balloon	kilotonne range

The seven nuclear explosions at Maralinga involved three different firing configurations, each of which imposed a characteristic, and different, behaviour on the close-in fallout. Thus two of the explosions, Kite and Taranaki, which were both airbursts, produced no significant close-in fallout and little or no evidence of these explosions remains at Maralinga. For one particular trial, Tadje, the close-in fallout was much richer in cobalt-60 as this nuclide had been incorporated in the trial. The official report says it had been included for 'diagnostic purposes'. What the cobalt-60 could diagnose that the abundant fallout could not, is hard to discern. It is much more likely the cobalt was included as a part of a study of a potential cobalt bomb, considered at one time to be the possible ultimate weapon.

For the four major trials conducted on towers—One Tree, Breakaway, Tadje and Biak—there was intensive activation of the soil around the towers caused by the massive flux of neutrons escaping from the explosion. In the ground surface explosion at Marcoo, neutron activation of the soil occurred and most of the ground area affected was removed and dispersed during the formation of the crater resulting from the explosion.

Thus all the radioactive materials we discussed in Chapter 3 (p. 95) were produced during the Maralinga tests—fission products from the bombs themselves and activation products from soil and tower construction materials irradiated by the massive surplus of neutrons from the bombs.

The layout of the village, firing range and its geographical relationship to the railway posed one very severe limitation on the bomb testers. They had to ensure that the fallout was blown north, north-east or north-west, but not under any circumstances south. This would contaminate the village, 15 kilometres away, make it uninhabitable and ruin all the expensive equipment.

There are two somewhat separate problems with fallout— the immediate, rather heavy, fallout downwind of the explosion, coming to earth within a few hours and kilometres of the blast, and the longer term return to earth of the material carried by the fireball high into the atmosphere. This radioactivity can take weeks, months or years to return to earth. Because the winds had to be southerlies or south-westerlies, it meant the long-term fallout was going to be blown over continental Australia and up towards the mining and pastoral towns of central Queensland. Putting the base village south of Watson and the firing range south of the village, would have meant the bombs could have been exploded when northerlies were blowing and they are not too uncommon. The radioactive clouds would then have been blown way down to Antarctica. The cloud would be so dilute and dispersed by the time it reached Antarctica, that it would not have posed too serious a threat to the penguins or the hardy scientists working there. The Antarctic continent does not have much fauna or flora, so the chances of any fallout entering man's food chain and being concentrated through it, as can occur in inhabited or agricultural areas, would have been much reduced.

It would be wrong for the reader to get the impression that things proceeded willy-nilly, with no thought for the consequences. There were two bodies set up following Federal Cabinet's approval of the 1954 agreement between the British and Australian Governments to establish the Maralinga test site. The Cabinet approval was given on 4 May 1955, and the two Australian committees formed were the Maralinga Committee, which met first on 9 May 1955 (either very good organization, or Cabinet approval had been taken as a foregone conclusion), and the Maralinga Safety Committee, which held its first meeting on 21 July 1955 under the Chairmanship of L. H. Martin, Professor of Physics at Melbourne University.

The Maralinga Committee later came to be known as the Maralinga Board of Management, and that pretty well describes its functions. Its main job was to co-ordinate the Australian response to the requirements of the UK team. The initial work was done by a private contractor (Kwinane Constructions), but from March 1956 onwards, more and more of the work was done by teams from the Australian Armed Services and the Commonwealth Department of Works.

The other committee, the Maralinga Safety Committee, is much more interesting. It lasted for about one and a half years and was reconstructed on 28 March 1957 as the Atomic Weapons Tests Safety Committee (AWTSC), with Professor Ernest Titterton as Chairman. Titterton had assisted Oliphant in Birmingham with the work described in Chapter 1, had worked on the Manhattan Project and had been the last British scientist to leave Los Alamos, and had worked closely with Penney at the Emu trials. The same Titterton who had spent much of his working life helping design bigger and better bombs was now responsible for the safety of the Australian population following the testing of such bombs. One way, perhaps, of finding out if poachers make the best gamekeepers. The Committee's name is also interesting—a *safe* atomic weapons test is an intriguing concept.

The role of the AWTSC was:

1. To examine information and other data supplied by the United Kingdom Government relating to atomic weapons tests proposed to be carried out from time to time in Australia. This examination was to determine whether the safety measures proposed to be taken in relation to such tests were adequate for the prevention of injury to persons or damage to livestock and other property as a result of such tests.

2. To advise the Prime Minister, through the Minister for Supply, of the conclusions arrived at by the Committee as a result of such examination, and in particular as to whether, and, if so, what additional, alternative or more extensive safety measures were considered necessary or desirable.

Thus the burden of the Committee's responsibility was clearly the health of the Australian population and the safety of stock and property outside the firing range. But they had to exercise that responsibility based on *information and other data supplied by the United Kingdom Government*. So the relationship between the potential malefactor and the actual watchdog had to be a close and cosy one. In the event, it seemed that the role of the AWTSC was to reassure the Australian public that all was well. The newspapers of the time trumpeted the success of the tests and quoted uncritically the self-satisfied governmental press release which stated that all was well and there was no danger from fallout. In his 1952 statement Menzies had said there would not be, so, of course, there could not be.

That was far from the whole story. Other investigations known to AWTSC and the Government were showing all too clearly that clouds of radioactive iodine released by the bombs had led to the contamination of large areas of Australia.

Before discussing the importance of that work it is worth noting that radiation safety within the Maralinga range was the responsibility of the United Kingdom. During test periods, health control was exercised by health physics teams from Aldermaston (Atomic Weapons Research Establishment). In the periods between the trials, health and safety control was the responsibility of the Range Commander, assisted by a radiological scientist, both of whom were Australian and resided at Maralinga. An Australian health physics team was formed to work with the British team, both during trials and in the inter-trial periods. Three members went to the UK for specialized health physics training and they in turn conducted training courses on their return to Australia. One of these was a seventeen-day course for members of the Australian Radiation Detection Unit, set up to carry out radiation monitoring in the region immediately beyond the boundary of the Range.

It should be remembered that radiation protection was at this stage the Cinderella of nuclear science — which makes nuclear weapons and nuclear power the ugly sisters? It was not until the Windscale reactor fire of October 1957 that health physics assumed the prominent role it has subsequently enjoyed. But for all the Australian involvement on the Maralinga site, the rules and regulations were British and the UK team had the final responsibility for radiation safety.

The exercise of that responsibility could in some cases have been improved. For instance, one of the Australians involved in the sampling programme, Lance Edwards, a former RAAF wireless operator, claimed that he had flown through the radioactive mushroom clouds to collect samples of bomb debris. Speaking on the Australian Broadcasting Commission television programme 'Four Corners' on 29 March 1980, Edwards said that on the first occasion he and the others in the plane had not worn protective clothing. After the flight, he had had to shower thirteen times to remove the radiation contamination. Edwards later developed cancer of the throat.

We wrote earlier on in this chapter that while Professor Martin, Chairman of AWTSC, and the others were making their categorical statements about fallout from Maralinga, or more correctly the lack of it, data were already available that the Monte Bello tests of mid-1956 had spread radioactive fallout over large areas of Australia. The information had come from the work of Dr Hedley R. Marston. A fellow of the Royal Society, Dr Marston was Chief of the Division of Biochemistry and General Nutrition, Commonwealth Scientific and Industrial Research Organization (CSIRO), Adelaide, and obviously a scientist of some standing and repute. The subsequent attempts to belittle his work and play down his findings seem strange until a newspaper report dated 16 May 1956 is read. In the Adelaide *Advertiser* of that date, Professor E. W. Titterton is quoted as saying:

> An Australian Safety Committee composed of six University and Defence Scientists has the hazard problem under continuous review and is responsible for choosing firing times so that weather conditions are favourable and no damage to life or property can result on the mainland, to ships at sea, or to aircraft which obey the instructions in prohibited areas.
>
> The Minister for Supply (Mr Beale) has stated that no hydrogen bombs will be fired in Australia and it was recently indicated that the *weapons tested would be 'small' relative to the American one which led to the accident to the Fukurya Maru* [our italics].
>
> The radioactivity will be far smaller—several hundred to a thousand times smaller.
>
> The radioactivity from the present Monte Bello test [it took place on the day of the newspaper article, 16 May] will be considerably less than that from the 1952 experiment . . .

A second bomb was exploded at Monte Bello on 19 June 1956. On 22 June, the *Advertiser* reported:

> Mr Beale said at Woomera yesterday: Professor Martin . . . has reported to me that conditions of firing were ideal, and there is absolutely no danger to the mainland.

Obviously from Minister Beale's statement of 16 May 1956, the spectre of the *Lucky Dragon,* and the burgeoning public antipathy to nuclear weapons it had produced, haunted politicians and scientists alike. But they were caught by their own mixture of bombs and bombast so Marston's data, when they became available, were anathema to those who had stuck their necks out too far.

Dr Marston's involvement in the biological monitoring programme dated back to August 1955, when his advice and assistance were first sought by Sir William Slater, then Secretary of the Agricultural Research Council of Great Britain. Subsequent communications between the Australian Department of Supply, the Chief Executive officer of CSIRO (Dr F. W. G. White), Dr R. Scott-Russell of the British Agricultural Research Council, Dr C. E. Eddy, Director of the Commonwealth X-ray and Radium Laboratory, Melbourne, and Dr Marston, resulted in the latter agreeing to conduct an 'iodine survey' and, in collaboration with the English team lead by Scott-Russell, to carry out experiments with sheep at Maralinga during Operation Buffalo, the code name given to the set of four explosions conducted towards the end of 1956 (see Table 4.1, p. 111). Little useful data was obtained from that particular venture but this lack was more than made up for by the other investigation. The iodine survey consisted of the collection of thyroid glands from sheep and cattle slaughtered for food supply from selected areas in central, northern and north-eastern Australia. The glands were sent to Dr Marston's laboratory in Adelaide where the iodine-131 content was determined.

Because of the need for security surrounding the bomb test preparations, Marston started his collection and measurement programme some time before the Maralinga explosions were due to take place. To his surprise, the iodine-131 content of the glands of animals killed after the Monte Bello explosions in May and June 1956, showed that a band of radioactive fallout had passed over a relatively large area of northern Australia. From and after about 8 June (i.e. after the first but before the second Monte Bello test) the findings of the 'Iodine Survey' were made known to both the Safety Committee (AWTSC's precursor) and the leader of the British Agricultural team, Scott-Russell.

So Marston was understandably surprised when the *News* of 21 June 1956 quoted Acting Prime Minister, Sir Arthur Fadden, as saying he had received a message from the Safety

Committee which said:

> We cannot overemphasize that the whole operation at Monte Bello was carried out without risk to life and property and absolutely no danger to the mainland.

The following day the *Advertiser* carried the statement by Beale quoted on p. 116.

On 4 July, Marston wrote to the Chief Executive Officer of CSIRO (White) as follows:

> These [our thyroid findings] taken in conjunction with various 'official' announcements in the press, can lead to one of two conclusions, viz. either the monitoring setup in use at present is incapable of doing what it aims to accomplish or someone is lying.

As he continued with the monitoring programme Marston obviously had faith in his equipment, so he must have reached his own conclusions about the use of what Churchill called 'terminological inexactitudes'.

On 18 September, the Chairman of the Safety Committee, Professor Martin, rang Marston and asked him to step up the sampling programme. 'I replied with some heat that the security imposition had rendered this impossible', Marston later (24 September 1956) wrote to his chief, Dr White. The next day Marston received the following message from Martin:

> We learn . . . that you forwarded a report on your measurements after Monte Bello experiments. This report has not been received by the Committee. Can you forward a second copy?

On the following day (26 September 1956) Marston replied, somewhat testily:

> All cogent findings of preliminary Iodine Survey have been passed on to the Safety Committee from time to time. Firstly about June 8 via White to a member of the Safety Committee for transmission to Eddy [a member of the original group that set up the programme] who was then in W.A. After I was in hospital [he had suffered a coronary occlusion in the interim]

and Eddy dead, data to mid July were given by my secretary, Packham, to Keam for delivery to you in person. At that period you seemed reluctant to receive data . . .

Four days later White wrote to Marston:

I have had the following message from Martin—'Discussions with Scott-Russell make clear that the UK authorities do not wish additional samples collected. In view of Marston's present state of health Safety Committee arranging own collection and counting of samples . . . The position is now completely under control.'

So within a week the wheel had gone full circle. Please can we have more measurements, please can we have another copy of the results, please do not bother any more.

Yet the levels of radioiodine detected by Marston, as disclosed when he was eventually allowed to publish in 1958, were not calamitous. Marston never claimed they were, never claimed they represented a major health hazard to the Australian public. All he said was iodine was detectable in quantities considerably above the levels suggested by official pronouncements, and it is important to note he said this privately.

Marston was no '50s deep throat, he was not causing official embarrassment by leaking documents to the press. Nevertheless, in November 1956, a member of the English monitoring team visited Marston's laboratory, reputedly on Martin's instruction, to reclaim the counting equipment which was being used for the iodine estimation and which had been lent to Marston by the Atomic Weapons Research Establishment [AWRE].

The blight of excessive secrecy that had afflicted the American programme had spread to Australia. The official paranoia regarding any mention of fallout continued, as reassuring statement after reassuring statement was faithfully reported by the Adelaide press.

The *Advertiser*, 29 September 1956:

Professor Martin, in his message to Mr Beale from Maralinga,

> said that all dangerous fallout had been deposited . . . The remaining fallout was 'completely innocuous' . . . There is no possible risk of danger or harm now or at any future time to any persons, stock or property.

The *News*, 9 October 1956:

> Thyroid glands taken from sheep up to 400 miles [640 kilometres] from the Maralinga A-bomb blast have shown no radioactivity. The Chairman of the Commonwealth Atom Test Safety Committee, Professor Martin said this today.
>
> Describing tests made last night at Maralinga, he said: 'Skilled men sent out by the British Medical Research Council worked through the night testing thyroids, and found no evidence of any radioactive iodine, or any other radioactive substances'. Professor Martin said today that thyroids tested were taken from sheep about the Hamilton Dams area.
>
> 'Sticky papers' laid before the bomb's blast showed there was no evidence of fallout anywhere in Australia outside the desert area which approached even one per cent of the natural background, he said.
>
> In the great majority of cases there was no evidence of fallout at all.

The *News*, 13 September 1957:

> Professor Sir Leslie Martin [having received the accolade, Sir Leslie became one of the early members of Australia's happy band of nuclear knights] said '. . . there has never been anything that could give you the slightest cause for concern about fallout from the Maralinga tests'.

By February 1957, Marston had finished two reports on the 'Iodine Survey', a full report for internal consumption, giving his complete findings, and an expurgated version for publication in the outside literature. In mid-June, advice was received via White (Marston's boss) that the UK authorities raised no objection to the publication, and towards the end of July the manuscript was sent to the editor of the *Australian Journal of Biological Science*. Two weeks later, word was received from Titterton via White that Sir William Penney wanted the paper either classified (and therefore unpublishable) or certain figures and certain related texts removed. This change of attitude, if such it was, is intriguing as White had earlier received advice that the British authorities accepted the expurgated version.

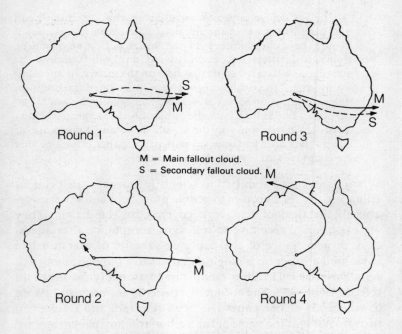

Fig. 4.3   Fallout trajectories of the 1956 series of tests.

However, Marston revised the paper. The abbreviated version was cleared for publication in mid-November and resubmitted to the same editor. This paper was published in March 1958 in the now defunct *Australian Journal of Biological Science*.

On 23 August 1957, Titterton who since 28 March had been chairman of the newly formed AWTSC, wrote to White:

> . . . if appropriate changes are not made we shall submit a parallel paper to the same journal to correct the mistakes and

misinterpretations that Marston has made.

Titterton's involvement surprised Marston and when he submitted his final version of the paper to the *Australian Journal of Biological Science* he wrote:

> There is of course no reason whatsoever why Titterton should not publish whatever the Editorial Board may accept, but it would be quite contrary to the usual policy of Scientific Journals if Titterton's demands were indulged. If, indeed, he has any new data to report that bear on the matter, or anything really cogent to say about how I have interpreted the findings, there surely is no sound reason why he should not wait, like any other individual, until the publication has appeared. There is in fact no reason why he should have any knowledge of where the paper has been submitted; the paper is not one that he could reasonably be asked to referee.

When papers are submitted to scientific journals, the prudent editor usually refers copies to people prominent and knowledge-able in the field of the work covered by the article. They are expected to recommend rejection, acceptance after altera-tion, or acceptance of the paper as submitted. Marston had submitted a paper on biological matters to a biological journal. As a physicist, Titterton could not 'reasonably be asked to referee' the article. The author of a paper is not normally aware to whom his or her paper has been referred, and referees in turn are not told the name of the author(s) of any paper they are asked to review. Anonymity in such matters, as in other fields, is an aid to scientific frankness.

There was one last round to go. In January 1959, Dr Marston received from the editor of the *Australian Journal of Science* (different to *Australian Journal of Biological Science*), a copy of a paper entitled 'Comments on a Paper by H. R. Marston Discussing the Take-Up of Radioiodine into the Thyroids of Grazing Animals Subsequent to Atomic Weapons Tests' (subsequently referred to as 'Comments'). The authors were L. J. Dwyer, J. H. Martin and E. W. Titterton. The paper was a destructive critique of Marston's paper and had been submitted for publication. Marston wrote a detailed defence of his earlier paper which he called 'Radioactive Iodine in the Thyroids of Grazing Animals as an indication of the Degree of Hazard Entailed in the Contamination of Terrain by Products of Nuclear Explosion Deposited from the Troposphere', and in February 1959, submitted it to the same journal as the Dwyer, Martin, Titterton paper. Neither title is particularly snappy, nor do they give any hint of the bitter scientific feud the papers represent. Both Dwyer and Martin (J. H. not Sir Leslie, note) were members of AWTSC, Dwyer was from the Bureau of Meteorology, Melbourne, and Martin was head of the Physics Department of the Peter MacCallum Clinic (Cancer Institute Board), Melbourne.

Marston also wrote, enclosing the relevant papers, to Professor Oliphant, now back in Australia and Director of the Research School of Physical Sciences at the Australian National University. He was also President of the Australian and New Zealand Association for the Advancement of Sciences (ANZAAS), the publisher of the *Australian Journal of Science*, and as such in a position to act as arbiter in the dispute. On 18 February 1959, Oliphant wrote to the editor of the *Australian Journal of Science* as follows:

> In my view it would be most unwise to publish these papers in the *Australian Journal of Science* as is contemplated at present. My reasons for this are several. In the first place Marston's paper was published in the *Australian Journal of Biological Sciences* and it would be only proper to publish a reply in the same journal. In the second place, there is a great sensitivity among the citizens of Australia to the possible effects of radioactive fallout upon the population and I believe it to be the duty of the Journal to publish nothing on those questions unless it is written by experts who know precisely what are the facts. Dwyer, Martin and Titterton are not qualified to discuss the biological hazards, although they are fully competent to discuss the distribution and magnitude of the fallout as they have previously in the Journal . . .

Both papers were submitted to referees and both papers were

pronounced not suitable for publication. So, after all the fuss and bother, only Marston's original (second version) paper was published. We have obtained copies of all three papers and they make interesting reading.

Marston's paper, published in March 1958, is entitled 'The Accumulation of Radioactive Iodine in the Thyroids of Grazing Animals subsequent to Atomic Weapons Test'. The summary (prepared by Marston) at the start of the paper is as follows:

> Radioactivity due to ^{131}I was found in the thyroid glands collected from sheep and cattle depastured on areas in various parts of Australia subsequent to atomic weapons tests conducted during 1956 at Monte Bello and at Maralinga. Thyroids from cattle were found to contain up to 830 nCi*^{131}I (37 nCi ^{131}I/g of tissue) and from sheep up to 144 nCi ^{131}I (70 nCi ^{131}I/g of tissue). The uneven degree of contamination of pastures was emphasised by the fact that some of the highest concentration of ^{131}I were observed in glands collected from individuals of flocks and herds grazing on terrain 1500-2000 miles [2400-3200 kilometres] distant from the site of the explosions. As the tests proceeded, fluctuations in the ^{131}I content of the thyroid glands of grazing stock indicated that many areas received repeated dressings of radioactive debris.
>
> Contamination of Adelaide and its environs with fallout from the third Maralinga explosion provided an opportunity to establish unequivocally that extremely little if any of the considerable amount of ^{131}I that became concentrated in the thyroids found its way to the glands via the lungs; and the occasion rendered possible a detailed study of the rates of rise and fall of ^{131}I in the thyroid glands of grazing animals in relation to the degree of contamination of the pastures.
>
> The value of the ^{131}I in the thyroid glands as a measure of the hazards imposed by contamination of terrain by troposphere fallout supervening on atomic weapons tests is considered in light of the findings.
>
> The speed with which grazing dairy cows gather radioactive

* Marston quoted his iodine levels in millimicrocuries or micromicrocuries, the units used at the time. To aid the reader the units have been changed to the more general nanocurie (nCi) picocurie (pCi) respectively.

debris that has been deposited on their pastures, as indicated
by the rise and fall of the ^{131}I in their thyroid glands, is
discussed in relation to the hazard entailed in the passage of
bone-seeking radioactive constituents of fallout via milk to
human populations.

Paragraph two perhaps gives a clue to the basis of the
controversy—this was the first indication that any fallout at all
had been detected in any Australian city. In his introduction
Marston spelt out his aims and the first of his disconcerting
findings.

> The primary purpose of this investigation was to assess the
> usefulness of the ^{131}I concentrating in the thyroids of grazing
> animals as an integrating measure of the degree of hazard
> entailed in the contamination of terrain by residue from atomic
> explosions. When it was undertaken, knowledge of the
> chemical state in which iodine isotopes exist in the airborne
> debris was uncertain, and interpretation of the chain of events
> responsible for the accumulation of activity in the thyroid
> tissue of the higher animals was confused . . .
> . . . The results of a survey of the amounts of ^{131}I found in the
> thyroid glands of animals grazing in various parts of Australia
> that are reported in this paper indicate that extensive areas of
> Australia have been contaminated, and that some of the more
> heavy precipitations occurred on terrain situated over 1500
> miles [2400 kilometres] from the site of the explosions, in areas
> more or less thickly populated.

Marston went on to review some American data correlating
increased iodine in the thyroid glands of slaughtered cattle
with the dates of Russian and American nuclear weapons tests.

Around Australia, Marston arranged twenty-six sampling
points lying within a wide arc of northern and eastern
Australia, ranging from Elliot, almost due north of Maralinga,
to Adelaide lying south-east of the test site. All Marston's
samples taken prior to mid-May 1956 showed less than 5 pCi of
iodine-131 (the lower limit of detection of the apparatus in use).
A few days after the Monte Bello explosion of 16 May 1956,

125

Marston's team started to detect contaminated thyroid glands collected from sheep and cattle depastured on areas distributed between latitudes 24°S and 30°S within a band approximately 800 kilometres wide, stretching from the western to the eastern seaboard. After the second Monte Bello test (19 June 1956), the levels detected increased a hundredfold or more. At Rockhampton, for instance, thyroids collected from cattle on 29 May and 22 June contained 3.2 and 2.5 nCi I-131 respectively, and on 12 May, 440 nCi I-131.

What appeared to surprise Marston was that some of the areas most heavily contaminated with fallout were 2400 to 3200 kilometres away from the test site. The subsequent effects of the June explosion were detected in the thyroids of grazing animals depastured within a band of terrain about 1600 kilometres wide, stretching west to east across the Australian continent. However, as Marston wrote, 'the variability observed within the band emphasised the uneven distribution of the deposited radioactive debris'. In his paper, Marston gives detailed tables of his findings and in his rather dry academic way he wrote:

> Areas on the north-eastern seaboard and in central western Queensland that received the relatively heavy dressings from the Monte Bello tests are within the sector over which prevailing winds tended to carry the plumes from tests conducted later at Maralinga. In these latter areas the observations indicate repeated dressings from subsequent tests.

From 28 June to mid-December 1956, thyroid glands were taken at approximately three-day intervals from cattle grazing within the vicinity of Alice Springs. The data showed clearly that the Alice Springs area had been subject to at least four dressings (to use Marston's word) of radioactive material during the period. The levels at Alice Springs ranged from 2.7 nCi I^{131}/g of thyroid on 4 July (after the second Monte Bello test) down to 0.02 nCi/g on 28 September just before the first Maralinga test. The levels were back up to 1.8 nCi/g by early November after the completion of the Buffalo series. The cattle had been taken from the Hamilton Downs area where 'skilled men . . . worked through the night testing thyroids and found no evidence of any radioactive iodine, or any other radioactive substance'. Perhaps it had been too dark to read the geiger counter dials.

At Longreach (Marston's site 15), the levels in Table 4.2 (below) were detected.

TABLE 4.2

Radioactivity detected in sheep thyroid glands at Longreach (from Marston)

Date of slaughter in 1956	Radioactivity of thyroid at time of slaughter	
	Total nCi I-131	*nCi I-131/g of tissue*
3 May	—	—
4 July	131.0	44.0
25 July	43.0	8.6
7 September	1.0	0.25
28 September	—	—
9 November	101.0	26.0

It was almost by chance that Marston got his evidence that the third Maralinga test (11 October 1956, officially classed as 'low yield') had contaminated Adelaide and its environs. Staff in Marston's laboratory had been interested for some time in the radon and thoron content of soil atmospheres and radioactivity in air due to their daughter products. Accordingly, they had a somewhat intermittent air sampling programme which, prior to 13 October 1956, never showed 'any considerable contamination from isotopes derived from explosions of nuclear weapons'. However, a 24-hour sample taken during 12-13 October showed clearly that the plume had passed close to Adelaide. The activity detected on the filter paper was 95 000 counts over 100 seconds. By 18-19 October, the figure was down to 62 counts/100 seconds. Marston did not attempt to quantify the degree of hazard this high count rate represented (at least not in the published paper) and it is difficult now to do the necessary sums with any degree of confidence. We do not know the counting efficiency of Marston's apparatus, whether he was counting beta and gamma activity together, the particle size efficiency of his filter papers. However, if we assume that Marston's counting efficiency was around 10 per cent (fairly optimistic) and his air sample volume was 20 m^3 his detected activity was around $1.5 \times 10^{-9} \mu$Ci/cc of air. (This figure is in reasonable agreement with the figure later published by Butement and others in their paper on fallout measurements following the Buffalo series of tests, *Australian Journal of Science*, Volume 21, 1958, p. 63.)

The maximum permissible levels for continuous (168 hr/wk) exposure for non-occupationally exposed personnel are around $3 \times 10^{-11} \mu$Ci/cc for strontium-90, $3 \times 10^{-10} \mu$Ci/cc for iodine-131, $2 \times 10^{-9} \mu$Ci/cc for caesium-137.

Obviously what Marston sampled was a complex mix of isotopes, many with short half-lives and, therefore, larger permissible levels than the ones quoted above. But if, as the authorities said, the plume never came anywhere near Adelaide, the concentrations of airborne radioactivity must have been pretty high wherever it did go.

In one way Marston benefited from the Adelaide fallout. By comparing the thyroids of pasture-fed and pen-fed sheep on his Division's farm at Glenthorne, he was able to show that the pasture-fed sheep contained over a thousand times the amount of iodine of the pen-fed animals. Thus the activity had been taken in by grazing, not by inhalation, so he was able to answer the question he had posed in the introduction to his paper.

Marston concluded his paper by speculating on whether iodine measurements could be used to estimate strontium-89 and strontium-90 intakes via grazing. He thought they might be useful for a period of three months or so after a nuclear explosion. Direct estimates of strontium uptake involved fairly complex radiochemical techniques which were both tedious and time-consuming. If a short cut could be found it would have much to commend it.

Nowhere in his paper does Marston attempt to quantify the biological hazard his data might represent and his writing is far from polemical in tone. Nevertheless, it must have touched some raw nerves among the members of the Atomic Weapons Tests Safety Committee as the Dwyer, Martin and Titterton paper shows. In their introduction, the authors state their clear intention.

> In a recent paper, Marston (1958) gives data relating to the take-up of radioiodine into the thyroid glands of cattle and sheep in the period immediately following weapon tests at the Monte Bello Islands and Maralinga during 1956. Although the phraseology of the paper suggests that the levels observed were high, he fails to make a quantitative assessment of the position. In this paper we shall rectify the deficiency, and show, from Marston's own data, that no damage could have occurred to man or animals from radioiodine.
>
> A number of errors of fact occur in Marston's paper—mainly of a type which suggests that the radiation levels were high; this inference is incorrect and the various points are discussed in the present communication.
>
> In the final section of his paper Marston raises an entirely new issue—that of the take-up of radiostrontium by human beings. He offers a number of opinions, unsupported by scientific evidence, on the route and rate of strontium take-up into the body and the 'probable' hazards. Measurements of Sr^{90} for the Australian environment are available and are included in the present paper. It is shown that Sr^{90} fallout in Australia is amongst the lowest in the world and that the contribution to it from the British tests in Australia is very small. The actual magnitude of the Sr^{90} risk can be computed following the

129

techniques of the UN Radiation Committee's report and is shown to be extremely low.

Nowhere in this paper do the authors take issue with Marston's data. Quite the contrary. They set out to show how low his figures are by quoting the average figure, 3.4 nCi/g, of sheep thyroid and contrasting it with the largest figure found by the Safety Committee's team, 56 nCi/g. This they said was measured during the 'close-in survey'. This figure would seem to contradict Professor Leslie Martin's statement about 'no evidence of any radioactive iodine'.

The paper goes to some lengths to downgrade the importance of iodine measurements. It states:

> It is well known that the radioisotopes principally responsible for the irradiation of populations as a result of weapons tests are the long lived Sr^{90} and Cs^{137}. They constitute almost all stratospheric fallout but only a small part of tropospheric fallout, which is made up mainly of short lived activity.

In fact it was not 'well known'; it was 'widely assumed'. Linus Pauling among others was in the process of taking the US Atomic Energy Commission to task for ignoring the biological significance of such radioisotopes as C-14 and I-131.

Australian attitudes to fallout in general and iodine in particular changed dramatically over the next fifteen years. By 1973, AWTSC had been replaced by another body with wider responsibilities. This was the Australian Ionizing Radiation Advisory Council (AIRAC). Its terms of reference were, 'To consider any problems referred to it by the government through the Minister for Environment and Conservation and to report through him'—and terms of reference don't come any wider than that. The initial convenor and later Chairman was R. J. Walsh.

In its first report, 'Fallout over Australia from nuclear weapons tested by France in Polynesia during July and August 1973', AIRAC No. 1 published May 1974, the Council members had no doubts about iodine-131. They wrote:

Measurement of iodine-131 in fresh milk and estimation of doses of radiation to the thyroid gland. This program is of importance because iodine-131 in fallout in pastures is ingested by cows and secreted in milk which could be drunk particularly by young children. Iodine-131 is concentrated in the thyroid gland.

In 1973, the Australian Government made application to the International Court of Justice seeking an injunction to stop further French atmospheric testing of nuclear weapons at Mururoa. In the application the Government draftsman wrote:

It is clear that if the French Republic conducts further atmospheric nuclear tests in the Pacific pending the ultimate decision of the Court, the consequences will be:

1. That further radioactive material resulting from such tests will be injected into the troposphere and depending upon the power of the device into the stratosphere.

2. That as a direct result of this injection some of the radioactive material injected will be deposited both in the short term and the long term on Australian territory.

3. That the material so deposited will be inherently harmful and potentially dangerous to the Australian people and could have deleterious somatic and genetic effects on them.

4. That notwithstanding that Australia objects to and sees no benefit to Australia in the conduct of tests by the French Republic in the atmosphere, Australia would be unable to prevent its territory and its people from being subjected to the ionizing radiation consequent upon the deposit of this additional radioactive material.

He went on to quote the 1962 UNSCEAR report at some length including the following:

The Committee therefore emphasizes the need that all forms of unnecessary radiation exposure should be minimized or avoided entirely, particularly when the exposure of large populations is entailed and that every procedure involving the peaceful uses of ionizing radiation should be subject to appropriate immediate and continuing scrutiny in order to ensure that the resulting exposure is kept to the minimum practicable level and that this level is consistent with the necessity or the value of the procedure. As there are no effective measures to prevent the occurrence of harmful effects of global radioactive contamination from nuclear explosions, the achievement of a final cessation of nuclear tests would benefit present and future generations of mankind.

On Tuesday, 1 May 1973, Prime Minister Whitlam tabled in the Australian Parliament a report prepared on behalf of the Australian Academy of Science. The Academy had been asked to report on:

The actual or potential harm to Australia including its human and animal population, its resources and environment, from the explosion of nuclear devices in the atmosphere, underwater or on or near the surface of the earth, with particular regard to the past and prospective explosions by France in the Pacific.

In its report, the following two conclusions, among others, were reached by the Academy:

3. It is assumed (as all official reports have hitherto done) that the responses to dose are proportional over the whole range. Australia, as the result of the French tests which have already taken place, could have 1 case of thyroid cancer per year due to isotope iodine-131 and 1 to 4 other cancer cases per year due to strontium-90, caesium-137 and carbon-14. Due to the same isotopes Australia could have one mutation in every 10 years leading to death or disability in the first generation, and up to 50-100 deaths or disabilities in all subsequent generations.

4. We draw attention to the improbable event in which the explosion of a high-powered bomb was combined with quite exceptional meteorological conditions giving a high fallout over Australia. Though this would be a singular episode, some increase in the above figures could be expected. Thyroid cancer cases due to iodine-131 could be about 10. Other cancer cases due to the other isotopes could increase to much higher figures than at present levels of radiation. Mutations could lead to two deaths and disabilities per year in the first generation and to more than a

thousand deaths and disabilities in all subsequent generations.

Conclusion 3 is based on the fallout arriving over Australia after being blown three-quarters of the way around the world (the prevailing winds are westerlies).

It is almost impossible to relate the 1956–57 figures to those of 1972–73. Marston measured iodine in the thyroids of animals; the Australian Radiation Laboratory (successor of the Commonwealth X-ray and Radium Laboratory — CXRL) team monitored iodine in milk directly. We can, however, make the not unreasonable assumption that the Academy's conclusion 4 would apply to the explosion of bombs within Australian boundaries.

The Academy finished its conclusions with the following observations:

> Further, with the long lived isotopes produced as the result of nuclear explosions in either the southern or northern hemisphere, the effects on the Australian population, though small, would be cumulative.

But we digress. We must go back to 1958 and the dispute between the AWTSC on the one hand and Dr Hedley Marston on the other. In their paper, Dwyer *et al.* argued that fallout contamination of Australia was greater from the massive testing programme in the northern hemisphere and that the British contribution in Australia was insignificant. They quoted data from the first UNSCEAR report to support their contention. Marston dealt rather unkindly with that line. Before accepting such reports he said he would like information on

> the chemical and physical nature of the soil that has been analysed, its topography, the vertical distribution of Sr^{90} within it, the nature of the cover and the agricultural usage, climatic conditions, means of sampling and above all the variations between samples . . .

He went on:

> And perhaps as suggested in the Report of the United Nations
> Scientific Committee on the Effects of Atomic Radiation an
> indication of who is responsible for the analytical figures that
> have been mapped might also be cogent when assessing the
> degree of hazard.

Dwyer *et al.* went on to chide Marston for not referring to a
report by Butement, Dwyer, Eddy, Martin (L.H.) and Titterton
giving figures for the Monte Bello tests (code-named 'Mosaic').
As Marston pointed out, that paper was not available when he
wrote his. The report by Butement and others was published in
the *Australian Journal of Science* in late 1957. It gave the official
figures based on the work of the Australian Radiation
Detention Unit (ARDU) covering fallout measurements up to
300 kilometres from the Maralinga site. A second programme,
measuring long-range fallout throughout the rest of Australia,
was operated jointly by the Bureau of Meteorology and CXRL
on behalf of AWTSC. And so the sniping went on. No wonder
Oliphant recommended against publication.

When discussing the data relating to Adelaide, the
'Comments' authors really went to town.

> In relation to Marston's discussion of what he calls the
> 'Adelaide Fallout', he states his filtration experiments 'clearly
> indicated that the plume from the third Maralinga explosion
> [11 October 1956] passed close to Adelaide and contaminated
> the city and surrounding countryside with radioactive fission
> products.' This is incorrect. As shown in the paper discussing
> measurements made at the time of the Buffalo operation [by
> Butement *et al.* but with the new CXRL Director D. J. Stevens
> replacing the deceased Eddy], the path of the radioactive cloud
> 'plume' from this explosion never approached within 160 miles
> [257 kilometres] of Adelaide. Before the weapon under dis-
> cussion was fired, the Safety Committee appreciated that a
> temperature inversion of 8°C just below the 6000 ft [1828 m]
> level would be capable of cutting off and trapping a very small
> quantity of radioactive material. Detectable quantities of
> activity, at a level far below that which could constitute any

hazard, were expected to be observed in South Australia, Victoria and NSW. In fact this prediction was confirmed and the veering of the lower-level winds in the post-explosion period led to a southerly drift of slowly setting material of low activity. Measurements of time of arrival and activity of this material in South Australia, Victoria and NSW are given in the paper referred to above. In the case of Adelaide the integrated whole body dose to infinity was less than 1 millirem.

Marston was rather sarcastic in his reply.

> The correctness or otherwise of the statement that 'the plume from the third Maralinga explosion passed close to Adelaide' depends essentially on a definition of what constitutes the edge of the plume—a definition which would be interesting to see. Nevertheless 'close to' is rather a loose expression in a precise scientific paper. One wonders how it escaped both the distinguished scientific referees and the extended attention of the Safety Committee. In an early draft of the paper the sentence was 'close enough to Adelaide to contaminate the city and surrounding countryside', which better expressed the author's meaning.
>
> In Adelaide on October 13—the day after this explosion—particular radioactive material suspended in the total volume of air (ca 20 m^3) that entered the lungs of each member of the population had an activity close to 1000 disintegrations per second $[\equiv 1.5 \times 10^{-9}\mu\text{Ci/cc}$—see p. 128]—an activity which perhaps may not be entirely negligible. If, as the Safety Committee claims 'the active cloud [*sic*] plume never approached within 160 miles [257 kilometres] of Adelaide', then so much the worse for the inhabitants of the areas it did traverse. The responsible shot was described as a device of low yield.

In his reply Dr Marston appeared to have no doubts as to who the principal author of the 'Comments' actually was. He wrote:

> In support of a preposterous calculation in another section, Professor Titterton and his colleagues state that 'global fallout put the entire population at risk, while local tests . . . cause irradiation of only a small and varying proportion of the population'; a further evasion that brings the matter into

sharper focus. This tendency to introduce means of associated data, and to weigh these means with population densities, evades the issue, which is the degree of contamination of certain areas of Australia with radioactive material deposited from the troposphere.

This scientific feud did not have the grandeur or longevity of the Teller-Oppenheimer rift, but in its own quiet way it was just as bitter. Perhaps the last word belongs to AWTSC. When asked recently by a *National Times* reporter to comment on the differences between Marston's paper and that of the Safety Committee, Sir Ernest refused to comment over the telephone on a 'highly technical subject which I do not believe the public has any chance of understanding, particularly delivered second-hand by someone without expert knowledge'.

5

Signs in the Desert

Three days after Malcolm Fraser was re-elected Prime Minister of Australia, the Melbourne *Sun* of 21 October 1980 carried, among the plethora of other election news, the following highly illuminating paragraph which read:

> News of the Fraser win was reported in the important newspapers, in their foreign news sections, without comment. One of the nation's [United States] largest radio networks, Mutual Radio, reported the re-election of the Australian Prime Minister, Mr Malcolm Wilson. After a call from an irate listener, worried about family ties, Mutual changed it to Mr Jack Fraser.

Given the Australian media's unfathomable obsession with what the rest of the world has to say about the country's doings and undoings, this must have come as a particularly unpleasant shock to the national pride. It was bad enough when, some months earlier, President Carter referred to 'my good friend John Fraser'. But this was far more disturbing. A double error, carried nation-wide across America on a leading radio network.

Around the same time the rest of the world was getting Mr Fraser's name wrong, another Australian title, much more difficult to spell and to remember, was doing the international rounds. It was Noonkanbah, and everybody was making sure they got it right first time. Not just the name, but the issues involved. The decision, by Australia's native people to take their case, over sacred sites, to the United Nations was a shrewd one indeed. Other indigenous peoples, most particularly the North American Indian, had travelled the same route years before, with similarly spectacular results.

Gradually the emerging voice of the Third World was gaining an audience and belated recognition for at least a percentage of its aims and objectives. If Malcolm Fraser found it hard to swallow that a centuries old culture was commanding more column space and respect than his latest electoral triumph, well so be it. What Mr Fraser, and a great many other opinion-makers in today's Australia are going to find even harder to stomach is just how much more significant the Aboriginal movement is going to become in terms of international recognition over the next decade.

Partly because of distance and isolation, and partly because of second-rate international public relations, Australia's internal politics still remain virtually ignored by the rest of the world. The same cannot be said of her native people and the treatment meted out to them by those who took over their land. Australia's track record in this direction is already earning much less than unqualified admiration. The bulldozing of sacred sites into an unrecognizable morass hardly stands for enlightened handling of a hugely sensitive issue in the eyes of the world.

If such conduct is causing eyebrows to raise around the world, it is interesting to conjecture what will be the effect when the real story emerges of how the Aboriginal people fared during and after Britain's A-bomb tests. Not that Australia should shoulder all the blame, but Britain did at least have the excuse of blind ignorance of native ways. Australia should have known better.

Ignorance really is the only justifiable description of the type of thinking that led to decisions such as the one to erect warning signs in the desert to keep Aborigines away from test sites. Even the esoteric thinking of the average British scientist of the time should have been no excuse for not realizing that, while the Aboriginal desert dweller reads his environment, its animal tracks and its open skies like a book, he does not read plain English. For most of those they were intended to keep away, the warning signs were meaningless.

Ignorance is also the kindest description one can put on the words of a British Air Vice-Marshal interviewed early in 1980 on an ABC radio current affairs programme. When it was suggested that Aborigines might have strayed on to one or more of the test sites, one could almost hear his moustache bristling in indignation. With the kind of dogmatism enjoyed only by those whose opinion is rarely, if ever, questioned, he said:

> This of course is nonsense. We rounded up the Aborigines and took them off to a safe area if my memory serves me right. We kept them there. We had the Australian regional officers to look after their affairs. They were there, and were responsible for their well-being, and when the tests were over, and the radiation levels had subsided, they were allowed back into their own particular areas, and they went walk-about again.
>
> I am satisfied that the safety precautions taken by the British, and, incidentally, the head of the Safety Committee was your Professor Martin, an Australian, a very distinguished man, and a great friend of mine, and a man I had the greatest possible respect for. It was his responsibility to see that nothing would be done that would endanger the lives of any human being or any livestock. We couldn't be sure about the odd kangaroo, but certainly human beings were not anywhere near the test site.

This statement, delivered to a nationwide audience, amounted almost to unintentional satire in its blissful disregard for either morality or facts, and bears closer scrutiny, if only to demonstrate the hideously inadequate approach to the value of human life it reveals. The Air Vice-Marshal begins by describing the 'round-up' of Aborigines, quite unperturbed by the concept of rounding-up people from their own land, for the

139

purpose of blowing it to the heavens. One wonders how he would have reacted had he and his family been 'rounded-up' from their country estate in Britain one fine morning by a tribe of painted Aborigines intent on using his backyard for a burial ceremony. The ceremony would have caused infinitely less damage to the environment. Next, one wonders, just how was the 'round-up' accomplished? A people adept at seeking cover behind a few grains of sand would have had little trouble, had they so wished, in evading the attentions of their would-be captors.

But perhaps most disturbing of all is the Air Vice-Marshal's blithe statement: 'When the radiation levels had subsided, they were allowed back into their own particular areas.' Who decided the radiation levels had subsided sufficiently for safety? Why, 30 years later, are those levels around Maralinga still considered hazardous enough for the Federal Government to warn visitors against staying longer than five hours? Who remained behind, weeks or months or years after the tests, to warn groups of Aborigines to break camp, to tell them they had been in a suspect area too long? It seems that apart from his practised use of the local patois—'they went walk-about again'—the Air Vice-Marshal did not learn a great deal about the Aboriginal people. His loss was undoubtedly theirs too.

Thanks largely to the intervention of the Australian Nuclear Veterans' Association (of which much more later), the plight of the Aborigine during and after the tests has not been as easily buried beneath the desert sands as the British and Australian Governments would, no doubt, have hoped.

The Federal Government in Australia made claims, initially, that were similarly emphatic as the comments of the Air Vice-Marshal. Nobody, including any Aboriginal peoples, had been affected by radiation from the tests. Those claims were amended after an ex-Army sapper named Kevin Woodland came forward with some embarrassing information. Interviewed by one of the authors at his desk in a country town north of Brisbane where he works as an estimator, Mr Woodland recalled the time in May 1957, when he was in the desert near Maralinga with an advance party of British scientists and Australian servicemen.

> Well, we were in a radioactive area. We were wearing protective clothing, and we had portable showers for decontamination. We came across this family of four Aborigines, they must have walked down from the Alice Springs area, passing through test areas and sleeping on the ground. The dirt was two inches thick on the bottom of the shower when we had finished with them. The warning signs were no good to the Aborigines, they couldn't understand them. They came to us with a billy for water, and we ran a geiger counter over them. The readings were pretty frightening. To begin with they couldn't understand what we wanted. There was a bloke, his woman and two young ones. The woman was wearing a potato sack, and we wanted them to undress. The bloke didn't want us taking her clothes off her, but in the end we got them in the shower, and they had to go through time and time again. There was a bit of a panic eventually, and about 50 scientists came down, and we were told to forget the whole thing. The Aborigines were taken back to Maralinga and that was the last we saw of them.

For years Kevin Woodland had done as he was told, and kept quiet. Then he heard the Air Vice-Marshal on the radio.

> I kept it to myself, because I thought it was covered by the *Official Secrets Act*, but when I heard this British Air Force bloke on the radio saying we put them all in a compound, that made me angry. I started talking about it, and then, in July this year (1980), my wife got a phone call at home, somebody asking for me by name. She said: 'Can I take a message?' because I wasn't there. The bloke on the phone said: 'You can take a message. Tell him not to say any more about Aborigines.' She told him to go to hell, and hung up. It doesn't worry me, I won't be gagged.

Not long after Kevin Woodland's statement was made public, Tom Uren, Labor's long-time spokesman on Maralinga, asked one of a number of embarrassing questions of the Government in Federal Parliament. One particular question, on 1 April

1980, read in part:

> Can the Minister say whether Aboriginal people were detained
> for decontamination at the Maralinga range; if so, how many
> persons were detained? Were any measures taken to monitor
> the subsequent health of these persons; if so, what measures
> were taken?

Another of Mr Uren's questions, on the same date, asked:

> Is there any evidence which suggests that Aboriginal people
> have suffered disease or disability as a consequence of exposure
> to radiation resulting from British atomic weapon tests in South
> Australia?

On 15 May 1980, Senator J. L. Carrick, the then Minister for
National Development and Energy, issued the following
statement:

> Our inquiries to date have identified only one recorded
> instance of Aboriginals entering a contaminated area. This
> occurred at Maralinga in May 1957, involving four persons.
> After appropriate washing procedures were implemented,
> radiation safety officials concluded that there was no possi-
> bility of any radiation injury having occurred. Nevertheless
> the Government is investigating allegations that other
> Aboriginals may have been exposed to radiation in the test
> areas. Information is being sought on any radiation associated
> health problems amongst these Aboriginals.

Despite the Senator's assurances, the Australian Nuclear
Veterans' Association was able to point to a number of alarming
discrepancies in his statement. In a paper headed: 'The
Layman's Case to Date for a Survey-Inquiry into Health of
Aborigines', dated 20 September 1980, the ANVA pointed out:

> The Senator's statement is disturbing. In it he admits that four
> Aborigines were able to enter a contaminated area during the
> test series, while the range was active, i.e. at full strength, not
> caretaker strength. This casts grave doubts on the effectiveness
> of the safety system, especially when we have been repeatedly
> told that all Aborigines had been removed from the possible
> danger areas prior to tests beginning.

If this group entered the contaminated area at the time, and while the range was active, how many did so once the range was out of use, and how much were they affected? The Senator admits that this group was contaminated, as others have reported to us. The fact that the radioactive dust on them registered on the equipment tells us that they must have been breathing contamination. Therefore it is unlikely that they failed to ingest some radioactive particles. It is well known that this form of contamination can take years to result in injury to the victim. This latency is ignored by the radiation safety officials who, the Senator says, concluded that no possibility of radiation injury had occurred.

Thus Tom Uren's question on follow-up monitoring of the health of the four Aborigines in question is answered. There was none. One hesitates to hazard a guess at the current state of health of that particular Aboriginal family.

Damning as this series of statements may be, it has nothing of the dramatic impact and horror of an interview one of the authors held with a 38-year-old Aborigine called Jim Lester, director of the Alice Springs-based Institute for Aboriginal Development.

As a young member of the Yankunyatjara tribe, Lester was living with his people at Wallatinna Station, north-west of Coober Pedy, when the British exploded an A-bomb in October 1953, at Emu Field. He remembers:

'I was a young kid then, about ten or eleven. We woke up early this day, about sunrise. I was just playing around . . . Then roughly, I suppose about seven in the morning, I don't really know, I heard this big bang, and everybody in the camp-site woke up talking and saying: "What was that?" I don't remember seeing any mushroom cloud, and we didn't think any more about it.

Later we went hunting, I think, and eating. I don't know how long after it was, we seen this smoke. Old feller from the camp reckoned it was the next day. It was black, greasy, sort of shiny. The sun was shining on to it, black and shiny with grey, like ash. It was rolling up to us through the mulga. We thought

143

it was a mamu, a devil spirit. The old people got their woomeras to wave it away, but it was a very strong mamu. I can't remember too well, but the old feller said it smelt very strong. We tried to bury ourselves in the sand, but it was too late anyway. It stayed around us for a while, I don't know how long. I don't remember how much later we started being sick, and we had diarrhoea. Pretty well all of us. Some were worse. There were about 40 or 45 of us, I'm only guessing I think about that. Some got pretty bad, some were more lucky. The old people and the children were the worst. I think some people might have died, I'm not sure. Some got really bad. It is our custom when a member of the family passes on, we move from the camp. After that we moved from the camp quite a lot, two or three times I think, maybe more. I don't know what they died from—young fellers are not allowed to see dead people.

It wasn't just our people. Others in the area had the same. It was a common known thing. Everybody knew about it. Army trucks come through, I remember seeing them. I suppose they were talking to the old people, telling them to get out of the area. I remember we had very sore eyes, very red and tears. I could not open my eyes, and I could not see again with one eye. Ever again. The other eye was very poor, and went altogether a few years later. Now I am blind, and the eye specialist, he tells me it is glaucoma and measles. I don't know. In the camp we talk about it a lot, about what happened. The Government tries to keep it a secret, for a long time we thought it was just one of those white feller's magic. They didn't know what they were doing.'

Jim Lester's story has been documented in several newspapers, magazines, and in Federal Parliament by Senator Cavanagh. There is far too much of the ring of truth about the way he expresses himself for his version of the events ever to be doubted. But if it needs verification, it can be found from people like Mrs E. L. Giles, a station owner whose story has also been raised in Parliament. In October 1953, Mrs Giles was living with her husband at Welbourne Hill Station, north-east of Wallatinna. She told her story to South Australian journalist Robert Ball.

I remember a cloud coming in—the dark girls ran to tell me, here comes a dust-storm. We shut up the house, closed windows and everything, and waited for the storm to hit. But it was unusually quiet. Normally a dust-storm roars, but this was quiet. There was no force. Yes, it was rather eerie . . . just a big, coiling cloud-like thing. We all stayed inside. Not even the black girls went out.

After it had gone we went outside and the orange and lemon trees were coated in this dust. It was an oily dust. You could see it on the walls too. We tried to hose the trees down, but they just withered and died.

The trees weren't all that died on the Giles' station. Mr Giles and two employees later fell victims to cancer.

Further corroboration, and perhaps the most disturbing evidence of all, comes from Perth businessman Patrick Connolly. Now a naturalized Australian, Connolly served with the British Royal Air Force as an Irish corporal at Maralinga from 1959 to 1962. He was interviewed at length in mid-1980.

We would see large numbers of Aborigines all over the restricted areas, they just went on walkabout around Maralinga and Emu Field, where the main testing was done. It was a never-ending problem where you had Aborigines walking on to the restricted areas unescorted. There was nothing to stop them, the signs were useless. During the two and a half years I was there I would have personally seen the best part of 400 or 500. I supervised when they were escorted from the area, or brought in for decontamination. This was a very small percentage of them, I wouldn't like to put a figure on it. The others were just shooed off like rabbits. In some cases we'd run a geiger counter over them, in other cases not. We just weren't that interested because we didn't quite understand the seriousness of the situation until some years later. The sad thing about it is that here in Western Australia there are about 14 or 15 blokes that I know who have cancer, and their families won't come forward for one reason or another.

There is a sort of intimidation going on at the moment, sort of pressure, whereby people are just being told to keep their mouths shut. It has happened to me many times. I have had personal visits from security agents. At that particular time, of course, I wasn't an Australian citizen. I was an Irishman, and they made it very clear that I should be careful what I said openly, and about rocking the boat. The inference was that, as an Irishman living in Australia, I could be deported. This worried me, why wouldn't it?

I have had calls from wives and widows afraid to come forward, just average people, businessmen and the like. They think they might be making fools of themselves. It's becoming too much of a hot potato to ignore now though. There are anything up to 20 people here who are affected with radiation because of Maralinga. Some would support what I say about the Aborigines, some wouldn't. Some have rung me back to say they've had second thoughts on it, they've just gone cold on it. My concern is for the people who are left behind, the wives and children.

On the Aborigines—there was a little bit of a round-up I suppose, but it wasn't so much getting them out then, it was after the tests were completed. How long do you keep them holed up? It's not safe to go there now except for a few hours. It was ridiculous to expect 20 or 30 of our blokes to police an area that size. It was just a token attempt. It was just a question of whistling at a guy two miles away to clear out. There was no real concerted effort made. We're not just talking about one specific area, we're talking about many areas.

Despite the pressure on him to keep his mouth shut, there is only one aspect of the affair about which Patrick Connolly is reluctant to talk. This is something he saw at the Yalata community, due south of Maralinga just off the coast of South Australia. During his RAF service, Connolly used to visit Yalata to take food to the Aborigines at regular intervals. Almost 20 years later, early in 1980, he made a return visit to the settlement, coming across something almost too disturbing for contemplation. This is all he will say of the experience.

About six months ago I was driving from Perth to South Australia on my own on business, and on an impulse I thought I'd drive off the track for a while and go and have a look at Yalata again.

What he saw shocked him profoundly, and the only detail he

will pass on is an encounter he had with 200 'very sick' Aborigines in the settlement. Many of them appeared to be partly blind, and 'seemed to have no life about them'. Questioned further, he said:

> Look, this is getting into a pretty sensitive area. We will just have to wait a bit longer to see what comes out. There are medical teams up there at the moment investigating the same thing. Whether it's still there now or not, I don't know. The Commonwealth Police have moved very quickly on that. They've gone up there and kept everybody away. I don't know if they've just dispersed all the Aborigines, or what. Just shooed them off to Arnhem Land or somewhere. There is a lot happening that is very underhand. There is one big hush-up. They are trying to cover the whole thing up. The word is, there is no cause for concern. That's what the authorities say, and that's what we have to go along with. It upsets me a great deal. I can't stand deception of any sort.

The Government's official line on this is provided by B. J. Lindner, manager of the Yalata community, who has denied all knowledge of Aborigines suffering radiation-connected sickness during his 20 years in the area. But there are others who prefer Patrick Connolly's version of events. A Queensland journalist, Philip Hammond, remembers staying at the Yalata Lutheran Aboriginal Mission in 1971 when, at the age of 22, he was travelling the Australian outback as a young British journalist, 'in search of experience'. In a letter to the Australian Nuclear Veterans' Association he wrote:

> During this time I made friends with mission staff, including a nursing sister whose husband worked in the area as a Flying Doctor. According to my diary of 20 June, the nurse mentioned to me the case of an Aboriginal woman who had strayed on to the Woomera testing range some years before. I recall this matter was dropped when I showed interest in knowing more. This is an extract from my diary: 'One woman, I learnt, repeatedly lost her children at birth because she was on walkabout in the Woomera Rocket testing area. Apparently everything was supposed to be safe, but radioactivity was

obviously present. Most of her subsequent children had died at birth, and the only survivor is sporting cauliflower ears, which look most odd on a snotty-nosed three-year-old.'

The rumours have even reached Federal Parliament. On 15 May 1980 Senator Cavanagh told the Senate:

We must have some clear investigation. The Aboriginals are deserving of consideration. We must find out whether that incident [high fallout levels recorded after one of the tests] is the cause of the blindness that one can track from Emu through to the north of Australia and Darwin.

There is more incidence of blindness among Aboriginals— what the medical profession is treating as trachoma—in that area than there is outside the passageway. [This refers to the path of fallout.] That is the position. Should not this be investigated? The Aboriginal tribes from the area have since been shifted to Yalata on the west [sic] coast of South Australia. When the Commonwealth made the decision to revert control of the site [Maralinga] to the State Government, it moved the Aboriginals in the area to Yalata. The mission at Yalata dismantled the materials on the site and took them to Yalata to build homes and sheds and so on at Yalata.

The British took the radioactive material back to Britain for disposal. On investigation they found that Maralinga was still a radioactive area. Watchmen still live in the area. Security guards see that no one enters the area. There is still some danger there. The danger is in the material on the property that is now at Yalata where Aboriginals are living. I suppose that Britain's ability to survive in the future was more important than the lives of a few Aboriginals, and the suffering they may go through.

Senator Cavanagh's concluding remark, unpalatable as it may be, perhaps comes closest of all to summing up the situation.

If there is ever to be an answer to the mystery of what Patrick Connolly saw at Yalata, it will most probably be provided by one or more of the teams of scientists and doctors which have been touring the outback since early in 1980. The purpose of these arduous fact-finding expeditions has been to attempt to establish exactly to what extent Aborigines have

148

suffered as a result of the tests.

When the information is collated, each and every Aborigine with a claim for compensation will be examined by an independent doctor, and the extent of his suffering will be gauged. The entire process, including the legal struggles which will almost inevitably follow the medical tests, is not expected to be completed until well into 1982. One of the medical men involved, Dr Trevor Cutter, of the Central Aboriginal Congress, a body funded by the Department of Aboriginal Affairs, spent weeks in the outback during 1980, tape-recording and documenting eye-witness accounts from Aborigines. One of his aims is to gain sufficient evidence for a World Health Organization inquiry, or a Royal Commission.

In September 1980, Queensland delegates to the National Aboriginals Conference in Toowoomba demanded that Aboriginal Affairs Minister, Senator Chaney, initiate such a Commission. They were told at the conference, by Australian Nuclear Veterans' Association National Director, Harold Crosbie:

> The Government has only ever admitted that four Aboriginals were affected by radiation. But we know that hundreds, and perhaps thousands, were. We're not just talking about those in the immediate vicinity of the A-bomb test sites of Maralinga, Monte Bello or Emu, but the huge areas in the paths of the fallout clouds.

Dr Cutter spoke to one of the authors early in 1980, at the time when the South Australian Health Commission was appointing its own team to go in search of evidence from Aborigines in the outback. He said:

> Jim Lester was the first person to put me on to this. He heard the veterans talking about it on the radio, and it brought back memories. We're still not absolutely sure what we'll do with the information when we get it, because it's up to the Aboriginal people concerned. But calling for a Royal Commission or something similar is probably the only way to get the information out and made public.

We hope to get a lot of stuff that is being kept secret. We know that during the later bombs, around 1957, they rounded everybody up and forced them off the area, and put them into big settlements, which were really exactly like prisoner of war camps. Places like Yalata, where they took people by truck and forced them to stay there, and they left on several occasions, and they were all dragged back again. They couldn't have got them all. I'm referring to the late 1950s, early '60s. They got a lot of them, and this probably killed more than the bombs, people just gave up the will to live. They weren't physically caged, but they were forced to live in these dormitories and what have you. A doctor, a friend of mine, who was there at that stage said it was worse than Belsen, people just dying like flies. He was a Health Department doctor, a Government employee, so he's not been allowed to talk about it. This is why we are arguing for a Royal Commission, because he would then be at liberty to talk to us. He wouldn't be otherwise. The Government is terrified about it, for that reason that the information would come out.

We've made approaches to various Government Ministers for a Commission but they've been completely negative, horrified; they say: 'That's an absurd idea, why would you want that? How would that help at all?' We see the Royal Commission as the only solution, it's the only way everything could be brought out. We've spoken to white station-owners who know what happened. They're unwilling to come forward publicly, but they would in a Royal Commission. One of the problems is that a lot of the witnesses are dead. It was 20 or 30 years ago, and they were adults then, so you can see why. We've had stories of groups of Aborigines being wiped out, and we've had a fair bit of publicity, and nobody has denied it so far. We're just frightened the whole thing won't come out for political reasons.

One of Dr Cutter's colleagues is Danny Vachon, a French-Canadian anthropologist with the Pitjantjatjara Council. He too has toured the outback, tape-recorder and notebook in hand. In his interview with one of the authors he said:

What we are basically doing is trying to determine not only how many people were affected, but how they were affected.

We'll then integrate that with what is known about radiation sickness at the present time. I've spent about a month asking questions in the Indulkana area of South Australia, where many people living there have provided me with quite a bit of information. We're planning on doing more work with people living at Yalata.

Questioned more closely about Yalata, Danny Vachon suddenly became deeply interested in the extent cf the authors' knowledge, and then cautious.

I know about the large hospital there, or rather I've heard rumours about things that occurred at Yalata in the past, but I've yet to research them. If you get the impression we're holding something back, here's one of the problems we're facing; I'm unwilling to release information that I haven't verified. The other problem is that we're in a dual process here, not only researching the extent of the effects of Maralinga, but we're also involved in negotiations with the Federal Government to provide certain services, one of which is an independent medical survey of the area to determine whether or not people are currently suffering from cancer, or possibly if in fact this is genetic break-down, if this is possible, I'm not even sure if it is.

Vachon explained that the whole issue of approaches to various Government departments is fraught with difficulties.

The Government's position is to tell us: 'If you feel that anybody has been disadvantaged in any way by the bomb tests, have them come up before us,' as Senator Carrick requested, 'and then state your case.'

Our position on that is that we're not going to do that — provide the Government with information which it will evaluate and then decide upon. We want to build our own case first. Scientifically I couldn't commit myself yet, and politically it would be disastrous.

One of the problems faced by researchers like Danny Vachon is the strict views Aborigines have on the disturbing of their burial sites. Confirmation that an individual has died from radiation-connected sickness can be found in his bones, and, quite possibly, Aboriginal graves across Australia contain exactly the kind of evidence scientists need to prove their case. Any researcher would look for the type of hard evidence that would certainly strengthen the case. However, the necessity to disturb the graves creates problems.

Philip Toyne, an Alice Springs lawyer representing Aborigines over the Maralinga issue, spoke to one of the authors over the importance of appointing a completely impartial doctor for the final examinations of potential compensation claimants. He explained that after lengthy meetings with Government officials it had been agreed that Aboriginal representatives would have the right of refusal of any doctor put forward for the examinations. 'It could well finish up that we'll have to bring in a doctor from Japan or America, because of the experience they've had of radiation-connected sicknesses in those countries.'

The Government's attitude to such examinations was given by Patrick Ryan, First Assistant Secretary of the Uranium and General Division of the National Development and Energy Department. He told the authors:

> What the Government has made quite clear is that where somebody claims to be suffering from exposure to radiation as a result of these tests, we have to find out what they are suffering from, and what their rights are.
>
> We are going into the outback with health and radiation people to try and find out from the Aborigines what they want us to do, and how we can meet their concerns. That matter has not yet been resolved, but we are leaning over backwards to work out a system. There are a group of Aborigines living at Ceduna, for instance, and we're bringing them to Adelaide to put them through a series of tests. I can only say that the Ministers concerned are very anxious to see that everything is done to ensure that people who have genuine claims for compensation receive what is due to them.
>
> There are real problems of chronology in dealing with the situation. We're looking at something that happened 20 or 30 years ago, and Aborigines in the desert don't have calendars. I don't know what I was doing in the '50s and '60s, and where I

was at any given time, so how can they be expected to remember their whereabouts in relation to the tests? We are obviously concerned to help the genuine cases, but at the same time, we don't hand the taxpayers' money out for nothing. The Government is using a vast list of resources in this—the Health Department, Aboriginal Affairs, the National Radiation Laboratory, the Atomic Energy Commission, the Department of the Environment, university people, like anthropologists, legal people, finance people, and so on. I would be confident that by the time we've finished, and that's going to be a long while yet, we will know everything we need to know.

Reassuring words. Only the events of the coming two or three years will reveal whether or not they indicate the Government's real intentions over the issue. The problem of arriving at a realistic figure for compensation for radiation-induced cancer, birth deformity or even death, promises to be a real stumbling block. If it is remotely possible to put a price on such sufferings, few would argue if it were to be in the hundreds of thousands of dollars in each case.

Given that there is some foundation in fact in the accounts of Aborigines themselves, servicemen and station-owners who were on hand at the time of the tests, the number of victims involved is going to amount, as Harold Crosbie said, to 'hundreds if not thousands' of Aborigines with legitimate compensation claims. So the overall figure the Government must face is, in all probability, going to be several million dollars. The handing out of such amounts is rarely approached by any Government with anything but reluctance, so the next question to arise is the possibility of buck-passing.

BRITISH RESPONSIBILITY

Since the British Government was conducting the tests, there must clearly be an argument for some contribution from it towards compensation claims. Melbourne lawyer, David Teed, who is a leading legal representative for the Australian Nuclear Veterans' Association, has already foreshadowed this. In the

153

early days of his representation of the ANVA, he mentioned the spectacular possibility of writs being hammered on to the door of 10 Downing Street on behalf of disadvantaged ex-servicemen. So why not disadvantaged Aborigines? It seems clear that some Anglo-Australian confrontation will develop over the tests at some stage in the future. The disposal of nuclear waste from Maralinga has already seen angry words flying across the world between the two Governments, but so far the subject of compensation has not been seriously broached with Britain. As outlined earlier in this chapter, the Aboriginal cause in general was considerably advanced by a visit to the United Nations. Perhaps the same thing will have to happen in Britain before any real progress can be made in this direction.

6

The Veterans

Warrant Officer William Cameron Jones could have had little idea of the chain events he was about to set off when he left his home base of Puckapunyal, in Victoria, in late 1953. He had joined the Army the year before, at the age of 25, and probably knew as little as most of his fellow servicemen about the deadly business of exploding atom bombs. All he was told, when the news of his transfer came through to Puckapunyal, was that he was going to Woomera in South Australia on a top secret mission. By the time he got there he would not have been a great deal wiser. W.O. Jones would have been told that the British were undertaking their first mainland atomic test at a place called Emu in a remote part of the desert, and he would have been told that he was to play an important role in the test. The terrible dangers that he would be exposed to were almost certainly not included among the information that was passed on to him.

By the date of the test, 15 October 1953, W.O. Jones had already completed the first part of his secret mission. He had helped drive a Centurion tank close to a place called Ground Zero. This is the technical name for the eye of the atomic hurricane—the site chosen for the explosion of the bomb.

W.O. Jones and his crew left the tank close enough to Ground Zero for it to catch the first waves of radioactive fallout from the blast, but not close enough for total destruction.

Those involved in the tests had decided it would be profitable to learn what damage would be caused to the Centurion by the bomb. They wanted it brought back out to civilization immediately after the explosion so it could be tested for the effects of the blast and radioactivity. Bushman, author and explorer, Len Beadell, touches on the incident in his *Blast the Bush,* a frighteningly naïve account of the events leading up to the tests. Published in 1967, the book deals in an inappropriately cheerful humorous way with Beadell's preparations and assistance in the choice of bomb sites. His reference to the tank reads as follows:

> The engines in the Centurion tank were started up for tests to observe whether they would continue moving or be snuffed out, and it was even equipped with 'Cecil', the straw dummy, propped up at the controls. It has been stressed before that this tank could have been placed in a position where it would have melted, but more knowledge could be gained if there was something left of it to study.

Beadell did not go on to describe what happened to the tank after the blast. How W.O. Jones travelled back horrifyingly close to Ground Zero, the air almost certainly still thick with radioactivity, and how he attempted to bring the Centurion back out with him. Not surprisingly, the tank refused to start, and spare parts were needed for the necessary repair work.

Because he was a good soldier, Bill Jones opted to stay with the tank while the spares were obtained. And because he had not been informed of the awful dangers of his task, he remained there for two days, until the Centurion was mobile again. His reward for his industry and determination to complete the job allotted to him was death from cancer 13 years later. The authorities can hardly have been surprised at his fatal disease, given their knowledge of his activities at Emu, but this did not in any way influence their attitudes towards his widow's subsequent action for compensation.

If Mrs Peggy Jones, of Clayton, Victoria, had not been as determined a fighter as her husband was a soldier, it is doubtful she would have got anywhere with her legal struggle. As it was, it took her eight long years to get the Government to admit it was in any way responsible for what happened to Bill Jones—and the value they put on his life was the princely sum of $8600. Appallingly inadequate as this was, it still represented a major breakthrough. To this day, it is virtually the only evidence of admitted responsibility by either Australian or British Governments for the sickness and suffering that has followed the tests.

On 20 March 1980, it was left once again to Tom Uren to detail the story of Warrant Officer William Jones to the Australian Parliament. As usual he did a thorough job. Here is the Hansard reference to his statement, made during the grievance debate.

> I want to raise further questions about the British nuclear weapons tests that were conducted in South Australia from the early 1950s to the early 1960s. In particular I would like to open up the question of the effect of those tests on the health of Australians who were involved in the weapons testing program at that time. I raise this matter because I have received further evidence which I present to the House that people who formerly worked at the weapons test sites have since contracted cancer, and some of them have died. I also raise this matter because there is more and more evidence in the United States that many have suffered as a consequence of the Nevada nuclear weapons tests. Yet, in this country, the Fraser Government still refuses to acknowledge that there have been people whose health has been affected by such tests. It even refuses to carry out or follow up any studies of health by the Australian personnel who worked at Maralinga and Emu.
>
> Last year I was approached by a Melbourne woman concerning her continued attempts to gain fair compensation for herself and her children for the death of her husband in 1966. The woman's late husband, William Jones, had been a member of the Army from 1952 to 1965, when he was discharged as medically unfit for military service. He died of

carcinoma nine months later in 1966 at the age of thirty-nine. Mrs Jones says that her husband was sent on a secret mission for several months from his home base at Puckapunyal to Woomera in South Australia in late 1953.

She says that his crew took a tank to be placed in the blast of an atomic explosion. She believes that after the explosion he went back to bring the tank out, but it did not work; so he remained in the blast area for two days waiting for parts. There is evidence to support her story in the book *Blast the Bush* by Len Beadell. It is the story of the first atomic test at Emu on 15 October 1953. Mr Beadell says that a Centurion tank was transported to Emu, and placed close to the bomb with a dummy inside to test the effects of the atomic blast. I believe that Mrs Jones' claims should be examined and investigated.

After her husband's death, Mrs Jones applied for compensation for herself and her four children on his behalf. After a long battle she was finally awarded compensation, in 1974, under the *Compensation (Australian Government Employees) Act*. The delegate of the Commissioner for Employees' Compensation determined that the disease William Jones had suffered from constituted a disease due to the nature of his employment with the Army. I want to stress that aspect. It was a metastatic carcinoma of the bone. He also determined that William Jones' death resulted from a disease due to the nature of his employment. I seek leave to have these two determinations incorporated in Hansard.

Having incorporated this document, Mr Uren continued:

Let us examine the evidence these documents present. The delegate has determined that some factor in William Jones' Army work caused him to get this cancer. . . . the evidence as it stands suggests that William Jones was a victim of radiation at Emu, and that this was reluctantly admitted, even within the bureaucracy. One of the features which stands out in this case is the frustration and secrecy which confronted Mrs Jones throughout her struggle.

William Jones tried to get compensation for his illness before he died, but failed. Mrs Jones says she then first sought compensation as far back as 1968, but from the start she was hampered by the secrecy. Everyone associated with her late husband's trip to Woomera had been told to keep quiet. . . . She persisted, despite knockbacks, until 1974, when she won the determination to which I have referred. Eight years after her husband's death a lump sum of $8600 and small weekly payments for each child were awarded. . . . The Army then haggled for three and a half years over how much should be paid for William Jones' medical expenses and lost wages. The amount of $585 that was awarded is still disputed by Mrs Jones. . . . Why has Mrs Jones had to battle so long for fair compensation? Why has there been so much delay and frustration? These questions should be answered.

We must also ask how many other people who worked on the weapons tests have cancer. How many of them have sought compensation? How many have been too intimidated to try? There is evidence that other people have been affected.

Mr Uren then went on to detail the cases of six Commonwealth Police officers who had worked at Maralinga, and were now dead, or dying of cancer. It was difficult to verify these allegations because former Commonwealth Police who guarded radioactive materials had been sworn to secrecy.

Three years later, on 20 August 1980, the ANVA's Harold Crosbie was to write to Commonwealth Police Commissioner, Sir Colin Woods, asking for specifics on members of the force connected with the tests. His reply, from Acting Assistant Commissioner W. L. Antill, said the force could not supply such information to an organisation like the ANVA, but was 'committed to affording every assistance and support to a properly constituted governmental inquiry'. The only problem was, of course, the Government had no intention of allowing such an inquiry.

Back to Tom Uren's address of 20 March 1980. He said that in 1978 he had asked the Health Minister for a complete health study of all Australians at Maralinga, but had been refused because, according to Health Minister Hunt, monitoring procedures were so stringent no one could have been harmed. That answer came in April 1978. Seven months later, Health

Minister Hunt reiterated, in answer to another Tom Uren question: 'For nuclear tests conducted in Australia by Britain, the most stringent safeguards to the health of personnel were implemented at every level.' Having incorporated these answers, Mr Uren continued:

> So the Government can give no greater assurance about the health effects of the weapons tests than its tired old rhetoric. The Government says that the risks were too small, and monitoring too stringent for there to be anything to worry about. The United States Atomic Energy Commission has said that for many years, but people in the United States are continuing to agitate. Many ex-military personnel have been located and found to be suffering from the effects of leukaemia and cancer. The evidence indicates that the incidence of these diseases is higher than normal. Ten people in the United States are receiving compensation for what they have suffered.
>
> I am now asking that the Government . . . re-examine Mrs Jones' case, and award adequate compensation if the facts I have outlined are as stated. . . . Not only should the Government have another look at Mrs Jones' case, but it should also undertake a thorough investigation into the health of those people who worked on weapons testing in the '50s and '60s.
>
> If a Government has made a mistake, whether it be the United States Government, the United Kingdom Government, or the Australian Government, it is about time they said: 'We were wrong. Let us now correct our mistakes.' The real issue is one of compassionate treatment by the Government. The Government should give greater consideration to these people, particularly those who are suffering so much.

Probably the most significant part of Mr Uren's lengthy speech was the finding in favour of Mrs Jones by the Delegate of the Commissioner for Employees' Compensation. Behind all the impossible civil service jargon, and all the 'also known as' circumlocutions, was the irreversible fact that Peggy Jones, at the end of a lonely and lengthy struggle, had got the Government to admit that her husband's cancer had been caused by his service at Emu. Forget for a moment, if that's possible, the 'mean and miserable' compensation she was awarded. Instead, contrast her victory with Health Minister Hunt's repeated assurances about 'stringent safeguards', 'strict controls' and 'constant monitoring'. The Government could not have it both ways. Either Mr Hunt was correct, and there were no dangers and no risks, or Peggy Jones' victory was a just one, and demonstrated that contamination could and did occur during the tests. Since Mr Uren's statement in March 1980, solicitors acting for Mrs Jones have been seeking to re-open the case.

Inexplicably the Government has made one half-hearted attempt to challenge the facts of the Jones case. In a letter to Pat Creevey of the ANVA, dated 19 September 1980, the First Assistant Secretary of the Uranium and General Division of the Department of National Development and Energy, Mr P. Ryan, wrote:

> Official records show that W. O. Jones was a member of an Army detachment sent to recover a tank which had broken down after being decontaminated and driven many miles from the Emu test site. W.O. Jones did not enter the active area, so it is not correct to say that he had been unprotected in a radioactive area for a dangerous period.

Harold Crosbie of the ANVA remains unimpressed by Mr Ryan's version of events. Among his members, he says, is more than one serviceman who was with Bill Jones when he volunteered to go in to the radioactive area around Ground Zero to bring the Centurion back out again. Crosbie further states that the men involved are ready, willing and able to sign statutory declarations, or give evidence before a court, totally refuting the 'official records' version of events. Equally significantly, Crosbie poses the question: 'Why did Peggy Jones win her case if her husband did not enter the active area?'

David Teed, the ANVA lawyer who also acts on behalf of Australian Vietnam Veterans in the Agent Orange controversy, told one of the authors, in September 1980, that 'if necessary the Jones case will be taken to any court in the land'. Mr Teed was obliged to ask Federal Attorney-General Senator Durack for advice on how best to begin common law proceedings against the Federal Government. And the problem of liability does not end there. Mr Teed believes there is a distinct possibility the British Government may have to be sued as well. So Peggy Jones' battle continues—a battle she started long before the concept of an organization to fight on behalf of nuclear veterans was first realized.

Another victim who began his fight single-handed, long before the advent of the Australian Nuclear Veterans' Association, was Rick Johnstone whose nuclear story began at the age of twenty-two. He was serving with the RAAF and, according to evidence given at subsequent court hearings, was a happy, well-adjusted individual. Then came the news of a posting to a place called Maralinga. This probably didn't mean a great deal to the young Johnstone, just that it was somewhere in the desert in South Australia, and the job had something to do with British arms tests. It wasn't long before he was confronted by unpalatable reality. Along with a number of other servicemen, he left Adelaide by train alighting at a god-forsaken spot called Watson's Siding.

From there the journey was continued across the desert by four-wheel drive vehicle to their destination. This turned out to be a city of tents pegged out in the middle of nowhere beneath the blazing sun, with only fellow servicemen, British scientists, and an even more formidable army of bush flies for company. In one of the many in-depth interviews Johnstone has since granted to various newspapers and magazines, he told Michael Hyde of *Nation Review*: 'The conditions were worse than any jail . . .' In the same article Johnstone spoke of the reaction of many of the men to the conditions and the work— constructing bomb towers and other preparatory work for the tests—which faced them on arrival at their new posting. The main aim was to get out; the methods they chose varied. One attempted suicide, others deliberately mutilated themselves in the hope of being invalided out. Another, more direct soul, simply loaded up a truck and set off across the desert in the general direction of Sydney. According to Johnstone, one of the most depressing aspects of the whole affair was the secrecy, so the soldiers and airmen were left with little choice but to assume that 'somebody must know what they were doing'. Johnstone's description of the first blast he saw—he witnessed four altogether—was graphic. He was eleven kilometres away from Ground Zero, and it was like 'the whole world going up in silence—like watching someone chopping wood from a mile away. You see the stroke and a few seconds later the chop. For some it's a traumatic experience'.

It certainly was for Rick Johnstone—he began to suffer vomiting, diarrhoea and nausea, all of which he attributed to tension. The tension was part of his new job. As a driver-mechanic with the Number One Radiation Detection Unit attached to the Royal Canadian Engineers, he had to drive into blast areas after the explosions as many as three times a day. The main purpose of this was to check, and sometimes retrieve, vehicles which had been deliberately left there, like Bill Jones' Centurion tank. Johnstone always had a geiger counter with him, and his instructions were to leave an area when the needle went past a certain point on the dial. Said Johnstone, in another interview with Nancy Berryman of the Sydney *Sun-Herald*: 'It was the tension of not knowing just how much radiation you were copping when the needle went off the dial.'

During a brief leave break in Sydney, Johnstone went into hospital for blood tests, and the idea that radiation exposure, not tension, might be causing his sickness and nausea first occurred to him. Around this time, early 1956, Johnstone underwent another experience the effects of which can only be guessed at. Len Beadell, the author and bushman referred to earlier, had gone missing on a survey trip in the desert, and Johnstone and another RAAF serviceman, whose name has since disappeared from memory, were sent out in a truck complete with supplies of water, oil and fuel, to find him. Johnstone and his mate did not find Beadell, but they stumbled across something else.

163

It was a ghost town, marked on the maps as X200, 240 kilometres north of Maralinga. The name it had been known by in 1953, when the first mainland tests were being conducted, was Emu Field. Half-way through their search for Beadell, Johnstone and his colleague drove into the deserted township, and to their amazement found about twenty-five buildings, in the middle of the desert. Even more unsettling was their discovery of kitchens stocked with food, eating utensils packed neatly in drawers, and several vehicles with their keys in the ignition. At the time, the two servicemen saw Emu as unnerving, certainly, but it also had a great deal more comfort to offer than the empty desert—so they spent two nights there while continuing their search for Beadell during daylight.

Back at camp, when Johnstone mentioned his strange encounter to a Warrant Officer, he was told: 'Forget it. You never saw it.' And forget it he did, until a chance encounter months later with Dr (later Lord) William Penney. The pair of them were inspecting a blow-hole on the Nullarbor Plain, where Johnstone recounted his Emu Field experience to the English scientist. 'You didn't go through that area did you?' Penney asked casually, before mentioning the tests which had been conducted there.

Finding a logical explanation for the desert-bound *Marie Celeste* which Johnstone and his colleague chanced upon, requires further reference to Len Beadell's *Blast the Bush*. Beadell found the site on which Emu was constructed, led the scientists to it, and helped design and construct the village. He included in his book an aerial photograph of the village, showing quite clearly the buildings to which Johnstone referred. Strangely there are no references, that the authors could find, in offical Government reports to these buildings.

Emu is discussed in the Australian Ionizing Radiation Advisory Council report No. 7: 'Radiological Safety and Future Land Use at the Emu Atomic Weapons Test Site, October 1979', but there is no indication of a village or any form of living quarters on the site. Reference is made to an airstrip and a road, but not to buildings. Why should the Government and the Warrant Officer who told Johnstone, 'Forget it!' be so keen to deny the existence of such facilities at Emu?

The answer lies possibly in that AIRAC Report No. 7. The problems of 'logistic support' are mentioned, and the resultant need to find a more amenable site. 'Accordingly few lasting facilities were developed at Emu,' states the Report. However, it does indeed reveal, albeit unwittingly, what may well have been the fate of those 'few lasting facilities'.

Only two tests were conducted at Emu; Totem I and Totem II, on 15 and 27 October 1953 respectively. According to AIRAC No. 7, fallout from Totem I drifted in a north-easterly direction, dispersing off the coast of Queensland. Unfortunately for Totem II the elements were not so co-operative. Immediately after the blast, wind sheer caused part of the fallout cloud to veer back in a south-south-westerly direction for two kilometres. Later the cloud 'broadened to south-easterly'. Is it assuming too much then, from this evidence, to suggest the following sequence of events on October 27.

Immediately after the bomb had been dropped from its tower and exploded, the fallout cloud began drifting, as in Totem I, in a north-easterly direction, away from Emu village and its living quarters. Then, to the dismay of the watching scientists, wind sheer took the cloud back on itself, heading it directly for their home base. It is not difficult to imagine the haste with which they would have packed and departed. Nor is it difficult to imagine the reluctance there would have been to own up to such an undignified flight. The questions of safety posed by such a confession would indeed have been difficult to answer.

If such educated guesswork is in fact correct, it gives a ready explanation for the evidence of hurried departure found by Johnstone. It also makes clear why Government reports have been so reluctant to acknowledge the existence of the buildings at Emu.

Taking the educated guesswork a stage further, one is

entitled to ponder why the tests were transferred to the Monte Bello Islands after Totem II. The order of sites for the tests was Monte Bello, Emu, Monte Bello again, and Maralinga. Why the move back to Monte Bello after only two tests at Emu? Surely a more logical progression would have been to complete the second Monte Bello tests at Emu, before moving equipment and manpower the comparatively short distance to Maralinga. But this, obviously, would have been impossible had Emu been badly contaminated.

Whatever the answer, Rick Johnstone's medical problems were worsening. Shortly after the Sydney doctor's diagnosis that he was suffering from the effects of radiation exposure, Johnstone was admitted to the RAAF base hospital at Richmond, NSW.

Here, predictably enough, such a diagnosis was found to be unacceptable, and was changed to a rare blood condition with nervous complications. On his way back to Woomera he suffered a relapse, and was admitted to the Daws Road Repatriation Hospital in Adelaide. Here Rick Johnstone underwent a different type of hell. He spent much of his time in a padded cell, and for a three-month period was given daily doses of insulin as shock therapy. At one stage this caused his heart to stop beating and, after revival by glucose injections, it was discovered he had forgotten much of his Maralinga experience. How convenient for the authorities treating his 'nervous disorder'! Shortly after this, the RAAF was happy and thankful to give him a discharge because of ill health.

Then followed a long series of anxiety attacks and visits to various psychiatric centres. Complicating his state of mind was the onset of a disease called agoraphobia, the morbid fear of wide open spaces. The real root of the problem, Maralinga and the bomb tests, had been pushed to the back of his consciousness by the shock therapy, so Johnstone rarely mentioned it to any of the doctors and psychiatrists who were seeing him during this period. And then, at the North Ryde Psychiatric Centre in 1968, Johnstone raised the subject of the tests during a group therapy session. Don't be ridiculous, he was told by the doctor, there have been no atomic tests in Australia. His strange ramblings were put down to schizophrenia, and another knock-out injection was administered.

Luckily for Rick Johnstone that particular doctor was an honest man with a long memory. Four years later, in 1972, the medical man watched a television documentary dealing with the atomic tests, and realized his mistake. He immediately contacted Johnstone by telephone, and apologized. The following year, Johnstone was awarded a fortnightly payment of $220 by the Commonwealth Employees' Compensation Board. But this still left him well below the poverty line in his attempts to support himself, his wife, and his two sons, one of whom he was trying valiantly to put through university. So a further fortnightly payment of $110 was coughed up by the Social Services Department, taking the Johnstones' weekly income to the niggardly sum of $165.

The most interesting point about the Compensation Board's award, however, was that it covered Johnstone for a pre-existing condition aggravated by his service. It was conveniently overlooked that the airman had been passed A-1 both physically and psychologically when he joined the RAAF. The next problem in the ongoing struggle for adequate compensation for his sufferings was the statute of limitations, which states that no action can be brought more than six years after the event. There was also a legal headache over whether an enlisted person is entitled to sue the Commonwealth. Since Johnstone's agoraphobia was so bad by now that he rarely, if ever, left his Sydney home, save for hospital visits, the answers to the two questions were becoming increasingly vital.

Today Johnstone believes his twenty years of ill health are directly attributable to what he saw and experienced at Emu Field and Maralinga. He believes the Government, through its medical services, deliberately tried to brainwash away all his memories of his role in the atomic tests. As long ago as October 1978, he told Tony Walker of the Melbourne *Age*:

> At the risk of being accused of sounding paranoid, I believe the

> treatment was a form of brainwashing aimed at dissuading me from speaking about the place [Maralinga]. I do feel a lot has happened which has been covered up.

More recently, in March 1980, Johnstone achieved something of a breakthrough in his legal struggle. The Commonwealth Government decided, after 27 years, to grant him legal aid. Johnstone believes this has made legal history, in that it is the first time an ex-serviceman trying to sue the Government has been granted legal aid to do so. At the time of this minor victory, his medical symptoms were listed as premature ageing, acute anxiety, agoraphobia, hypertension, allergic asthma and neurodermatitis.

More legal history was made towards the end of 1980, when Johnstone's first court appearance took place—in the television room at Alanbrook Private Hospital, Mosman, Sydney. For one day that room became the Supreme Court, with Mr Justice Cantor presiding. The issue at stake was whether or not the airman should be allowed to proceed with his action, although it fell well outside the statute of limitations.

At the time of publication of this book, Rick Johnstone's legal battle is continuing.

ANVA

Harold Crosbie of the ANVA is a man who feels immeasurably for those who have suffered from their service for their country during the bomb tests. He conveyed the depths of this feeling in October 1980 when he was invited by the Uranium Advisory Council to present his submission on the Commonwealth Government review of the Atomic Energy Act. Crosbie was only too ready to accept the invitation. He wrote back:

> This Association [the ANVA] believes that all citizens of Australia have well established rights to prevent life-threatening harm from damaging themselves or their children. Under the Australian constitution, this right to life is

fundamental. It is known that ionizing radiation is harmful to living things, and causes adverse health effects. It is known that the nuclear fuel cycle as a means to generate electricity produces enormous quantities of long-lived ionizing radiation, much of which cannot be, and is not, isolated from the biosphere which mankind inhabits. Life-threatening experimentation on citizens without their consent, and the wilful causing of disease, death and deformity within a large number of people over a long period of time are crimes against humanity. It can never be maintained that sound public policy would permit Government or non-governmental agencies to deprive human beings of their lives in order to obtain energy for other human beings.

It is both interesting and instructive to contrast this statement with one made by Professor Sir Ernest Titterton earlier the same year during a lecture series at the Australian National University. It was an equally emotional outpouring, but one that came from a mind frighteningly unfettered by considerations of humanitarianism.

Sir Ernest was touting the advantages of nuclear power as the cheapest, safest and most environmentally desirable means of power generation yet devised by man.

> Unless we harness other energy sources [i.e. nuclear power], national economies will fail, there will be no commerce, trade or employment, nations will fight to obtain the remaining, dwindling energy supplies, standards of living will collapse, and man will return to the Dark Ages.

And then, for a flash, he allowed the real extent of his arrogance to show through. Those opposed to high energy consumption, he said, were 'long-haired, sandal-footed, do-gooders'.

Harold Crosbie certainly could never be described as long-haired. He generally dons footwear appropriate to the venue and occasion, and would oppose bitterly any description of himself as a do-gooder. But then he is also not entirely convinced that national economies, commerce and trade are the highest pinnacles to which man can aspire. With less than a year struggling for the ANVA cause behind him, Harold Crosbie has built up a formidable catalogue of invaluable contacts and allies, ranging from many of the servicemen who were at Emu and Maralinga to the politicians who will now decide their future. He is prepared to use any weapon at his disposal, whether it be his considerable media contacts, his softly-spoken persuasive manner or his hugely impressive grasp of his subject, to further the aims of his organization. These were outlined early in 1980 and attached to membership applications sent to every nuclear veteran of whom Crosbie had knowledge. The aims were, and still are:

1. To establish a national register of all people concerned about their ill health, relatives' ill health, and genetically deformed unborn children, which may be as a result of service in Hiroshima and Nagasaki, or working as a civilian or serving in Australia in the 1950s during the atomic tests.

2. To gather scientific and technical information on the harmful effects of radiation on mankind.

3. To liaise with interested organizations here and overseas to gain information and assistance.

4. To make this information available to claimants, so they can lodge claims with compensation bodies and/or courts of law.

5. To produce a newsletter to keep members informed.

6. Eventually to get the Commonwealth Government to conduct free, comprehensive and routine medical examinations on those members who can establish that they have been exposed to radiation because of Government negligence or ignorance.

7. To gain compensation for those entitled.

One of the first hard lessons Crosbie had to learn after the drawing up of these aims was that the Australian Government was not particularly interested in helping establish a national register of potential nuclear victims as suggested. His request for a list of the 2000 Australian servicemen at Emu and Maralinga, needed for compilation of the register, was turned down out of hand. He remarked at the time: 'We knew then they really did have something to hide.'

Because of that refusal, the first of a number the ANVA was to receive at the hands of the Federal Government, the organization was forced to start finding out names the hard way—by word of mouth. Despite this, Pat Creevey was able to boast, in his first president's report, filed a few months after the statement of aims:

> You now have, for the first time, a national organization to find the answer to this question: 'Am I, or my children, or my friends and theirs, suffering any effects because of duties in radioactive situations?'
>
> This organization consists of solicitors, scientific and medical advisers . . . It is based in Brisbane now, and is taken seriously by the Federal Government, its departments, the RSL and other ex-service bodies, civilian associations and union groups. It is an apolitical welfare association which seeks help from both sides of the political fence and favours neither.

Creevey then went on to list the seven original aims, and the progress achieved in each:

1. The national register is well established, with between three and four hundred names here, and over one hundred on the way from WA. These men are POWs, occupation force veterans, atomic test veterans . . . reporting the same range of complaints. The raw data show cancers, sterility, nervous disorders, tumours, blood diseases, skin disorders of unusual nature, premature ageing and problems in children. From the tests veterans' reports there are 90 cases of cancer, 77 of these have died, most between 1970 and 1980. This is raw information which needs confirmation by death certificates, doctors' certificates, etc.

2. The gathering of information on radiation effects has been well begun.

3. Liaison with other organizations here and overseas has been established.

4. This information is available to claimants now through our solicitors . . . Legal aid has been applied for on your behalf as an association.

5. The newsletter is established.

6. We have written to the Federal Government to gain free regular medical monitoring of those who it can be shown may have been over exposed to radiation. Currently you can get such a check-up by submitting a claim for compensation. We don't regard this as satisfactory.

7. To gain compensation for those entitled. The solicitors have begun preparation on cases involving Veterans Affairs for a man and a widow of a Japanese veteran, a Defence Forces Retirement Benefit case for retroactive invalid pension benefits, a common law case, and an appeal against a Commonwealth Employees' Compensation decision.

Later in his first report, Creevey was able to point to other progress. Previously atomic test veterans had been dealing with up to seven Government departments in their struggle. The ANVA managed to get it narrowed down to one, the Department of Development and Energy, which had agreed to co-ordinate the hunt for relevant information.

Creevey then drew members' attention to the growing media interest in their cause. Television shows such as 'Willesee at Seven', 'Sixty Minutes' and 'Four Corners' ran news features on the issue during 1980. Countless radio stations, newspapers and periodicals further widened the coverage. Members still concerned with breaches of the *Official Secrets Act*, or the revealing of classified information, were even given a Canberra phone number where they could check if their story constituted a breach of national security! Since Defence Minister Jim Killen had already ruled, with uncharacteristic magnanimity, that security was not a problem, there seemed little point in such a precaution, other than to ensure the Government of the ANVA's good faith.

Mr Killen's ruling came in the form of a letter, dated 12 June 1980, in which he drew Harold Crosbie's attention to a statement from Senator Carrick issued on 15 May 1980.

The Government is concerned at suggestions that some Australian personnel who believe that they have been exposed to dangerous radiation, or believe they know of others who may have been so exposed, may be inhibited in coming forward because of uncertainty as to the present security significance of their involvement in the atomic weapons tests. Their continuing sense of responsibility in this matter does them credit, but the particular circumstances of any possible exposure (as distinct from information about the tests themselves), should not be of any security significance. If these persons remain in any doubt, however, they are urged to contact the Department of Defence for advice.

By this time, the ANVA's Radiation Exposure Profile and confidential medical record questionnaires were receiving wide circulation among nuclear veterans. When the ANVA first makes contact with a potential member, it informs him of the aims, and invites him to join, for the $10 fee. Whether he decides to join or not, he is asked to fill in the medical record and the radiation profile, and a letter is sent to his GP, where known, requesting that certain medical tests be undertaken.

The radiation profile is prefaced by the following brief:

> Today acceptable levels for radiation exposure are much lower than they were in the 1940s, and 1950s. This means that, even if all was done well at Maralinga, Monte Bello Island, Amberley, Hiroshima, and Nagasaki, and other places involved, that people have been subjected to radiation levels which are dangerously high by today's standards.
>
> If you and your family desire to be thoroughly checked for possible ill effects from radiation exposure (we include family because we have medical proof that three generations may be affected), we need to have the enclosed forms filled out by you. This Association intends to make submissions to the Commonwealth Government to support our demand for an open judicial inquiry. Therefore we must tabulate and compute all available information from you and other sources to establish exposure patterns.

Initially the profile requests details of names, age, address, service number, rank, corps or department, date of enlistment and discharge, units to which posted, code names and places of explosions witnessed, dates of explosions, duties performed, number of times and/or periods of exposure. It then goes into more detail.

The next questions deal with the subject's proximity to Ground Zero at the time of detonation and exposure, and asks for details of any decontamination procedures experienced. Ill effects such as vomiting, nervousness, listlessness, unexplained bleeding, loss of hair, anaemia or frequent headaches are listed with requests for dates when first experienced. 'Were you ever told by qualified people that you were suffering from radiation sickness?' asks one question. Another seeks to know: 'While at the test or firing areas, were you ever hurriedly evacuated? If so describe the area and circumstances as best you can.'

Other, similarly vital questions ask:

> What time after detonation did you enter the fallout area? Did you approach near to, or work at Ground Zero? Were you issued with a protective mask or clothing? Were you monitored for radiological contamination after every exposure or only occasionally? Were you issued with a film badge or dosimeter? What other methods of recording radiation dosages or readings were used? Have any of your children or grandchildren shown signs of abnormalities? Were you briefed on the dangers of the work you were carrying out, or the protective measures you were to take? Did you ever go into or work in a contaminated area without the direct supervision of a scientist, qualified technician or officer?

As can be seen, the radiation profile was designed to give as complete a picture as possible of safety procedures in use during the tests.

But when the completed papers started coming in, and that picture began taking shape, the results were far more alarming than encouraging. Sixty per cent of those filling in the profile were not issued with protective masks; sixty-four per cent were not issued with protective clothing; forty-four per cent were not monitored for radiation; thirty-six per cent were not issued with a film badge; sixty-two per cent were not issued with a dosimeter; fifty-seven per cent did not sign for either film badge or dosimeter; and fifty-nine per cent reported that the readings of their dosimeter went unrecorded. An embarrassingly second-rate safety record by any standards, and one that would almost certainly bring any commercial company under the close scrutiny of the law.

The medical questionnaire was similarly thorough, and elicited similarly disturbing results. It wanted to know of any children fathered before or after the possible exposure situation, and of any abnormalities they suffered. Details of all medical problems associated with radiation exposure possibilities were also requested, as were details of medical treatment during and since service. Information was requested on pensions and compensation received, and incidences of miscarriage or cancer among wives. Also, importantly, subjects were asked whether they have or had any souvenirs from possibly contaminated areas. The completed questionnaires, with the individual medical histories, were sent to the ANVA's honorary medical officer, Dr L. S. S. Lau.

Within their first three months of operation, Harold Crosbie and Pat Creevey had enlisted 400 test veterans in the ANVA, and within three months of the first medical questionnaires, 68 cases of cancer had been turned up, 54 of them fatal. By September 1980, the figure had increased to 90 cancers, 77 of them fatal. Even before computer analysis of statistics, Harold Crosbie announced that the final survey would surely reveal a massive disparity between ANVA members and a control group without experience of radiation contamination. In addition to the abnormally high cancer rate, other radiation sickness-related problems were cropping up. These included blood and bone disorders, sterility, tumours, nervous disorders to the point of suicide, and various handicaps and abnormalities in veterans' children.

Around this time, Pat Creevey posed a highly pertinent question. Six veterans had claimed they were treated for radiation sickness as a result of the tests, but there is no Government record of this. The ANVA want to know why, and

175

also what follow-up monitoring was done by the Government on people considered sick enough for treatment. The ANVA also wanted to know to which safety levels the British and Australian Governments worked during the tests. As explained earlier a rem is a biological measure of radioactivity absorbed by the human body. The international permissible exposure level dropped from 15 to 5 rems per year during the late 1950s, so it is vital to know to which level, if any, they were working during the tests.

It was around this time, when the first results from the questionnaires were coming in, that Harold Crosbie had an experience that banished once and for all any lingering doubts he might have had over whether he was doing the right thing. This experience centred around a 48 year-old test veteran called Lester Stephens, possibly the most tragic individual of the many encountered by Crosbie and Creevey.

During his twelve years with the Royal Australian Navy, Stephens spent time at Maralinga, where he witnessed four of the tests, three of them from relatively close range. Later in life, he contracted cancer of the lip and bowel, but did not connect his illness with the tests until he heard of the existence of ANVA. Shortly afterwards he joined the Association and was examined by Dr Lau. The honorary medical officer reported that there were definite grounds to suggest the sickness was caused by radiation exposure.

After Dr Lau's initial examination, Stephens made an appointment with Harold Crosbie to discuss his case. The veteran had already attempted, on three occasions, to obtain a 100 per cent pension for his sickness, but had been turned down each time. The Government was prepared to accept his lip cancer as service-related, but refused to make the same connection for his bowel cancer. A letter from Veterans' Affairs Minister, Evan Adermann, to Mr K. G. Schultz, national secretary of the RSL, dated 8 May 1980, spelled out the position.

The letter noted Stephens had first lodged his claim for benefit on 24 October 1973, and had had his lip cancer

WARNING

YOU ARE APPROACHING

A RADIOACTIVE AREA

READ ALL NOTICES

Warning sign . . . completely incomprehensible to most Aborigines who happened upon them.

Top: The same aircraft pictured in the photograph opposite page 65 with Staff Sgt Smith at the controls. This photograph was taken at Emu in December 1956, three years after the aircraft had been contaminated.

Warning sign at Watson rail sidings with police guard.

accepted, and his bowel cancer rejected by the Repatriation Board on 30 April 1974. Then followed two appeals, first to the Repatriation Commission, and then to the Entitlement Appeal Tribunal. Both appeals centred on the bowel cancer, and both were disallowed.

It was about this letter that Lester Stephens made his appointment to see Harold Crosbie on the morning of 8 July — an appointment Stephens did not keep. Instead, he telephoned Crosbie in the early hours to tell him he would not be coming, he would be dead from the overdose of sleeping tablets he had just taken. Less than a week after the call, Crosbie described the incident as follows:

> It was two in the morning when the phone rang, and I wasn't thinking too straight. He apologized for the lateness of the hour, and said it was a matter of urgency. He then said he didn't have much time to talk, because he had taken a massive overdose of sleeping tablets. I kept trying to get him to tell me where the phone box was he was calling from, so I could get help to him, but he refused to tell me. He spoke for a few minutes about keeping up the good work for the ANVA, apologized for not being able to make the appointment the next day, and then said: 'Goodbye and God bless.'
>
> It was clear from what he said that he wanted his death to be used as a means of drawing attention to the problems of surviving bomb-test victims. He hung up before I could find out where he was. I rang the police and gave his address in Brisbane, and told them to look in nearby phone boxes. Two hours later they called me back to say they had found him, but he was dead. . . .

7

Untruths
and Half-truths

Nineteen eighty was in every way a vital year for Australia's nuclear veterans, and one of considerable advancement for their main hopes and aims. It was also the year that saw the entire issue of Britain's A-bomb tests, in the South Australian desert and at Monte Bello, become the subject of regular debate in Australia's Federal Parliament. Labor's Tom Uren was the champion for the veterans, and the main source of embarrassment for a Government unaccountably more concerned with suppression of the facts than with the granting of justifiable compensation to those who had genuinely suffered through Britain's need to join the nuclear arms race, courtesy of another's backyard.

Long before Crosbie, Creevey and the ANVA came on the scene, the tests had been brought up in Parliament for a variety of reasons. During the early 1970s, there was a brief flurry of controversy over whether or not Britain had told the whole truth and nothing but the truth about exactly what her scientists had left behind. That issue was later to become considerably more involved, and will be dealt with in full in Chapter 9.

As far as the veterans were concerned, possibly the first hint of what was to follow came on 9 March 1977, when Bill Hayden, later to become Opposition Leader, asked Defence Minister Jim Killen for 'a full list of all nuclear explosions which have taken place in Australia, giving the date, the size, location and purpose of each'. On 31 March, Mr Killen provided the following list.

Date	Location	Approx. size
2 October 1952	Monte Bello	Kiloton range
15 October 1953	Emu	Kiloton range
27 October 1953	Emu	Kiloton Range
16 May 1956	Monte Bello	Kiloton range
19 June 1956	Monte Bello	Kiloton range
27 September 1956	Maralinga	Kiloton range
4 October 1956	Maralinga	Low yield
11 October 1956	Maralinga	Low yield
22 October 1956	Maralinga	Kiloton range
14 September 1957	Maralinga	Low yield
25 September 1957	Maralinga	Kiloton range
9 October 1957	Maralinga	Kiloton range

He added: 'The purpose of each explosion was related to the development of a British nuclear deterrent.' It may not have meant a great deal at the time, but it provided a neat cast list for the drama that was to follow.

Fourteen months later, on 11 April 1978, Mr Uren asked two questions of the then Health Minister, Ralph Hunt. They were:

1. Has the Minister's attention been drawn to the United States Government's follow-up study on personnel who were involved in their past atomic testing programmes?
2. Will the Australian Government institute a similar inquiry amongst all persons who worked at Maralinga, South Australia, during the years 1950 to 1965, in order to ascertain what ill effects they have suffered?

Mr Hunt's reply to the first question was a simple 'Yes'. The second he answered as follows:

> All personnel working at Maralinga were subject to stringent
> health procedures. Their activities in the field were strictly
> controlled, and they were constantly monitored to ensure that
> they were not exposed to dangerous radiation. The majority
> . . . were UK personnel. Any follow-up studies . . . would be a
> matter for the UK Government . . . Because of the stringent
> monitoring procedures undertaken at the time, and the fact
> that they were not exposed to dangerous radiation, there is no
> proposal to institute studies on Australians who were in
> support of the UK activities at Maralinga from the rear areas.

Even given that this was 1978, and there was no ANVA around
with embarrassing evidence that monitoring was either
neglected entirely or done on a haphazard basis, this was still a
shamefully lame effort on Minister Hunt's part. What he was
saying in effect was that nobody got hurt because everything
was completely safe, but if anybody did get hurt, they would
have been British anyway, and that was their problem. Fair
enough in a way, but what about his parting shot about
Australians 'in support . . . from the rear areas'? What would
Warrant Officer Bill Jones, and all the other Australians who
ventured perilously close to Ground Zero after the explosions,
have had to say about that? Probably that it simply was not
true, and the Minister was either misinformed or, more
probably, was under instructions to play the whole affair
down. Either alternative had disturbing implications, and gave
an early indication of what the Government's official stand was
to be.

Later the same year, on 11 October 1978, Tom Uren was on
his feet again in the House of Representatives, this time to
deliver a relatively lengthy address on the tests. Too long to
reprint in full, it contains much which, pithily and
unarguably, states the case for the nuclear veteran. The speech
began:

> There is one certain thing which can be said about Maralinga—
> this Parliament and the Australian public have not been told
> the whole story—instead a succession of Liberal-National
> Country Party Ministers have made misleading and con-

tradictory statements to the Parliament and outside the Parliament about Maralinga. Public concern has been answered with a series of untruths and half-truths about what testing took place at Maralinga, and about the waste which now remains, and the hazards at present.

He went on to say that many unanswered questions and unresolved problems were associated with Maralinga. These questions concerned the health of Australian citizens (especially Aborigines), Australia's sovereignty, and whether the Australian Government had always been kept informed of events on Australian soil. He asked about the hazards of the waste remaining at Maralinga, and the cost to Australian taxpayers of policing this waste for the 300 000 years it will take before it loses its toxicity. The Opposition asked for a full public inquiry to answer these questions.

Uren went on to give a detailed attack on Jim Killen over statements he made in 1976 over the exact nature of the British tests between 1958 and 1961. Quoting from *Scientist at the White House,* the private and later published diary of George Kistiakowsky, erstwhile explosives expert from Alamogordo, Uren attempted to prove Killen's statements were 'more than misleading'. They were in fact, deception, said Mr Uren, 'if not by the Minister, then certainly by his departmental advisors'.

The list of tests obtained by Bill Hayden was then touched upon. The Defence Minister had issued, on 31 March 1977, a list of nuclear tests held at Maralinga, numbering seven.

A letter from the British defence Minister to a Member of Parliament, Russell Kerr, which Uren had in his possession, spoke of nine tests.

Next on Tom Uren's chopping list was the Atomic Weapons Tests Safety Committee, referred to earlier (p. 113). He questioned the reliability of the committee, claiming that it was

a group of nuclear hawks[who] consistently supported French nuclear weapons tests in the Pacific, and said that they represented no health risks. That view has been totally discredited. It is well known that the Ranger Inquiry Commissioners were less than happy with the objectivity of the

181

committee's most prominent member, Professor Sir Ernest Titterton.

Uren quoted the case of a group of men who had been Commonwealth policemen at Maralinga in the 1950s. Four of their group of seven had died of cancer since Maralinga. This small sample, while not proving anything, raised serious questions which needed further investigation. The Government had refused to do this.

> The United States Government is now engaged in a study of the health of personnel previously involved in atomic tests. I asked the Minister for Health on 11 April this year if he would institute a similar inquiry, but he refused. He tries to brush the issue aside by saying that strict monitoring procedures were undertaken at the time. This is irrelevant — cancers do not show up for many years after the cause.

After discussing the effect of the tests on Aborigines, Mr Uren concluded that the whole Maralinga story was one of 'negligence, dishonesty and secrecy on behalf of Liberal-National Country Party Government'. Nothing of the serious, unresolved problems associated with Maralinga would have become public if it had not been for the courage of a few people, who previously worked at Maralinga, and some public servants who had made details public. The whole affair, said Uren, demonstrated vividly the Government's assurances about uranium were not to be trusted. The same people who asserted that nuclear waste is not a problem had continually lied about Maralinga. They were culpable for leaving the awful legacy at Maralinga.

The following month, 9 November 1978, Tom Uren was back in the fray, this time with more questions for Health Minister Hunt. He wanted a comparison between the health risks encountered at Maralinga, Emu and Monte Bello, and those encountered during the American atomic weapons testing programme. He also wanted to know how safety precautions differed between the two series of tests. Mr Hunt replied that there was insufficient knowledge of what happened in

America to make a comparison, but reiterated that for nuclear tests conducted within Australia, by Britain, the most stringent safeguards had been implemented at every level.

Tom Uren's next questions, on 27 March 1979, were aimed at finding out the incidence of cancer among Commonwealth Policemen who served at Maralinga. Administrative Services Minister, John McLeay, told him the problems in researching answers to these questions were insurmountable. Then, on 1 April 1980, Mr Uren asked Defence Minister Jim Killen about compensation claims received from individuals working on the tests. Some weeks later, Mr Killen was able to answer that there had been seven such claims. The first two were in respect of Bill Jones and Rick Johnstone.

Claim Three was received on 6 June 1972 for a 'malignant melanoma of the back' allegedly attributable to radiation exposure at Maralinga. It was disallowed by the Commissioner for Employees' Compensation on 26 November 1975 on the basis of specialist medical opinion.

Claim Four was received on 18 August 1977 for 'chronic myeloid leukaemia', allegedly attributable to exposure to radiation while on seagoing duties 100 kilometres off Monte Bello Island. It was disallowed by the Commissioner for Employees' Compensation on 30 November 1979 on the basis of specialist medical opinion.

Claim Five was received on 4 May 1978 for gout, allegedly attributable to radiation exposure at Maralinga. It was disallowed by the Commissioner for Employees' Compensation on 31 August 1979 on the basis of specialist medical opinion.

Claim Six was received on 19 March 1980, for 'hurthle cell carcinoma of thyroid gland' allegedly attributable to exposure to radiation while on flying duties at Woomera. At the date of Mr Killen's reply, the case was still under investigation.

Claim Seven was received from a widow on 27 March 1980 for death of her husband resulting from 'cancer of the oesophagus', allegedly attributable to radiation exposure while at Woomera. It was still under investigation on the date of Minister Killen's reply.

On 16 April 1980, Mr Uren asked another eleven questions, dealing with the bizarre and dangerous practice of sending aircraft into and through radioactive mushroom clouds to monitor fallout. These questions were based largely on a statement on the ABC programme 'Four Corners', on 29 March 1980 by former RAAF wireless operator Lance Edwards. Edwards had claimed that the throat cancer he was suffering had developed after such flights, on the first of which he had worn no protective clothing, and had been forced to shower thirteen times to try and rid himself of radioactivity.

Also prompting Tom Uren to bring up the subject was a statement made to the media by a former RAAF corporal called Ray Donald. He alleged that about 100 servicemen had come into contact with contaminated aircraft in 1953 and 1954. Donald, from Ipswich, said he had helped overhaul Lincoln bombers fitted with special canisters to collect radioactive dust samples by flying through the mushroom clouds immediately after the explosions. With other maintenance men, he claimed he began servicing the planes, without the protection of any special clothing, for two days after the blast programme began. When an English officer tested the aircraft for radioactivity with a geiger counter, and the pointer 'went wild', safety measures were introduced, and the aircraft were flown to Amberley, Queensland, where they were quarantined. Donald further alleged that he and many of his colleagues unwittingly took home their heavily contaminated clothing for their wives to wash.

The equally disturbing story of what happened at Amberley was traced by one of the authors to a small town, an hour's drive north of Brisbane. Here a man with close-cropped, iron-grey hair spoke for the first time about a subject he had been keeping secret for an uncomfortably long time. Former Warrant Officer, Noel Freeman, works in a real estate office but still carries himself swagger-stick straight, with the kind of military dignity peculiar to the ex-serviceman who still looks back with nostalgia on his period in uniform.

Noel Freeman's story, related quietly in his comfortable

living room, begins with the arrival in 1954 of four Lincoln aircraft at Amberley. It was fully a year later before he and three other servicemen, plus a hygiene officer, had cleaned the four planes of radioactive contamination.

His recollections began thus:

> I was in charge of the decontamination centre, I was sergeant then. The aircraft were parked on the big apron. It was inside a compound with the gates kept locked. Nobody else was allowed in but us. It was an enormous saucer-shaped concrete area, and as we cleaned the Lincolns everything ran down into the dip. It was drained into storage tanks and pumped into an evaporator. If you got 1000 gallons going in, you'd be left with 100. You'd boil it up and the steam went out through vents into the atmosphere, but only after it'd been monitored. It was never released while it was active.

What was left in the bottom of the tank was the concentrated essence of 1000 gallons of radioactive liquid waste. This was taken off and poured into a number of 44-gallon drums, between twelve and fourteen in all. Another dozen similar-sized drums were filled with parts of the aircraft which had proved too heavily contaminated to be cleaned. These solid parts were thrown into the drums, and liquid concrete poured over them. Noel Freeman's secret was what happened to those drums.

> We loaded the drums aboard an aircraft. There were two occasions. I didn't go out myself, but I think it was the same pilot and the same plane both times. We heard him say afterwards that the drums with the solid parts had gone straight down to the bottom. But the ones with the liquid in burst when they hit the ocean. That's understandable when you think about it, they'd have to. The pilot said the ocean changed colour, it was like pea soup.

Mr Freeman is not so frank when asked about the exact location of the drop-off. Initially he claimed it was 'some way north-east of Brisbane'. But the ANVA has a record of Mr Freeman mentioning a distance of 200 miles [322 kilometres] off the coast. A spot such a distance north-east of Brisbane is almost due east of Rockhampton, on the southern edge of one of the world's richest and most valuable natural resources, the Great Barrier Reef. Later, Mr Freeman denied he was emphatic about the figure two hundred. 'It could have been anywhere between two hundred and six hundred,' he said.

This grossly irresponsible attitude towards the environment displayed by the authorities contrasts strangely with the stringent safety procedures they insisted that Noel Freeman and his team observed during their cleaning duties. They always wore safety overalls and rubber boots when in the active area, and if they went out, even for a sandwich or a break, they would strip off and leave their clothing inside. They would run geiger counters over themselves, sometimes running geiger counters over geiger counters. They even did all their own washing. Despite such precautions, and regular blood checks for two years after the decontamination exercise, Noel Freeman began experiencing an unidentified stomach disorder some years later. 'It's a worry,' he said. 'Nobody seems to know what it is. It could be attributable to my service.'

Noel Freeman's Lincolns were not the only aircraft to fly through atomic clouds. The Melbourne *Sun* of 28 September 1956 reported:

> Eight minutes after the burst, Canberra jet bombers flew right into the atomic cloud to take test samples, and to track the atomic cloud . . .

The Melbourne *Argus* of 27 September 1956 confirmed:

> Immediately a flight of Canberra jet bombers roared overhead straight into the cloud to collect radioactive samples.

Thus the experts were guilty of repeating old mistakes, they were not learning. The hazards and inconvenience of having to clean the Lincolns which flew into the clouds in 1953 had taught them nothing. Three years later, they were doing precisely the same with Canberras.

Almost equally significant is the following extract from the coverage provided by the Melbourne *Herald* of 28 September 1956:

> In Brisbane today the weather bureau chief, Mr Newman, said the winds above 10 000 feet [3050 metres] were blowing across almost all Queensland from the general direction of Maralinga. Civil Aviation officials in Brisbane said a Queensland Airlines DC3, on a flight from Brisbane to Cunnamulla, 450 miles [724 kilometres] west, will end its flight at St George, 280 miles [450 kilometres] west.
>
> A grazier, Mr C. W. Russell, has delayed a private flight from Dalby, 120 miles [193 kilometres] west of Brisbane, to Bourke in New South Wales. Officials said these measures were merely a precaution, and the bans would be lifted later today.

This last paragraph illustrates, perhaps as well as anything, the inconsistency of the authorities towards safety matters. It was seen fit to send servicemen flying straight into the mushroom cloud minutes after the blast, but civil aircraft were banned from approaching the remnants of the drifting radioactivity many hours later.

Given this wealth of evidence, it was hardly surprising that when the answers to Tom Uren's questions finally came, on 19 August 1980, they contained a great many more Government admissions. The answers were read to the House of Representatives by Deputy Prime Minister, Doug Anthony. They were provided by Senator Carrick, Minister for National Development and Energy. Mr Anthony began: 'Yes, I am aware of statements made by Mr Edwards on "Four Corners"'. The answer to question two, on the number of aircraft and personnel involved was:

> There were approximately 150 Air Force personnel present in RAAF aircraft which flew through, made contact with, or tracked radioactive clouds. Some of these personnel entered or contacted the cloud on more than one occasion. No civilians were carried on these flights. The estimate of total personnel is based on a normal Lincoln crew of seven persons.

Mr Anthony said some 80 Air Force crew would have been

subjected to decontamination procedures 'such as repeated showers' after such flights. He said 21 RAAF Lincoln aircraft flew through or tracked radioactive clouds during the 1952–53 tests, and were decontaminated at Woomera, Richmond and Amberley. More significantly, he admitted the aircraft had landed at Townsville, Queensland, Williamtown, NSW, and Parafield, SA, before decontamination.

Senator Carrick's answers side-stepped the all-important question of follow-up monitoring of the health of those involved in such flights, and it was no surprise that the debate received considerable media coverage the next day. Australians could hardly have been happy to learn of the appalling risks run by their countrymen in the cause of developing Britain's nuclear deterrent. Predictably, the ANVA had something to say about Senator Carrick's reluctance to answer the questions on follow-up monitoring of health. In a statement issued late in 1980 by Harold Crosbie the Association claimed:

> The Government has been misinformed again. No veterans' medical or personal records yet to hand contain any information on levels of exposure received. None contain any information on this matter as a guide to Unit Medical Officers, to assist in any follow-up monitoring of the members' possible radiation-related illnesses. However, cases have come to hand in which the documents reveal that exposure has occurred to the point where injury has been sustained. In one case in 1952, the Medical Board passed a man A-1 medically fit. Three months later, after duty in an atomic test, this man was evacuated. The diagnosis was: 'suffering from severe radiation exposure'. Blood tests showed a severe red/white blood cell imbalance. The Medical Board convened later remarked that this man had received severe radiation exposure of UNKNOWN quantity, and that he should, in future, avoid all unnecessary exposure. The radiation information just was not available to them from the man's records.
>
> Some veterans state that they had a blood test before leaving Maralinga in 1957. One states that he had a test three months after Maralinga in 1957. Another states he was followed-up

after being contaminated in the decontamination centre at Amberley in 1956.

The statement claimed that no veterans were asked about previous exposure to radiation before the tests, meaning that progressive doses could not have been calculated. Some veterans claimed they were working on radioactive aircraft for 14 days before they were told the planes were contaminated and precautions were introduced. Fifty-nine per cent of the veterans who had answered questionnaires by this stage said readings had not been recorded, to their knowledge. Other allegations included the absence of facilities for measuring internal radiation, and inadequacy of instruments in the aircraft—the monitoring needle often went off the dial and stayed there.

In addition, no radiation level recording devices were provided for the fitters who checked the sample canisters on the wings after landings. 'Before and after' medical checks were far from routine, and no limits were laid down for a 'turning back' point when radiation reached a certain level. One officer claimed that when the needle went off the dial it was decided that they 'might as well carry on and keep track of the cloud as required'.

Crosbie also pointed out in his statement that safety limits during the tests were three times higher than those used today. He disputed Carrick's figure of 150 servicemen being involved in the flights, mentioning instances where ground crew were taken along in case servicing were needed. Decontamination of aircraft was often inadequate, he continued, and at Amberley, before the specially designed facilities were introduced, the planes were merely washed down and then used for normal training flights.

These included occasions such as the Queen's visit in 1954, when the Lincolns flew as weather scouts for the Royal Yacht from Mackay, south. Veterans state the planes were later used for the Maralinga series of tests, then decontaminated in the designed centres. Mr Anthony's statement says in part that the numbers involved in decontamination cannot be ascertained. Yet in a letter from the Department to the ANVA, dated 19 September 1980, it is stated: 'Radiation records were kept on those who worked in contaminated areas.'

Veterans state that during the tests they detached the sample canisters from the aircraft bare-handed in ordinary clothing and, in one example, handed them into the care of a protected British scientist. Other veterans state they flew in aircraft in ordinary flying suits to monitor clouds, then flew long-distance home in the same aircraft. There were many variations in decontamination procedure standards. One case involved the use of the same towel shower after shower until the subject was clear. Another veteran states quite seriously that he wore an oxygen mask for respiratory protection on a cloud monitoring flight, and took it off only to eat. A veteran, employed in a designed decontamination centre where all was done properly, admits that, while steamcleaning radioactive parts of planes in a steam room, he was not required to wear respiratory protection.

Other veterans used steam cleaners overhead on aircraft in the open, and the resultant slush came down on them. They were wearing ordinary clothing.

Much of this statement demonstrates that either large numbers of veterans had extremely vivid imaginations, or Senator Carrick was badly misinformed, or guilty of telling less than the whole truth.

The period between 16 April, when Tom Uren asked his questions on decontamination procedures and the practice of flying aircraft into radiation clouds, and 19 August, when Senator Carrick provided the answers, was one of considerable activity for the ANVA. The organization received encouraging news during April from the New South Wales Cancer Council, whose director, Dr Gordon Sarfaty, suggested individual examinations for all test veterans. He added that once these examinations were concluded the results should be compared, in group form, with the results of similar examinations among servicemen who had not been exposed to radiation. Dr Sarfaty also advocated the use of medical records from Hiroshima and

Nagasaki as another yardstick.

The same month, the Melbourne *Age* ran the story of James Barry, an Irish immigrant employed by the Department of Supply to build houses and other constructions as targets for the A-blasts.

According to his widow, Mary Jane Barry, he developed cancer while working at Maralinga and underwent an operation. He died in 1966, aged 50, after leaving Maralinga in 1962, having worked there for seven years. Mrs Barry told the *Age:*

> He wasn't supposed to tell me anything, because of the Secrets Act and all. But he told me bits and pieces. He said things were very lax up there, they didn't take enough precautions.

Mrs Barry said that after her husband's operation for removal of a stomach cancer, he returned to Maralinga because, 'the money was so good'. She continued:

> When he came home we had this mortgage on the house, and he had to go back. That's why he stayed as long as he did. I'm happy it's all come out now, because I thought James' case was the only one.

By now increased media attention to the aftermath of the tests had prompted Sir Ernest Titterton to throw what he obviously hoped was some calming oil on troubled waters. Asked by the *Age* whether he felt new evidence was beginning to cast doubts on the adequacy of safety precautions used during the tests, Sir Ernest said:

> As far as this is concerned nobody has brought forward any evidence that has any validity. Radical precautions were taken, and they were absolutely first class, there were no significant radiation doses to any individual.

How anybody, even Sir Ernest, could afford to be so emphatic should perhaps be left to the wisdom of hindsight.

At the forefront of media investigation of the British bomb tests around this period was the Adelaide *Advertiser*. During April 1980, that newspaper ran a superbly researched and compiled series on every aspect of the tests and their aftermath. Several journalists were involved, but the two by-lines appearing most regularly were those of David English and Peter De Ionno. During the following months television programmes, such as 'Sixty Minutes', and magazines, such as *Penthouse,* helped step up the media focus on the controversy, but it is doubtful whether Maralinga would have become an instantly recognizable catchphrase without the groundwork laid by the *Advertiser* series.

Among the stories the *Advertiser* broke in April was the Labor Party's call, at Federal Government level, for a thorough investigation of the tests and their aftermath. Shadow Health Minister, Dr Neil Blewett, called for a complete epidemiological study of all Australians involved in the tests, an examination of safety standards in use during the tests, particularly in the light of latter day improvements, and an investigation of the subsequent health problems of both Aborigines and British servicemen. Even at this early stage, Dr Blewett foresaw possible problems over compensation. While he felt the Australian Government should be the one to cough up, he also felt that there were grounds for a claim against the British. 'I would hate to see this sad business develop into a five or ten year battle between governments while people suffer,' was the way he put it to the *Advertiser*.

In one of the newspaper's first articles in the series, English and De Ionno came close to summing up perfectly the dilemma caused by the controversy. They wrote:

> If they [the veterans] succeed in getting a hearing from Government, and perhaps ultimately compensation, they will change the way governments and the military think about the casualties of developing military technology. . . . No one can say cancers were caused conclusively by radiation exposure, and equally no one can say they were not. What can be established is that the cancer dead and many others were exposed to radiation far in excess of that experienced by average Australians. Without a full-scale medical survey of the Maralinga men, no one can say whether exposure to nuclear-

fission radiation has resulted in a higher rate of cancer than that experienced in the general and unexposed population. 'We have had thirty years of looking at the damage the enemy did to the sons of Australia, and now we have to look at what we did to them ourselves,' Pat Creevey says.

Among the first veterans interviewed in the *Advertiser* series were Lance Edwards and Ray Donald, already mentioned on p. 184. Donald told the newspaper:

> We all got a fair dose of radiation, but we didn't know it until an English boffin came over and checked the planes, and discovered they were red hot with radiation. After that they gave us white gloves, and made us have showers.

Edwards confirmed:

> We only had our normal flight clothing on the first flight, but for the second one they backed off a little and gave us white overalls with hoods. As soon as we went into the clouds the aircraft and everything in them took up the radiation level, and we flew back to Woomera with it.

In the same article, many veterans were traced and gave their stories. They included Robert Dash, from Brisbane, a radio technician in the ground crew servicing the Lincolns. 'The geiger counters were off the dial on the highest setting,' he said, recalling how the men were ordered to burn their contaminated overalls after it was realized precautions should have been taken. Another member of the ground crew, Maurice Bradford, died of cancer of the oesophagus in 1972. His widow, Vera, remembers how he used to insist it was the contaminated aircraft that ruined his health. Another Maralinga widow, Anne Clarke, of Adelaide, lost her husband Terry when he was 37 from cancer of the pancreas. He worked at Maralinga from 1962 to 1964 as a mechanical engineer with the Royal Navy.

Bob Cassidy, also of Adelaide, told the *Advertiser* of his role in the clean-up operation at Emu. He was employed as a fitter by the Department of Works. He claimed no warnings were passed on about radiation, and describes the hundreds of tonnes of waste littering the site from the bomb blasts. He has since contracted cancer of the gullet and stomach, but his doctors assure him it is in no way connected with radiation contamination.

English migrant, David George Fountain, worked on the same clean-up operation, and died of cancer of the bladder and genitals eight years later. Another civilian worker was Tom Brougham, of Mallala, South Australia, who built showers in the decontamination centre. He told the *Advertiser*: 'The wind blew the sand in every direction, the dust was over everything, the whole place would have been contaminated.' After his work was completed, he contracted huge abscesses under his arms which bled freely.

Another person interviewed in the same article was Avon Hudson of the South Australian town of Balaklava. He had already played a prominent part in exposing the haphazard nature of clean-up operations and burial of waste after the bomb blasts. He told the *Advertiser*: 'All the rules laid down were not enforced and some were broken outright.' He remembered a stand-up argument between a British Army captain and a scientist over whether or not a particular area was too heavily contaminated for safety. 'The officer ordered the men in anyway,' said Hudson. He claimed that the protective overalls and hoods were much too hot to wear in the blazing desert, and were discarded by most men, even when working in contaminated areas.

The day after the newspaper ran its first list of interviews with A-bomb casualties, the floodgates opened, and many others began making contact. Their stories were published during the following days. Among these were Frederick Sanders, from Adelaide, who worked as a plumber at the test site in 1956 when four bombs were exploded. He remembered a visit to Ground Zero where fellow workers pilfered articles, including a pair of boots and a boomerang left in an obviously heavily contaminated area.

Terry Flinn, of Adelaide, told the story of his father, Herbert, who died from cancer of the stomach at the age of 58 in

1971, after returning home from Maralinga a changed man. Other surviving relatives with stories to tell were Ian Wilson, whose father Thomas Robert Wilson died of cancer in 1975 after serving with the Army as a captain at Maralinga in 1955 and 1956; and Florence Finney, whose husband Albert died of cancer of the stomach, bowel, chest and throat, in 1978, after working at Maralinga as a barber with the Department of Supply in 1956; and Fay Nabes of Adelaide, whose husband Richard died of heart disease at the age of 40 in 1973, also after service at Maralinga, in his case with the Royal Australian Navy.

Over the next few days, other names and case histories filled the columns of the *Advertiser*. Coincidences all? The Government would probably have liked to think so, but the case against the authorities was mounting fast.

As the casualty list mounted, the *Advertiser* continued its series with an article that turned out to be somewhat premature in its optimism. Public service sources contacted by the newspaper seemed to think that the Government was on the verge of announcing an inquiry. However, when Federal Ministers were contacted, a masterly exercise in buck-passing resulted. The following ministers all directed reporters elsewhere: Defence, Veterans' Affairs, Health, and National Development and Energy. Finally Senator Carrick, of the last-named ministry, issued the following statement through an aide.

> Senator Carrick won't be making any statement in the immediate future. It is not clear whose responsibility this is. There are a lot of portfolios involved, including National Development, Health and Defence. The Government will not be responsible to journalists. If the Opposition makes approaches, it may or may not respond. I would not ever expect they will respond by way of newspaper coverage. I don't think you can expect anything from Senator Carrick in the near future. We will take next week as it comes.

The arrogance contained in parts of this statement must have shocked the journalists working on the story, particularly given the wealth of damning evidence they had discovered.

The statement turned out to be an advance notice of what was to follow from Senator Carrick himself in Parliament. On 15 May 1980, he addressed the Senate on the issue, in a speech which became something of a watershed for the veterans' movement. The essence of the speech was to announce the Government's intention to deny what everybody involved had predicted they were about to allow—a full-scale investigation of the tests and their aftermath, either through a Royal Commission or a judicial inquiry. But if the Government anticipated this refusal to face up to their responsibilities, blinkered and demonstrably unjust as it was, would have the effect of weakening the veterans' resolve, it was to be sorely mistaken. It achieved precisely the opposite. The veterans no longer had any illusions about what they were up against, and were no longer naïve enough to imagine they had anything but a long, hard fight on their hands.

THE AMERICAN EXPERIENCE

In the United States, the battle is just as difficult, as both citizens and veterans seek recompense from a government equally reluctant to atone for past mistakes.

The Nevada test sites have been the scene for dozens and dozens of both above and below ground nuclear tests. The latter in fact are still continuing. While the tests appear never to have disturbed the hardy gamblers of Las Vegas, the residents downwind of the sites continue to count their losses.

Shakespeare almost had it right when his Henry V rallied his troops before the Battle of Harfleur with the cry, 'God for Harry! England and St George!' The modern call should have been 'God save (New) England and St George from Harry'. For Harry was the code name for a particularly dirty bomb exploded at Yucca Flats, 160 kilometres north of Las Vegas, on 19 May 1953. As the result of an unspecified error, most probably a misreading of potential wind changes, inhabitants of the small town of Saint George, 240 kilometres east of the test site, were exposed to 6000 millirems of radiation in just one day. The residents of the town, now known locally as Fallout City, were not told of the high fallout levels. The exposure figures were only released in 1979. All they were given were the usual soothing affirmations that their exposure was far below hazardous levels. At the time, the permissible level for radiation workers was 300 millirems per week; the current figure for exposure of members of the public is 500 millirems per year. The residents of the towns of southern Utah were told in a US Atomic Energy Commission pamphlet published in 1955, 'You are in a very real sense active participants in the nation's atomic test programme.' Although they did not know it, they were, in a very real sense, *radioactive* participants in the nation's atomic test programme.

The first American 50 kilotonne bomb was 'Simon' (detonated 25 April 1953), already noted in Chapter 3 as having contaminated areas as far away as Troy in northern New York State. It also produced very severe local contamination. Nine hours after the explosion, monitors reached record levels and roads leading into the testing zone were blocked for hundreds of kilometres. Of the 250 vehicles that were examined coming out of the fallout zone, 40 needed total decontamination. A bus on its way to Los Angeles, with 30 passengers on board, is reported to have given a reading of 250 millirem/hr on the outside and 160 millirem/hr on the inside.

The official assurances continued, and it is only now, with the declassification of previously withheld documents, coupled with the enlightened US *Freedom of Information Act,* that the extent of bureaucratic deception has become apparent. The Atomic Energy Commission (AEC) appeared to be much more concerned about continuing the tests than about the welfare of the exposed populations. One AEC memo, written in 1953, the year of 'Simon', 'Harry' and nine other US atmospherically tested bombs, said in part

> . . . in the present frame of mind of the public, it would take only a single illogical and unforeseeable incident to preclude holding any further tests in the United States.

Maralinga

Apart from the first warnings, given by the detection of fallout way out on the east coast, a more tangible indication that something might be very wrong came in the spring of 1953 when 4200 sheep that had been wintering 80 kilometres north of Yucca Flats were found dead. In 1955, the sheep farmers failed in a lawsuit claiming damages from the Government. The judge somewhat reluctantly ruled against them, largely because the Atomic Energy Commission had classified all the relevant information, and because the farmers had no expert witnesses to testify on their behalf. They were caught in a classic Catch-22 situation. The only people who knew anything about fallout and its effects worked for the Government; the Government classified the data so that the farmers were cut off from any scientific assistance. It was early 1979 before fresh evidence about the sheep appeared. The Governor of Utah, Scott Matheson, along with many other residents, used to get up early to watch the nuclear fireworks in the Utah Desert. The people were encouraged to do so by the USAEC, which had even made a film of St Georgians watching the tests and talking about how the tests had no effect on them whatsoever. Ten of Governor Matheson's relatives had died of cancer so, when the stories of the unusual deaths of sheep in 1953 and now of people came to him, he was a more than sympathetic listener. He instituted a detailed search of the State archives to find out just what information there was concerning those fallout-laden years.

One of the first papers found was a 1953 US Public Health Service autopsy report on some of the dead sheep, showing very high iodine-131 concentrations in their thyroid glands. The AEC had at the time claimed that the dead sheep had shown no thyroid abnormalities, nor exhibited effects experimentally induced in pregnant ewes deliberately fed large quantities of radioactive iodine. The official AEC line was that the 1420 lambing ewes and 2970 new lambs (out of a sheep population of 11 700) had all died from the effects of bad weather and lack of forage.

Governor Matheson's findings prompted a former AEC

Fallout Studies Branch scientist to look further into the story. Using his spare time, Harold Knapp put together a report which concluded

> . . . the unusual and unexplained deaths of thousands of sheep in areas downwind of the Nevada test site in spring 1953 can be attributed to the fallout from two nuclear tests. The simplest explanation of the primary cause of deaths, not considered at the time, is irradiation of the sheep's gastro-intestinal tract by all the fission products present in the fallout particles which were ingested along with open range storages.

Knapp contends that the new-born lambs died from prenatal accumulation of radioactive iodine in their thyroid glands. He also says that most AEC measurements were made of sheep that were not in the areas of highest fallout!

Hard as it was for the sheep farmers, the effects on people give us greater concern. A medical epidemiologist at the University of Utah Medical Centre, Joseph Lyons, decided in 1978 to conduct a survey of leukaemia rates in children under 15 in southern Utah. He observed that it was 2.4 times higher in children born after the atomic tests than in children born in the same area before the test programme. Lyons is reported as saying his study was prompted by annoyance.

> I was getting tired of too many questions I couldn't answer. I run the Cancer Registry in the State and people were making wild statements that the apparent high rate of leukaemia must be related to the fallout. My general reaction was, how do we know that? There's no data, no evidence, but after a raft of phone calls and news stories, I thought maybe it was time we found out. Unfortunately the answers weren't what we expected. I had expected that the results would be negative, but they weren't.

It now seems that by the mid 1960s the United States Government had strong evidence that excessive cancers were occurring among the people who lived downwind of Yucca Flats. The report for the Public Health Service, released only in late 1979 under the *Freedom of Information Act*, was prepared by Edward Weiss. Weiss looked at the incidence of leukaemia in southern Utah between 1950 and 1965. The expected number was 19, whereas 28 cases of leukaemia had been identified by 1965—a 47 per cent increase which Weiss attributed to living in the fallout zone.

There is a rather sad irony about the high rate of leukaemia in southern Utah. In 1976, Joseph Lyons had published a study showing that the overall cancer rate in the area was 22 per cent lower than in the rest of the nation. Lyons attributed this to the rural environment and the Mormons' lifestyle, involving abstinence from tobacco and alcohol.

In 1969, Professor Ernest Sternglass, of the Department of Medical Physics, University of Pittsburgh, produced a series of papers linking reduced birthrates and smaller sized babies in the areas downwind of the test site to the fallout levels. Attempts were made to discredit his work and he had great difficulty getting his paper published. Yet at the time, both the AEC and Public Health Service were sitting on data showing increased leukaemia rates.

The controversy caused by Sternglass had an interesting consequence. The Atomic Energy Commission put two of its most senior medical researchers, Drs John Gofman and Arthur Tamplin, on to destroying Sternglass' credibility. After careful study of his data, they concluded that Sternglass had overstated his case, but that he was basically correct. Population figures showed there had been a reduction in the number of babies born in the fallout states.

The USAEC considered this to be classified data and stopped Gofman and Tamplin publishing in the open literature. They resigned their jobs and published anyway. They have since become, Gofman especially, stern critics not only of the weapons testing programme but of the whole nuclear industry. Gofman has argued long and hard against the use of plutonium as a nuclear fuel, not only because of its possible diversion into bombs but because of its extreme toxicity. The Atomic Energy Commission must oft times have wished it had never heard of Sternglass, or set two of their best people out to destroy his scientific reputation. In one of his papers, Gofman argues that much of the epidemic of lung cancer sweeping the northern hemisphere is caused not only by cigarette smoking, but is added to by the plutonium particles everybody carries around in their lungs as a result of the atmospheric weapons tests. As plutonium counts are not carried out on people dying of lung cancer, no data is available to support his calculations.

Sternglass is still fighting fallout battles. At the 1979 meeting of the American Psychological Society, he presented a paper showing that the Scholastic Aptitude Test—the standard academic yardstick taken by all would-be US college entrants—fell 26 points in Utah in students born during the testing period. The Sternglass hypothesis is that the high levels of iodine-131 in the thyroid and strontium-90 in the pituitary gland have led to a slow-down in the development of these children which ultimately affected their SAT scores. Sternglass noted that the Utah SAT scores had risen 10 points in the last few years, something that couldn't have happened if socio-economic factors alone had been responsible for the initial fall.

The steadily accumulating data, on both the Government's mendacious attitude concerning fallout levels and the high incidence of cancer among the people living in the fallout zone, have led to the biggest single lawsuit against the US Government. Over 1000 people have filed for damages, claiming the Government acted negligently in encouraging their participation. They will have to show that their fallout exposure led directly to the hundreds of cancers and deaths. All the plaintiffs are either themselves suffering from cancer or are the surviving relatives of cancer victims. A US House of Representatives Committee, after looking at the data and hearing from Knapp about the sheep deaths, concluded that 'sufficient evidence exists for the government to accept at least compassionate responsibility, if not strict liability' for human injuries. A final settlement could reach $A1 thousand million.

Given the documents that have been released, it would appear that 'strict liability' extends all the way to the White House. One paper quotes Eisenhower as suggesting that the

Maralinga

Atomic Energy Commission 'confuse' the public about the size of the bomb due to be let off the week after the Harry test that contaminated St George so badly. A catchphrase popular in Truman's time, Eisenhower's predecessor, was 'give 'em hell Harry'—it certainly took on a sinister new meaning for the people of Utah. Eisenhower also advised that the words 'thermonuclear', 'fusion' and 'hydrogen' be left out of press releases and speeches.

In 1955, one of the Atomic Energy Commissioners said, 'People have got to learn to live with the facts of life and part of the facts of life is fallout.' So compassionate responsibility would seem to be the minimum possible response.

During the tests, a total of 103 000 soldiers participated in experiments to test their physical and psychological response. Some of them were as close as 2000 metres from Ground Zero. Apart from some limited data showing increased leukaemia rates among the soldiers involved in the 'Smoky' test (p. 90), the US Department of Defence is keeping its records of cancer rates secret. There were, however, 22 rhesus monkeys exposed, along with 3000 servicemen during that particular test. The medical centre that has cared for the monkeys since their exposure has reported that to date exactly half of them have contracted cancer of one sort or another.

The US Veterans' Administration has dismissed most of the nuclear test related claims it has received. Out of 290 claims lodged by the end of 1979, only eight had been granted and 18 were pending appeal.

Thus, like their Australian counterparts, the American veterans have no doubts about the long, hard and bitter struggle ahead as they too seek redress from a grudging Government. The foot-dragging attitude of the Australian Government and the gradual disillusion of ANVA members is discussed in the next chapter.

8

No Illusions

Senator Carrick, Minister for National Development and Energy, began his history-making address of 15 May 1980 by summing up the position to date on the tests controversy.

> The Government [he said] has given careful consideration to recent expressions of concern that Australian personnel were exposed to high levels of radiation during the atomic weapons test programme conducted by British authorities at Maralinga, Emu and Monte Bello, and to calls for an inquiry into the current health of the Australian personnel involved.

He then summarized the eight compensation claims already received, taking great care to point out that only two had been successful. Of these, one had been granted (Rick Johnstone), 'for a psychological disorder resulting from the aggravation of a pre-existing condition'. The other (Bill Jones) was granted 'on the grounds that there could have been a connection between an officer's death from cancer and his exposure to radioactive dust . . .'

In one breath, Senator Carrick was attempting to take away everything, however miserly, the Government had already conceded. He conveniently forgot Rick Johnstone's condition had been graded A-1, with no sign of a 'pre-existing condition' before his service. And, more importantly, he altered completely the findings of the Delegate of the Commissioner for Employees' Compensation who sat on Bill Jones' case. In announcing his findings in 1974, Mr D. E. Rumble had twice used the same phrase—Bill Jones' sickness had 'resulted from a disease due to the nature of his employment', and the cancer had 'constituted a disease due to the nature of his employment'. But in Senator Carrick's words 'there could have been a connection'. Any nuclear veteran listening in could have been excused for walking away in disgust at the outset.

Worse was to follow. The Senator continued,

> I also understand that during the past decade about six claims attributing the onset of cancer to atomic weapons tests in Australia have been examined by British authorities. In none of these cases have the authorities found evidence of exposure to nuclear radiation significantly above the natural background level, or that cancer arose from other than natural causes.

So there it was, spelled out for all to see, the Government's official view. All those deaths, all that suffering . . . nothing more than natural causes. He went on:

> The Government is satisfied on the basis of reports submitted at the time that all personnel working at Maralinga were subject to stringent health procedures, and that their activities in the field were strictly controlled and monitored to ensure that they were not exposed to dangerous radiation. On the basis of evidence presently available the Government is not convinced that the need has been established at this time for a full survey of the health of those Australians who were involved.

Up to this late stage, many of the veterans and their families had been of the same mind. Everybody knew politicians occasionally played with the truth, juggled statistics and facts to make them paint the desired picture. But this, surely, was not going to be like that. This was not about statistics and facts; it involved human lives, human suffering, and, in some cases, the suffering inflicted on young babies that had committed no sin other than to be born to the wrong father. And the fathers, what was their crime, other than that of serving their country and obeying the orders of men they should have been able to trust? So there could hardly be any doubt, could there, that the politicians would do the right thing, and attempt to shoulder the responsibility for the terrible wrongs that had been done? The veterans were doing no more than saying: 'Here's the situation, this is what we say. Check it out, and if your findings coincide with ours, please help us.'

That was the issue as the veterans saw it. What Senator Carrick's words meant was that the Government did not accept the catalogue of sickness and death that had been trotted out in the media; was not interested, even, in surveying the health of those involved. The veterans, by inference, were a bunch of malingering, whingeing malcontents, determined to blame their trivial aches and pains on an incident long in the past and best forgotten. The bitter taste of betrayal filled the mouths and hearts of many veterans that day.

It is interesting to reflect on the motives of the Government for perpetrating such a betrayal, particularly since there are two good reasons why they never need have done so. The first reason, quite simply, was that it wasn't their mistake—the men who had made and condoned the errors had been in power some 25 years earlier. The second reason is a logical follow-on from this, and one that, given the nature of politicians, is all the harder to understand. Here was a group of around 2000 men, and/or their surviving relatives, asking for compensation for a wrong done to them by a government which had long since relinquished its power. What a golden opportunity for the successors, 25 years on, to earn some rare and welcome kudos for an act of selfless humanitarianism. 'We know it wasn't our fault, but that doesn't matter, we're going to put it right.' Just the kind of language politicians love to hear themselves spout.

Given this, there are perhaps no more than three logical reasons why Fraser's Government opted for betrayal rather than the righting of a wrong they hadn't committed. The first, and perhaps most obvious, was the potentially huge expense of compensation payments. The second was the distinct possibility of the emergence of an embarrassing animosity between Britain and Australia over the issue. And the third was the potentially bad image the publicity over the whole affair would impart to the future of the uranium mining industry, at a particularly vital stage in its development.

Even the sugar Senator Carrick used to disguise the poison on 15 May could not have fooled many. His speech continued:

> We fully appreciate the concern and uncertainty of many of the Australian personnel who believe that they may have been exposed to dangerous levels of radiation, and may now, or in the future, suffer resulting injury or disability. The Government will ensure that full consideration continues to be given to all claims for compensation put to it under the Compensation (Commonwealth Government Employees) Act. To facilitate this consideration, persons who are concerned about the possibility of injury having been suffered as a result of involvement in the tests are invited to come forward for interview and, if appropriate, medical examination.

In closing, Senator Carrick passed on the doubtful consolation that 'the Government will seek the expert advice and experience of . . . the National Health and Medical Research Council'. Ironically, the NHMRC was at this stage revealing its true colours in another, almost parallel issue—the Agent Orange controversy involving some of Australia's 40 000 Vietnam veterans. First there was the disturbing case of Dr Barbara Field of Sydney University, whose research had linked 2,4,5-T (one of the herbicides contained in Agent Orange) with the birth defect, spina bifida. Dr Field claimed she had received a letter from the NHMRC urging her not to publish her findings. The Council had already given its official stamp of approval to 2,4,5-T, stating it could find nothing 'in any way convincing' about the contamination sickness claims of American veterans.

Most disturbing of all, the Council had revealed, in a statement issued in June 1978, that it based its unshakeable convictions on the herbicide issue on a catastrophic misunderstanding of a detail central to the entire controversy. By 1978, anybody who read their newspapers knew that 2,4,5-T contained a hideously lethal chemical known as dioxin, officially listed as one of the world's most deadly substances, and one million times more potent than thalidomide in causing abnormalities in foetuses. Dioxin, the public had learned through almost daily newspaper coverage, was unavoidably present in 2,4,5-T. Nothing could be done to eradicate it; only the level could be controlled. The NHMRC knew differently, however. Their statement, corrected at a later date, read in part: 'During the manufacture of 2,4,5-T, traces of TCDD (dioxin), a highly toxic substance, *may* [our italics] be found.' So, flying in the face of international science, the NHMRC had decided dioxin was a hazard that cropped up occasionally in the herbicide, not an ever-present and deadly factor of its existence. So much for the 'expert advice and experience' of the NHMRC. The nuclear veterans could take cold comfort from that direction.

After Senator Carrick had resumed his seat, Senator Cavanagh (South Australia) rose to say he felt that leaving the onus of proof of contamination to the individual concerned was perhaps less than just. He went on:

> The figures to date indicate that there is a greater incidence of cancer among those people who worked at Maralinga than in people in other sections of the community. How one proves that the cancer one may have has resulted from employment at Maralinga, I do not know. But it is reasonable to accept, I think, that if the incidence of cancer is out of all proportion, there is some significant connection between the employment and the disease. I think greater consideration should be given to the fact that these people were employed at Maralinga, and that as a result of their employment there, they have had diseases which could arise from an over-exposure to radiation.

Senator Cavanagh outlined the effects of the tests on Aborigines and the formation of a nuclear veterans' organization. He asked whether there should not be a full investigation into the possible ramifications of this exposure, and who may have been affected by it. He hoped that the Government would pay compensation, not on the basis of 'beyond reasonable doubt', but on the basis of probability.

> This matter is something about which we know little, and it needs full investigations . . . We do know from the Adelaide *Advertiser* reports of evidence stated and names given that at least 52 of the 2000 Australians who took part in the Maralinga test died of cancer, and that seven others are living with the disease at the present time. Is this a higher proportion than the normal death rate among Australians from cancer? If it is, should we not have an investigation to establish the incidence of cancer? It may have spread to a further area than the actual area of Maralinga, and I state the truth when I say that the cost to Australia and the health of Australians of the development of the British nuclear arsenal is still obscure, and that is for reasons relating to security in Australia.

Senator Cavanagh touched on the security aspects of the bomb tests, saying he felt the Government should issue an invitation, with a guarantee of immunity, to anyone with information on the danger aspects of the tests to come forward and make them public. He cited the example of an RAAF corporal:

> Here is a man who, for security reasons, is afraid, and who would be prepared to say that there was a large number of people wandering freely through the area [of the tests]. There were 800 to 900 people living in the area affected by radioactivity at Maralinga. Why can he not be given the freedom in the Minister's statement to state these beliefs publicly, and give details of where the incidents occurred?

Senator Cavanagh told Parliament of Jim Lester, the blind Aborigine whose experiences were detailed in Chapter Five.

> In one incident associated with the Emu test in October 1953, 45 Aboriginals were enveloped in a rolling black mist for several hours following an atomic bomb explosion. Within 48 hours, they had uncontrollable vomiting and diarrhoea. Soon after a skin rash like measles covered their bodies. The Aboriginals were left too sick to even gather food for themselves and almost

COMMONWEALTH of AUSTRALIA
MARALINGA ATOMIC WEAPONS TEST RANGE
PROHIBITED AREA
DEFENCE (SPECIAL UNDERTAKINGS)ACT – 1952
SUPPLY & DEVELOPMENT ACT 1939–1948

BEFORE PROCEEDING TO MARALINGA ALL PERSONNEL MUST
REPORT TO THE WATSON CONTROL CENTRE
SITUATED TO THE REAR OF THIS NOTICE

BY ORDER
RANGE COMMANDER

Warning sign erected at Watson rail sidings.

These four 44-gallon drums were supposed to be a barrier between
the claypan at Emu and the inhabited homestead of Mabel Creek.
The road separating the two ran for 160 km and the unmanned,
impromptu barrier was the only indication of the inadvisability of

starved. This is the incident which Dr T. M. Cutter is now examining.

The Senator called for the Government to find out who suffered as a result of Maralinga, to pay compensation and to make sure that such a situation did not happen again. Next on her feet was Senator Jean Melzer, of Victoria, who had some equally strong words to say about Government failings over the issue.

> One of the things that terrifies me [she began], in this report, and in so many of the reports we are getting lately, is the air of cover-up. We are told to accept assurances that all is well. We are told that everything is under control, and that the procedures we are using are quite safe.

Drawing a parallel with the Agent Orange issue, Senator Melzer said there was little point in putting great faith in official assurances of safety. In 1977, the Government had said that there were no problems.

> Yet in February 1977, Professor De Bruin in Adelaide was calling on the Department of Defence to give details of any material buried and the possible side effects of the tests. Why was he concerned? He was concerned because he had received an increasing number of reports from people who had worked in the Maralinga area and who were ill. He received an increasing number of reports of contaminated material that had been distributed from the site at Maralinga. But at that time we were told that there were no problems, and we were not to worry, as the tests had been safe and the people of Australia had nothing to worry about.

Senator Melzer went on to place some disturbing statistics before the Senate, of cancer sufferers living downwind from the Rocky Flats Nuclear Weapons Establishment in Colorado, USA. She said medical experts had found that men living up to 20 kilometres downwind of the plant had a testicular cancer rate of 140 per cent higher than normal; throat and liver cancers were 60 per cent higher; lung and colon cancer and leukaemia were all 40 per cent higher; and the overall cancer rate for men was 24 per cent higher and for women 10 per cent higher. She then drew the debate back to Maralinga.

In 1956 [she continued] we had major explosions of atomic bombs on Monte Bello and at Maralinga. The men who were involved in those experiments were not given special clothing and did not take precautions in any way. On record is the evidence of a man who flew one of the Canberra bombers through the resultant clouds several times without wearing any sort of protective clothing. Three years later he found that he had cancer of the thyroid. . . . The men involved at the time were not the only ones who suffered the effects of radiation, and who came down with cancer. We do not know how much of the material that was contaminated went out of the area. . . . There is evidence that windborne contamination can cause cancer. We have evidence that material that has been contaminated cannot be used safely by human beings, and that it might cause cancer. The report [Marston] that was suppressed shows that the contamination from the experiments at Monte Bello and Maralinga had much wider consequences than we were led to believe.

. . . People have been concerned about the rates of cancer in some very small settlements in those areas. Nobody knew why in small areas of 2000 or 2500 people, up to 50 people were suffering from cancer at about the same time.

Some of those people felt six years ago that the cancer from which they were suffering might have had something to do with Maralinga. They pointed out . . . that the prevailing winds in their area came from Maralinga. When the question was raised with scientists at the time they said they did not think . . . that Maralinga could have caused that sort of contamination. They thought it was more likely to have been caused by chemicals. Now that this report [Marston] has come to light, now that diagrams show where the material was blown . . . I do not believe it is good enough for the Government to say that it will have a selective inquiry. . . . We want a full, wide-ranging inquiry into the matter. For one thing we want to know why the report of the Government's inquiry into the allegations of health effects resulting from atomic weapons tests was suppressed. What has it got to do with security? Every time a problem such as this arises we are told that we cannot inquire into it, and that we cannot be told the facts because of security.

What about the security of the people who have lived in the area so long? What about the people who worked there? We will not uncover any extraordinary secrets now, by inquiring into the matter. . . . What other material has been suppressed? What have been the results across the country of the fallout from those experiments? Where is the contaminated material? Where did the trucks, shovels and radios go? Who has been working in them, and living beside them since, because the Federal Government did not care enough to make sure they were buried or taken away?

What has happened to the Aboriginal people living in the centre of Australia? What has happened to the men and women who were involved in the area? What has happened to the people who lived in the area? I ask the Government to reconsider the matters it has raised in the statement it has put down today. I ask it to conduct a full and far-reaching inquiry for the sake of the health of the people of Australia. I ask it not to hide behind the excuse of security. I ask that there be no more cover-ups in this area. I ask it to get down to the truth once and for all of what really happened when we experimented at Maralinga and Monte Bello. I ask it to tell that to the people of Australia, and to look after the health of the people who may have been contaminated.

And there the debate ended. It hardly constituted the smooth passage that Senator Carrick had hoped for. The realization, in all probability, must have dawned on the Government then that, if concealment and suppression were what they had in mind, they had a hell of a fight on their hands. There was little comfort for them to derive from the following day's papers either. Inexplicably, there was little or no coverage of the statements from Senators Cavanagh and Melzer, but the Melbourne *Age* ran a relatively hard-hitting editorial to go with its lengthy story on Senator Carrick's rejection of demands for a full-scale inquiry. The editorial, headed 'The

Maralinga Paradox', described government response as 'unsatisfactory', and stated:

> The issue is not so much whether the prescribed procedures were carried out at the time, as whether, in the light of later knowledge, those procedures were adequate to protect the people directly involved in the tests, or any Aborigines who happened to wander into the area.
>
> . . . By what criteria is it decided whether a claim [for compensation] is valid? According to what scale is the amount of compensation computed? And there remains the basic paradox presented by a government which insists on the one hand that health procedures at the test sites were satisfactory, but concedes, on the other, that at least two people, perhaps many more, may have suffered damage to their health as a result of these tests. The case for a proper and independent inquiry into the whole messy business was in no way answered by Senator Carrick's statement yesterday.

If nothing else, the Government's attitude towards 'the whole messy business' taught the veterans one invaluable lesson. Quite simply, any advances they were going to make in their fight for compensation would be won despite, not because of, the powers that be. Taking on a foe as formidable as a Federal Government means that sooner or later some reasonably high-powered legal advice is going to come in handy. Around this time, two lawyers, Bill McMillan, from Brisbane, and David Teed, from Melbourne, were fast establishing themselves as the champions of the Vietnam veterans' cause over the Agent Orange herbicide issue. A number of close parallels existed between the Vietnam veterans' struggle, and that of the nuclear veterans, so, perhaps logically, McMillan and Teed began acting for the victims of Britain's A-bomb tests.

The necessary approaches were made and, less than a week after Senator Carrick's address, Bill McMillan was outlining to Pat Creevey of the ANVA the three paths to compensation he felt were open to members. These were, first, to go before the various boards and commissions set up under the Repatriation Acts; secondly, to lay a claim with the Commonwealth

Employees Compensation Tribunal (as had already been done in a number of cases), and thirdly, and most significantly, to take legal action, either in Britain or Australia, against either the British or Australian Governments, or both.

McMillan explained that, where possible, veterans' court expenses would be covered by legal aid. He also envisaged the possibility of test cases being employed to fight the veterans' cause against the two governments. Under Australian law there is no provision for a group, such as the veterans, to band together in an action before the courts. This procedure is known as a class action, and was at the centre of the tactics used by McMillan, Teed and various American lawyers to gain considerable advances over the United States Government and chemical manufacturing companies on behalf of the Vietnam veterans. The absence of such a process made the task facing McMillan and Teed in Australia so much harder, and the outcome so much more unpredictable for the nuclear veterans.

McMillan outlined the position thus in a circular sent to ANVA members in mid 1980:

> At this time we envisage a representative action being commenced against the Commonwealth in the names of a handful of people who will represent and sue on behalf of all claimants. In this way we hope to keep the number of separate writs to a minimum, whilst including everyone in the action.

On 14 August 1980, McMillan wrote to the Federal Attorney General's Department applying for legal aid for the veterans. The irony of a group of men applying for financial assistance from a body against which they were intending to take legal action could not have escaped those involved.

The application listed eight causes of action:
1. Failing to warn the plaintiff of the dangers represented by atomic radiation.
2. Failing to take proper measures by way of shielding and protection both during and after an atomic explosion.
3. Failing to adequately dress and clothe the plaintiff compatible with the state of the art at the time of the explosion.

4. Failing to instruct the plaintiff in the precautions, care, management and safeguards in relation to atomic radiation having regard to the responsibility which the Commonwealth owes to the plaintiff.

5. Failing to provide a safe place and system of work.

6. Exposing the plaintiff to a risk or damage which the Commonwealth ought to have known.

7. Failing to warn the plaintiff of the medical condition that would develop following exposure, and failing to adequately treat the plaintiff.

8. Failing to adequately treat the plaintiff consistent with his medical condition.

The application also foresaw the need to retain a number of atomic radiation experts and leukaemia therapists, and also to travel to the sites of the atomic blasts. Although McMillan pointed out the difficulties in arriving at a figure for legal aid, he suggested that $60 000 would suffice for the first year. It was fully five months later, in January 1981, before the Attorney General's Department responded favourably. By this time, Harold Crosbie had on file 250 applications for compensation waiting the go-ahead for legal action.

Bill McMillan greeted the news with the caution peculiar to his calling. He said it would at least enable·submissions to be completed on a number of vital points leading up to the compensation actions. These, he added, included the veterans' right to have their cases heard outside the statute of limitations. He told one of the authors: 'This is a breakthrough, and represents a change in thinking by the Government. I don't imagine they particularly want to go down in history as being the Government which said "No" to a group of loyal soldiers on a legal technicality.' Bill McMillan also warned there could be delays of something like two years before the first case went before the courts.

Three days after Senator Carrick's address the ANVA's first general meeting was held at New Farm, Brisbane, in premises owned by the RSL's south-eastern District. Forty-seven veterans attended, and a couple of television stations sent along camera crews. Right from the outset, the Association's unique make-up was agreed upon—it was thought to be the first ex-serviceman's group designed to embrace civilians (Aborigines, Commonwealth Police, construction workers and administrators) with similar aims and problems. The need for unity was spelled out to members. Those attending were told: 'We are a self-help group with a problem we must help solve ourselves. No one else is going to do it for us if we sit back.'

The long and impressive list of organizations which had pledged support for the ANVA was detailed. It included the RSL, the Air Force Association, the Naval Association of Australia, the British Commonwealth Occupation Forces Association, the Regular Defence Forces Welfare Association, Legacy, War Widows, Civilian Widows, Leukaemia Foundation, Cancer Fund, the Queensland Ecumenical Council, Action for World Development, National Aboriginal Council, and legal, medical and scientific personnel. The list of correspondence received included letters from Malcolm Fraser, Bill Hayden, Jim Killen, Tom Uren, Don Chipp and Bob Hawke. The ACTU also wrote pledging circularization of relevant unions to aid identification of exposure victims.

The organizers of the ANVA had been busy themselves with pen and paper. On 21 July 1980, Pat Creevey wrote at length to Senator Carrick, outlining initially the health problems most regularly encountered by members. These included cancers, blood and bone diseases, nervous disorders 'to the point of breakdown and suicide', tumours, sterility, handicapped children, and children with blood disorders. Creevey also had a number of questions for the Minister over his 15 May offer of interviews and medical examinations for those who felt they were suffering ill health as a result of the tests. Where, Creevey wanted to know, would the interviews and examinations be held? What would they consist of? Who would pay for them? Would the results be available to members and the Association? Would the medical tests be standard throughout Australia? Would the results be collated to enable comparison with a control group not subject to exposure?

Creevey also wanted to find out if the interview and examination offer was open to those serving at places such as RAAF Amberley, individuals who had worked on contaminated equipment, but had not served at the test sites. More importantly, he asked:

> Does this offer mean, in effect, that everyone who was involved in the Atomic tests can come forward and be checked out? If the answer to this question is 'Yes', why not say that, and make it a survey, include the deceased and settle the matter?

Creevey had honed in on the ambiguity of Carrick's offer, and the confusion it was causing among veterans. If the Government was prepared to grant medical examinations to anybody who feared his health had suffered during or after the tests, why not make the same offer to the survivors among the whole 2000 involved, thus accomplishing the full-scale survey the ANVA had requested?

Creevey also asked the Minister if records could show amounts of radiation received by individuals, thus demonstrating (perhaps) to those involved that their exposure was below the maximum permissible total dose. He wrote:

> It follows that the progressive total exposure would have been recorded to ensure that no one exceeded his maximum permissible total dose. Therefore finding this information would be a worthwhile exercise to reduce the number of those concerned. . . . The Association is concerned about members who have reported that their records show nothing about their service in the test areas, or their medical treatment at the test sites. There must be lists available on who was cleared by security to enter these sites. They may be the only way the Government has of establishing who was there. Can this be checked please?

For good measure Creevey ended with another batch of difficult questions:

> Where [he asked] are the records of those treated for radiation at the hospital at Maralinga, Health Physics at Maralinga, the hospital ship at Monte Bello and the isolation ward at

Amberley? What safety procedures were routine at the test sites and off-site, where people worked on contaminated equipment, e.g. aircraft, vehicles, etc? What was the type and range of geiger counters and dosimeters used? What follow-up monitoring was done on the health of anyone who had been contaminated to the extent that treatment was warranted and given at the time? When the international safety level for radiation exposure was dropped to five rads per annum after the series was over, did the Government consider this in relation to the permitted exposures during the tests? The international standard was three times higher, (15 rads) during the tests.

When the case of *Jones* v. *the Crown* showed that a man had been unprotected in a radioactive area for a dangerous period, did the Government consider the possibility that others may have been exposed as well? If consideration was given to this possibility, what were the Government's findings and actions, if any?

Carrick himself wrote back on 5 August, but the Government did not reply in full until 19 September, when P. Ryan (see page 161), First Assistant Secretary of the Uranium and General Division of the Department of National Development and Energy, sent detailed answers:

A check of service and medical records will be carried out on individuals participating in these investigations [Government interviews of veterans]. All medical treatment of servicemen in service institutions is recorded in personnel medical records, and there should be no need to refer to hospital records for this information. Where service records conflict with statements by individuals, every attempt will be made to verify such statements through other channels, for example by examination of extant security records. Radiation records are also available for Australian personnel who worked in contaminated areas, and these will be checked. Information regarding radiation exposure and service records will naturally be made available to individuals.

So far so good. Ryan also promised interviews and medical examinations in each state, to be carried out by Commonwealth

Medical Officers, and paid for by the Government.

The letter went on to say that results would be collated 'for evidence of exposure of specific groups, as a result of involvement in the tests'. At Maralinga, wrote Ryan, responsibility for radiological safety lay at all times with Britain. In periods between trials, responsibility for implementing safety regulations was shared by the Australian Health Physics Representative and the Australian Health Physics Team. During trials, the British Atomic Weapons Research Establishment exercised health control. Following trials, radiological surveys were undertaken to classify areas as either active or non-active. Signs were displayed at the entrances to active areas, and film badges and protective clothing were compulsory within them. Access to the contaminated 'forward' area at Maralinga was through security checkpoints, manned observation towers and roving patrols. Access also required permission from the Health Physics Group. And so it went on, right down to types and number classifications of instruments used for radiation monitoring. The system of radiation exposure levels was outlined in great detail. Everything, in fact, according to Ryan's letter was about as foolproof and safe as mother's milk. It is only when the letter is read side-by-side with the veterans' questionnaires that the true picture emerges of how often these stringent safety measures were observed, and how often they were ignored.

Around this time ANVA headquarters in Brisbane received a visit from two members of the Police Special Branch. What they wanted was a quick glance at some of the Association's literature. This accomplished they went their way, having imparted a little well-meant advice on the way through the door. At the time Creevey said he had shown them what they wanted to see. It seemed to be an amicable visit, more in an advisory capacity than anything else. The officers told him that there were subversives around who try to infiltrate organizations like his, to use them for their own ends, and generally cause trouble. Creevey thought they might also have been a bit worried that the Association might be planning to hold a march. He assured them this was not so. This may, of course, have been the only motive behind the visit. At that time street marching in Brisbane was about as well-advised as babbling sedition from a soap-box in Red Square.

Less than a month later, in September 1980, the Association again came into contact with Special Branch. This time the ANVA made the initial approach. Harold Crosbie had received a late-night international phone call at his home, from an individual not anxious to reveal his identity. He did say he was a representative of a British newspaper empowered to offer Crosbie and the ANVA $20 000 to stop releasing information on contamination of Aborigines during and after the tests. Crosbie left the caller up in the air, with no option but to ring back if serious. Whether or not he was a crank did not emerge, but Crosbie felt sufficiently concerned to alert the Special Branch who agreed to investigate the matter. The practice of journalists, particularly Americans, doubling as agents for their Governments, is well documented. Given the obvious source of embarrassment to Britain that the Aboriginal issue was rapidly becoming, it is not beyond the realms of possibility that the offer was bona fide.

The same month, Opposition spokesman on Veterans' Affairs, Dr Everingham, caused a minor stir at the 65th National Congress of the RSL in Canberra by calling on the Government to provide immediate compensation for all Vietnam and nuclear veterans whose health had suffered as a result of their service. He said such compensation should be paid immediately before it was proved either way that there was or was not a connection between the men's sickness and herbicides and radiation. 'Give them the benefit of the doubt,' was Dr Everingham's generous proposal. Needless to say it fell on deaf ears.

Early in October 1980, the Association issued a press release carrying what it hoped was a convincing statistical argument. Commonwealth statistics showed that for the year 1975 Australians between the ages of 25 and 54 were dying from cancer at the rate of one in a thousand. During that same year,

1975, seven members of the Association within the 25 to 54 age group had died from cancer. Since there were 2000 servicemen at Maralinga, this worked out at a cancer death rate of three and a half per thousand, significantly higher than the national figures. Using this argument as a springboard, Harold Crosbie appealed to all widows of ex-servicemen involved in the tests to make contact with the Association.

Around this time, Crosbie informed members through a newsletter what most of them had no doubt long suspected — that the Association had given up trying to negotiate with the Government outside the courts. Wrote Crosbie:

> In the past, we have asked the Commonwealth to negotiate with us to try to resolve our claims for compensation without resort to courts and legal action. We have got nowhere, and it is now time for the lawyers to take over. I hope that you will give them all the help you can.

This was a reference to the ongoing case being mounted by Bill McMillan and David Teed.

Around this period Crosbie also issued a detailed statement attacking Senator Carrick's 15 May speech. The reason for the delay was the time needed to receive and collate the statutory declarations, letters and questionnaires flooding in from veterans. Crosbie used information gleaned from this correspondence to attack Senator Carrick's statement that 'stringent health procedures' had ensured that all those involved in the tests were adequately protected at all places and at all times. Crosbie ripped into this demonstrably ludicrous and badly misinformed view with a fourteen-point attack. His research, he claimed, had turned up the following:

1. A lack of a uniform high standard of safety in the range areas.
2. Men were sent officially into forward (contaminated) areas to recover stores, and in one case food, for use at their rear camp.
3. Men went unofficially into forward areas to souvenir and look at craters, etc.

4. The second and third points were often performed without protective measures being laid down and followed, either in the contaminated areas, or on return.

5. It was common knowledge that the above was happening.

6. Tradesmen serviced vehicles for the contaminated fleet, which had been retrieved from the forward areas. They did so without precautions, except that the bodies of the vehicles had been decontaminated.

7. A refrigerator mechanic was sent to a forward area to retrieve components for repair at camp. He was not briefed or equipped for a contaminated area. When he mentioned the job to Sir William Penney, he recollects Sir William said the area was still a hazard.

8. Aborigines gained entrance to contaminated areas.

9. An unprotected man gained access to an active laboratory. He states he was carrying a sample canister from a monitoring aircraft into the lab for a scientist. When the scientist measured the radioactivity he left the lab 'as expeditiously as possible'. The serviceman describes this as his briefing on radiation in his questionnaire.

10. Radioactive material was carried in containers not designed for it. This concerns the radioactive sludge from the Amberley decontamination centre, where the material was carried away and dumped at sea off Queensland in 44-gallon drums.

11. Respirators were not used as often as they should have been, and were used incorrectly, due to poor or little instruction on site. They were not always part of the protection in the dusty forward areas.

12. The issue, control and identification of film badges was not consistently done in accordance with laid-down procedures. One man still has his film badge, another states he had his after discharge.

13. Due to an inadequate power supply the decontamination measuring machine was difficult to operate efficiently. The power supply was not consistent, as needed, due to load variations.

14. Time limits for being in contaminated areas were assessed and laid down, but due to work commitments were occasionally broken.

Crosbie completed his submission with a list of radiation-connected sickness recorded among Association members. This included cancers, blood disorders, tumours, bone diseases, problems in children, and so on. Over 90 cases of cancer, 77 of them fatal, had also been recorded, although some of these were awaiting confirmation by death certificates and doctors' reports. The case of an unnamed serviceman at Maralinga was quoted. He had fathered a healthy child prior to his posting, and three with blood problems since. Crosbie wrote:

> The Association is not interested in finding someone to blame for their problems. They are concerned to find an answer to this question: 'Have I or my children been affected by my duties in radioactive areas?' The best way to answer this is to have a survey done on the health of those concerned. [He then quoted the late American President J. F. Kennedy]: The number of children and grandchildren with cancer in their bones, with leukaemia in their blood, or with poison in their lungs, might seem statistically small to some, in comparison with natural health hazards, but this is not a natural hazard, and it is not a statistical issue. The loss of even one human life, or the malfunction of even one baby, who may be born long after we are gone, should be of concern to us all. Our children and grandchildren are not merely statistics towards which we can be indifferent.

A few days after completing this submission, Crosbie posted it, and three others completed earlier the same year, to four people—one to Prime Minister Malcolm Fraser, one to Opposition leader Bill Hayden, one to Australian Democrats leader Don Chipp, and one to RSL national president Sir William Keys. His timing was immaculate—just four days before the Federal election of 18 October 1980. The three political leaders were sent a short accompanying statement. It read:

> I, the Director of the Australian Nuclear Veterans' Association, hereby make it the will of the members that you should state categorically before the election whether or not

> you will order a full and open judicial inquiry into the current
> health of Australians involved in the British nuclear tests held
> here in the '50s and '60s.

To make sure he squeezed the last drop of influence from his
manoeuvre, Crosbie also issued a nation-wide press release
briefly setting out the Association's case to date. Almost
immediately the replies started coming in. Dr Neil Blewett,
Shadow Health Minister, replied in a telegram on behalf of Mr
Hayden.

> Dr Blewett said he would take up as a high priority with
> officials of the Department of Health the possibility of
> mounting an epidemiological study of all those who were at
> Maralinga, funded and organized by the Department. Dr
> Blewett said that he considers the current approach where the
> initiative must be taken by the individuals themselves is totally
> unsatisfactory.

Senator Chipp also sent a telegram, which read:

> In answer to your telegram, answer is yes.

Predictably, the Government's response was a resounding
silence. Accordingly Crosbie issued a second press release the
day before the election. In this he pointed out that both the
Opposition and the Democrats had given full support to the
holding of an inquiry, while the Government had not
responded. He added: 'Service and ex-service men and women
should bear this in mind when voting tomorrow.' Another few
days passed and the Democrats' telegram was followed up by a
press release stating that the Party was seeking an early public inquiry into the complaints of Australian ex-servicemen affected by
nuclear testing and herbicide contamination in Vietnam.
Senator Colin Mason said the two problems involved 'a failure
of justice to men who had a right to expect it from the
community'. He added: 'The approach so far to these problems
has been far too leisurely', and made it clear the matter had a
high priority for the Democrats in the Senate.

The Labor Party's commitment was re-affirmed in January

1981 by Senator Don Grimes, Shadow Minister for Veterans' Affairs and Social Security. He wrote pledging continued support, and observing:

> It is utterly inconsistent for this country to complain about the effects of the nuclear explosions by the French in the Pacific, and yet show such lack of immediate concern for the welfare of our ex-servicemen . . .

Three months after the original sixteen-page submission had been sent to Malcolm Fraser, he had still not replied, despite Harold Crosbie's flow of reminder letters and telephone calls. Then, in mid-January 1981, a letter on the Prime Minister's notepaper, but signed by Wal Fife, Minister assisting the Prime Minister, arrived. It began by thanking Crosbie for his letter of 20 November, one of his reminders, but completely ignored the contents of the sixteen-page submission. Mr Fife's letter was basically an updated re-write of Senator Carrick's address of 15 May. As Pat Creevey pointed out: 'It looks as if they haven't even bothered to read our submission.' Nothing had changed.

The RSL's response to receipt of the Association's submission was almost as late coming as the Government's, but infinitely more significant. Traditionally, the RSL had always been less than vitally concerned with the problems of ex-servicemen who had never seen action, and this was the category into which almost all of the British test veterans fell. Crosbie and Creevey had long been aware of the inestimable value of getting the RSL behind their movement, but had achieved little in this direction, apart from getting national president Sir William Keys to act as patron. 'There is no more influential group in Australia,' Crosbie told one of the authors. 'We need their help badly.'

So, in January 1981, when Crosbie received a letter from Sir William, he was, not surprisingly, jubilant. The letter called on the Government to institute a full inquiry into the health of all servicemen involved in the tests. Said Crosbie: 'This is possibly the single most important advance we have seen since the ANVA came into being.' Sir William's letter read in part:

Following consideration of this matter by the national
executive at its recent meeting we have now made a further
submission to the Commonwealth Government asking that the
Department of Veterans' Affairs conduct a medical survey of
any personnel involved in the tests.

Going back to the period of the Federal Election in October
1980, one of the most bizarre, and potentially sinister, aspects
of the entire affair had emerged briefly in the national media,
and then passed virtually unnoticed. Crosbie had been
conducting research into the actual construction of buildings
at the test sites, mainly as a result of receiving a number of
compensation queries from civilians who said they had been
involved. All reported similar problems . . . proving they had
worked on the sites. None had tax records or employee pay-roll
numbers, or any other documented literature to prove their
connection with the tests. They were, to all intents and
purposes, a ghost army. The next common factor to emerge was
that many of the civilian workers were newly arrived migrants
when they were sent out to the deserts of South Australia.
Crosbie's research told him that between 50 and 100 civilian
workers, most of them immigrants had been employed at the
test sites.

He also turned up the name of a company called Morag Pty
Ltd, registered in Melbourne in the early fifties, which had
been involved in flour milling. The company, operated out of
an address at Barkly Street, East Brunswick, in Melbourne, had
advertised in immigrant newspapers, including *New World*, in
March and April 1956, for prospective employees. Of the 100
or so migrants who replied, many were employed in
construction work on the bomb sites, and were retrenched two
years later. Many of them had been asked to sign the *Official
Secrets Act* before beginning work, and a number had since
died of cancer.

Mrs Anne-Marie Ratcliffe, of the Melbourne suburb of
Balwyn, was listed as a Morag director, and was interviewed at
length by one of the authors. She said that her husband had left
the British Army in 1949, and had come to Australia the

following year. She agreed that her husband was an ex-British Army major, and that she and he had both been listed as Morag directors. The company had been wound up in 1968, shortly after her husband's death. Mrs Ratcliffe was insistent that Morag was involved merely in flour milling, and had no connection with the bomb tests. Then she let slip the information that her husband was involved with MI5, the British spy organisation. Questioned more closely, Mrs Ratcliffe said: 'My husband would never discuss this side of his life with me.'

She would be most surprised, she added, to learn that her husband had continued his work for British intelligence after moving to Australia. Further research into the Morag company revealed a second, parent company, called Miag, which was based in West Germany and, according to Harold Crosbie's sources, involved in the manufacture of munitions.

The news made a brief flurry in the national media, but was almost immediately and conveniently buried. Even so, the ANVA undertook to pursue the compensation claims of civilian employees of Morag who had worked on the test sites, and since incurred health problems. This undertaking included the promise to continue to search for the missing tax records, payroll numbers, etc., connected with their employment.

Three years earlier, on 8 September 1977, another, perhaps even more sinister, example of the background to the tests came to light. A small literary magazine, published in Melbourne and titled *Overland,* had been about to run an article containing some disturbing allegations about the role of Sir Robert Menzies in the tests, when something highly peculiar happened to the raw copy. The 2500 word article dealt with a period in 1956 when Russia was in the process of invading Hungary. A Security Council meeting had been scheduled for 5 October 1956, to discuss the growing crisis over the Suez Canal. It was important from Britain's point of view that her representatives at the meeting be able to provide evidence of the country's nuclear capacity. A bomb test had been scheduled for 27 September 1956, eight days before the Security Council meeting. And since both American and Russian observers had been invited to the tests, it was important all went well.

Unfortunately, on the eve of the test, the winds were blowing in the wrong direction and, according to the *Overland* article, scientists on the safety committee decided that a bomb explosion in these conditions could endanger Australia's east coast population. The scientists advised against the test. The article went on to allege that Sir Robert Menzies overruled this advice, and authorized the British to go ahead with the explosion as they wished. The bomb was duly set off on 27 September, and the fallout spread north-eastwards across Queensland and over the Pacific. Included in the article was information that Brisbane's milk supply was dumped, and replaced with milk from unaffected sources during the relevant period. No documentation was included in the article on any adverse effects on the health of those over whom the fallout cloud passed.

This article was due to appear in the September issue of *Overland* and, according to the magazine's associate editor, John McLaren, was being re-typed for that purpose when two men appeared at the publication's offices.

> After the article had been prepared [wrote McLaren], one of the secretaries who was re-typing it was visited by gentlemen who introduced themselves as members of the Department of Meteorology. The explained that they just wanted to check the article for its factual accuracy.

The copy was taken away—and never seen again by *Overland*. A check with the Department of Meteorology revealed a complete lack of knowledge of the men or the article. Stranger still, individuals who held documentation supporting the article, suddenly found themselves unable to supply their information as originally promised.

Interviewed in 1977 over the *Overland* allegations, Sir Ernest Titterton, a member of the Safety Committee reportedly overruled by Sir Robert Menzies, commented:

> It is absurd to imagine such a thing happened. You are asking me to recall something that happened more than 20 years ago, but I am certain that the Safety Committee had made no such recommendation to the Prime Minister.

Sir Robert at the time refused to either listen to the *Overland* allegations, or comment on them.

Given this type of background, it is hardly surprising that Britain has remained sensitive and prickly over their Australian atomic experiments. Witness the frigid tones of a letter Harold Crosbie received from Col. G. Stocker, C.B.E., secretary-general of the British Commonwealth Ex-services League. Crosbie had written an innocuous, politely worded request for assistance to the League in April 1980. All he had wanted was any details of British forces serving during the tests, and 'any literature that you consider may help us in any way, however infinitesimal it may seem'. The reply he received a week later was couched in the same bristling terms of indignation that were used by the Air Vice-Marshal of the Royal Air Force who had so scathingly denied that any Aborigine could have been affected by the tests (see Chapter 5). The League's letter read in part:

> Neither ourselves nor the Royal British Legion have the information you seek, *nor is it believed that any (or indeed the need for any) exists.* [Our italics, their brackets.] It may interest you to know that the signatory of this letter was much involved with the Maralinga tests with no ill effect, which was to be expected, in view of the great safety precautions taken.

As Harold Crosbie remarked at the time: 'Methinks the colonel doth protest too much.'

Contrast this letter with another one, from the American Legion, that Crosbie received six months later:

> Thank you for your splendid letter introducing yourself and your organization. . . . I am sure that exchanges of ideas can be beneficial to all veterans, and we are grateful to you for

thinking of us. We are referring your letter to our Veterans
Affairs and Rehabilitation Director. I am sure he will be in
touch to convey any ideas we may have on disabilities due to
nuclear exposure.

It is interesting to theorize why there should be such a gulf
between the attitudes of two organizations, one British and one
American, on the same subject, particularly when both groups
share the same aims and motives for the benefit of ex-
servicemen. It may be over-dramatic to suggest that those in
the know in Britain are already gearing themselves for an
avalanche of highly expensive and embarrassing compensation
claims, and are acting accordingly. On the other hand, it may
not. Either way, there can be little doubt that Maralinga is
going to become a name well-known in Britain, if it is not
already so.

The mass circulation newspaper, the *Daily Mirror,* carried a
screaming banner headline 'A-Deaths Shocker' on to millions
of British breakfast tables on the morning of 22 April 1980. The
front-page story began:

> Hundreds of former servicemen risk death from cancer
> because of nuclear bomb tests by the British Government, it
> was claimed yesterday. The deaths of 37 people have been
> blamed on the tests, and the toll is expected to greatly increase.

The report went on to detail a promise by Britain's Defence
Ministry to investigate 'relatives' complaints of bomb-linked
deaths'. Within days, Defence Secretary Francis Pym was
being asked a series of questions in the House of Commons by
Shadow Defence spokesman, William Rodgers. And the death
toll was climbing into the fifties.

During the Adelaide *Advertiser's* excellent series on the
effects of the tests, two journalists were contacted by a British
non-commissioned officer from the RAF, who said he wanted
people to know that mistakes could be made. 'We could not
predict everything that would happen with those bombs,' he
added. What followed was a chilling account of the night a
radioactive cloud 'went missing' for several hours. According

229

to the RAF officer, who asked to remain anonymous, the incident happened after the fourth Maralinga explosion on 22 October 1956. He told the *Advertiser*:

> Conditions were perfect for the test—so it seemed—but at the last minute cloud cover came right over. When the bomb went off it rolled the clouds back like a carpet, and then the weather clamped back in. They literally lost it. We could sense there was concern, because there was a maximum flying effort, and whenever a plane came down to refuel, it went straight back up again.

The officer said it was several hours before the cloud was traced, and then it was by accident. A Hastings transport aircraft landed at Maralinga, and was discovered to be highly radioactive. Putting two and two together, the scientists sent up a team of tracker jets to retrace the Hastings' flight-path, and eventually found the cloud drifting towards Darwin. An official report put out by the Australian Weapons Safety Committee two years later confirmed the cloud had reached the coast close to Darwin, but mentioned nothing of its having been 'lost'.

The same officer spoke to the *Advertiser* men, evidently with some bitterness, of his experiences at Maralinga. 'They asked us to put our lives on the line for nothing more than an experiment to keep up with the Russians and the US.' He then told of the occasion on 11 October 1956, when the third Maralinga bomb was detonated, and he and a group of his men were ordered into a forward area about two and a half kilometres from Ground Zero. At the actual explosion stage, the men had turned their backs and covered their eyes for fear of being blinded by the flash. When they opened them they were greeted by the macabre sight of scores of blinded rabbits scurrying helplessly around them. 'Half of my team were so terrified they turned and ran,' he said. 'The rest of us didn't move, but only because we were so petrified. When the other blokes came to their senses and came back, nobody pulled their legs about it—we understood.' Two other Britons involved in the tests contacted the *Advertiser* at the same time, and spoke in detail of the grossly inadequate decontamination procedures in operation for the aircraft used to track, and fly into, radioactive clouds.

It is perhaps reasonable to assume, then, that when and if Britain does face a flood of compensation claims from Australian test veterans, there will be a similar action, or series of actions, already underway from British servicemen. This, seemingly, would be of considerable assistance to Australians seeking belated financial aid for their ills.

9

Buffalo to Brumby and Beyond

> Penney reached independently the same definition as I did regarding the one point safety tests, namely that so long as the total explosive force [of high explosive (HE) and nuclear charge] is due predominantly to the HE explosion and the nuclear reaction is just observable by instruments, this should be called an experiment and not a weapons test.

So wrote George Kistiakowsky (the excited explosives expert at Alamogordo) in his book *Scientist at the White House*, describing his years as President Eisenhower's scientific adviser.

Thus both Britain and the United States rationalized their continued programme of nuclear weapons experiments. They complied with the letter of the partial test ban treaty, if not necesarily with its spirit. Many of the smaller experiments, 'kittens' they were called, produced extensive local contamination.

Typical of the sorts of experiments that went on were dropping a nuclear assembly from a high tower to see what happened; or putting a bomb inside its casing and building a large fire around it. From the pattern of residual contamination, extensive experimental work was done with plutonium-239,

232

that highly toxic metal that readily burns when exposed to air, producing a dangerous aerosol. Other work involved the use of thorium-228 and the non-radioactive but hazardous element beryllium. Work of various sorts continued at Maralinga until 1963, even though the last nuclear explosion as such took place on 9 October 1957. (One witness of some of the 'kitten' experiments says that at least one produced a small fireball—presumably that nuclear reaction was only 'just observable' by the instruments.)

The tests were of two broad types:

1. Scientific and military experiments to assess the behaviour of uranium, plutonium and beryllium under impulses produced by chemical high explosives, i.e. the continuing search for improved 'triggers'.

2. Safety experiments to assess the behaviour of nuclear weapons under accident conditions.

The AWTSC assessed the safety provisions of these minor trials and the approved firing conditions so that the fallout of radioactive debris would occur on the Range and none would escape the Range boundary.

In 1963 the British Government decided it no longer needed to use Maralinga. A more formal ban had been placed on atmospheric nuclear weapons tests and the Christmas Island site had been developed for H-bomb tests. Much of 1964 was spent cleaning up the site and burying the most contaminated equipment. Operation Hercules, as it was called, was carried out by staff from AWRE and on its completion the Range was considered safe for occupancy on a care and maintenance basis. Most staff, including the health physicists, had left by November 1964.

In 1966, Britain decided to relinquish the site entirely and a more comprehensive decontamination programme was instituted at Maralinga and at Emu Field where the explosions code-named Totem I and Totem II had taken place. The project was named Operation Brumby and the details were worked out in conjunction with AWTSC. The actions taken by the decontamination teams at the major sites are summarized in Table 9.1.

TABLE 9.1

Decontamination procedures during Operation Brumby March-June 1967

Major trial   Treatment of the Ground Zero environs

	glazing and other debris	grading and ploughing	fresh soil: free from contamination
One Tree	all larger pieces hand-scavenged; smaller fragments ploughed in and covered with fresh soil	circular area of 250 m radius	Circular area of 100 m radius covered with about 4 cm of soil
Marcoo	no action required (Marcoo crater filled and levelled)	not required	not required
Kite	no action required	not required	not required
Breakaway	all larger pieces hand scavenged; smaller fragments ploughed in and covered with fresh soil	circular area of 240 m radius	circular area with 180 m radius covered with about 4 cm of soil

Table 9.1 cont.

Tadje	metal debris, and fallout pellets with cobalt-60, hand scavenged fragments of glazing and remaining pellets ploughed in	circular area of 140 m radius	concrete tower base covered with about 15 cm soil
Totem I *Totem II*	all larger pieces hand scavenged, smaller pieces ploughed in and covered with fresh soil	circular area of 125 m radius	circular area with about 125 m radius covered with about 4 cm of soil
Biak	all larger pieces hand scavenged, smaller fragments ploughed in and covered with fresh soil	circular area of 200 m radius	concrete tower base covered with about 15 cm soil circular area 160 m radius covered with about 40 mm soil
Taranaki	no action required	extensive ploughing and introduction of fresh soil to part of the environs for other purposes.	

From: AWRE 0-16/68 'Final Report on Radiological Containment of the Maralinga Range and Emu Site'.

The details of the actions taken were written up in Atomic

Maralinga

Weapons Research Establishment report AWRE O-16/68 entitled 'Final Report on Radiological Containment of the Maralinga Range and Emu Site'. It was classified 'Restricted', one of the lowest levels of security classification, and became known as the Pearce Report after its author, N. Pearce. An unrestricted version was finally released in May 1979 by the Australian Department of National Development under the imprimatur of Kevin Newman, the then Minister. The only difference between the restricted and unrestricted reports are the deletion of any references to cobalt-60, beryllium and natural uranium contamination. Obviously, the British wanted to keep quiet about any work they may have been doing on a possible 'cobalt bomb', hence the deletion of references to cobalt-60. Beryllium, apart from being a major hazard when inhaled, is an efficient slower down of neutrons and can be used to increase bomb efficiency. Natural uranium is used to increase fallout from fission-fusion-fission bombs, so obviously all the potential 'dirty bomb' tricks had been studied. The release of this information was obviously not considered to be in the public interest in May 1979. Yet a report published in January 1979, AIRAC No. 4, referred to on page 238 gives considerable information on the cobalt-60 hazard at Maralinga. Strange are the ways of government.

Pearce wrote:

> Hence, at the present time, even a permanent inhabitant of the Range, free to move about at will would not be exposed to a significant hazard unless he chose to spend most of his time at or near Ground Zero. This eventuality is most improbable now and the likelihood of its occurring in the future should be considered in the light . . . of the decaying gamma dose rates.

But not only the gamma dose rates presented a hazard. Relatively large areas were found to be still significantly contaminated with plutonium; both plutonium-240 and 241 and, most especially, plutonium-239. These were the areas that were graded and ploughed. This seems to have been a strange approach, because as early as 1958 evidence of wind dispersal

236

of radioactive debris at Maralinga was observed and later on studies were made of the movement of fallout and glazed pellets at Biak. To plough and grade contaminated land was one way of breaking up the soil into sizes for easy wind dispersal, so, far from consolidating the activity which was the professed aim, Operation Brumby turned into a classic dilute and disperse exercise. The effects of wind erosion were noted first in 1972 when the area was revisited to inspect possible revegetation. The results observed during the inspection are shown in Table 9.2.

TABLE 9.2

Observed conditions of Ground Zero environs, November 1972 at various Maralinga sites

Site	glazing and other debris	graded and ploughed areas	soil top dressing
One Tree	glazing in abundance on surface	heavy loss of top soil; limited regrowth of vegetation	top soil lost from centre area around Ground Zero revealing limestone stratum
Breakaway	glazing in abundance on surface	advanced regeneration of native flora and no obvious evidence of heavy loss of soil	
Tadje	no obvious evidence of remaining fallout pellets or fragments of glazing	total loss of top soil revealing bitumenised area immediately around central concrete pad; poor regrowth of vegetation	soil cover loss from concrete pad

237

Table 9.2 cont.

Biak	glazing in evidence on surface	total loss of top soil revealing b i t u m e n i s e d area immediately around central concrete pad; beyond this advanced regeneration of vegetation	some soil cover remains over concrete pad
Taranaki		heavy loss of topsoil throughout the treated area; limited regrowth of vegetation	

From: AIRAC No. 4 'Radiological safety and future land use at the Maralinga atomic weapons test range'.

The most comprehensive official review of the present state of Maralinga and Emu Field comes from two reports published by the Australian Ionizing Radiation Advisory Council (AIRAC) — AIRAC No. 4, 'Radiological safety and future land use at Maralinga atomic weapons test range', which was published in January 1979, and AIRAC No. 7, 'Radiological safety and future land use at the Emu atomic weapons test sites', published in October 1979. AIRAC No. 4 reports the extensive survey and monitoring work carried out by teams from the Australian Radiation Laboratory and other places in 1977. As the authors of the official report put it:

> The main evidence now available for dispersal by wind derives from the data obtained in the present survey on the neutron activation product, europium-152. Initially induced in the soils of the Ground Zeros and still abundant there, this nuclide distribution in surface soil in 1977 extended up to a kilometre from the Ground Zeros. In areas even remote from the ground zeros europium-152 is present, not only in surface soils, but also uniformly distributed with depth down the soil profile of

the deeper sand drifts. There is little doubt that grading and ploughing in the Ground Zero environs in Brumby in 1967 rendered the activated soil available for dispersal by wind. The massive loss of surface soil from most major trial sites, observed in the November 1972 survey, accords with this information.

We couldn't have put it better.

The aim of Brumby was to render the sites as featureless as possible. All external evidence of testing was removed, and the fences torn down (with the exception of those round the burial sites at Taranaki and TM 101). The hope was that revegetation would take place, the test sites would disappear from sight if not from mind. In fact Pearce wrote:

> With the passage of time and the eventual removal of the high cyclone mesh fence at Taranaki and TM 100-101 the debris pits will have lost their identity. It is of importance, therefore, to have an accurate record of the locations of pits and this was achieved by a survey made by the Survey Section of the Department of the Interior, August 1967.

So the official anticipation was that before too long the bush would have reclaimed the sites and all would be as before. But, in 1977, the AIRAC authors wrote:

> In spite of high hopes of revegetation expressed in 1967, the major test sites at Maralinga remain clearly identifiable. Although non-identification or anonymity of the test sites may formerly have been a rational approach to its future, it is not now practicable. This is partly because nature has not yet obliged us by healing the scars, but principally because of the public interest and emotion which have developed about the issue.

Given the singular failure in the past to serve the public interest and the long history of equating 'public interest' with the need to preserve as much secrecy as possible, the 'emotion' is understandable. If the generation of such emotion leads to adequate compensation for those who developed cancer and other diseases as a result of their enforced exposures, and if it prevents further such experiments, it is to be heartily welcomed and further encouraged.

The environs of Maralinga are still contaminated with radioactive materials. The 1977 survey found isotopes present at various places as shown in Table 9.3.

TABLE 9.3
Significant long-lived isotopes in 1977

Nuclide	Half-life radiation	Origin(a)	Principal organ at risk	Pathway
^{90}Sr	27.7 yr	FP	bone	ingestion
^{137}Cs	30 yr	FP	whole body	external irradiation
^{155}Eu	4.65 yr	FP, A	whole body	''
^{60}Co	5.3 yr	A	'' ''	''
^{152}Eu	12.4 yr	A	'' ''	''
^{154}Eu	7.84 yr	A	'' ''	''
^{239}Pu	24 390 yr	W	lung & bone	inhalation
^{240}Pu	6 580 yr	W, A	'' ''	''
^{241}Pu	13.2 yr	W, A	'' ''	''
^{241}Am	458 yr	W, A	'' ''	''

(a) FP = Fission product
A = Activation product
W = Weapons material

From: AIRAC No. 4

It will take another fifty years or so before the external radiation fields will no longer exceed the allowable limits. The levels of plutonium in soil will not change except as further wind dispersion occurs and the activity migrates slowly downward through the soil.

The pits present a different problem. Because of the amount

of activity present in them, plus the long half-life and high toxicity of at least one of the contaminants, plutonium, no access can be allowed virtually for evermore. The surrounds will have to be checked periodically to see if material is leaking out of them. Just how carefully this must be done is demonstrated in AIRAC 4. In annexe 4, the author, W. R. Ellis, reports high plutonium readings for a bore hole drilled at 45° beneath Pit 6 at Taranaki. After describing tests to determine the chemical nature of the plutonium, Ellis concludes the core sample was contaminated by any of the following:

1. the samples being left in an open core box in a high plutonium area;
2. the drill intercepting the pit at its lower level and becoming directly contaminated by the contents; or
3. the area around the pit being contaminated at the time the pit was excavated as it had to be partially blasted out of limestone.

Ellis concludes:

> It is virtually certain that there has been no leakage of plutonium from the pit, whatever may be the correct explanation of the anomalous findings.

What is certain is that Maralinga and Emu with their buried wastes will keep scientists and politicians occupied for a long time to come. The self-perpetuating Maralinga industry is hardly an appropriate solution to the unemployment problem, however.

The role of politicians and the way they have perceived the 'public interest' is a classic example of 'tell the public as little as possible as infrequently as possible', and a perusal of Hansard proves most illuminating.

A minor bombshell was dropped in the House of Representatives on 14 September 1972 when the Deputy Leader of the Opposition, Lance Barnard, suggested that Britain might have been using Maralinga as a dumping site for nuclear waste from British nuclear establishments. He asked Supply Minister, Vic Garland, whether lead-lined boxes of waste had been flown from Britain for that purpose, how much had been dumped, and why had it been kept secret.

Clearly there was no truth in Mr Barnard's allegations, but they did serve the useful purpose of drawing Mr Garland on some other interesting points concerning Maralinga. His initial reaction to the questions was to ask for time to prepare his answers. He did let slip, however, that he understood the radioactive material present at Maralinga had a 'half-life of 15 or 20 years', an error which was to be thrown back at him some time later. Later the same evening, Mr Garland's inquiries enabled him to tell the House there was no truth in the allegations, and no request had ever been received from Britain to bury her nuclear waste in Australia.

Next, on 9 December 1976, Mr Uren asked questions of Defence Minister Killen over secret atomic 'trigger' tests at Maralinga between 1958 and 1961. Mr Killen's reply, in a letter dated 3 February 1977, pointed out that details of such tests were classified. Mr Uren was quick to point out that such 'classified' information had already been made public in the book *Scientist at the White House*, by George Kistiakowsky (see p. 181).

Then, on 16 February 1977, Gough Whitlam entered the debate, asking Mr Killen if earlier assurances that Britain was not flying her nuclear waste to Australia for dumping were still valid. Yes, said Mr Killen, they certainly were. On 9 August 1977, Environment Minister Kevin Newman announced a scientific study on the radioactive material at Maralinga. The bodies involved, he said, would include the Australian Ionizing Radiation Advisory Council, the Department of the Environment, the Department of Defence, the Australian Radiation Laboratory, the Australian Atomic Energy Commission, the Bureau of Meteorology and, from South Australia, the Department of Mines and the Environment. Mr Newman then inadvertently clouded the issue by referring to 'low yield atomic tests at Maralinga from 1955 to 1963'. The latter date sounded alarm bells with Tom Uren, who later claimed it was at variance with dates given by Defence

242

Minister Killen on 9 December 1976. 'The Environment Minister admits that there were low yield atomic tests through to 1963, but the Defence Minister says there were no explosions after 1956,' he told the Parliament. The public was left in the dark, and the Government, 'in its usual arrogant manner' chose to give no explanations.

Mr Uren also wanted to know how much radioactive waste lay at Maralinga. His sources told him 41 kilograms of plutonium; the Government figure was 20 kilograms. Despite all these contradictions, the clean-up issue at Maralinga did not start attracting headlines until late 1976. At this time, a former RAAF aircraftsman called Avon Hudson (see p. 194) started the rumours that nuclear waste from Britain had been buried at Maralinga. He spoke of witnessing the burial of 26 lead-lined boxes of plutonium, each weighing two to four tonnes, beneath three metres of red sand beside the airstrip. He suspected the waste was from Britain, because the words 'Calder Hall' were printed on the side of one of the boxes. (Calder Hall is the name of a British atomic power station.) Within days, the South Australian Mines and Energy Minister, Hugh Hudson, had announced that 800 tonnes of radioactive waste were buried at Maralinga, and it was his feeling that the area should be regularly monitored. Mr Hudson claimed his approaches in this direction to the Government were floundering on the Prime Minister's objections, despite Mr Killen's agreement-in-principle.

Unaccountably the issue was allowed to fade into obscurity over the next twenty-two months. Then, in October 1978, the Australian Foreign Affairs Department sent a telegram to the British Foreign Office requesting that Britain remove the plutonium she left at Maralinga. Reason behind the sudden move was a submission to Cabinet by Defence Minister Killen that the plutonium was sitting there waiting for the first international terrorist with the wherewithal to steal it, and hold the world to ransom. Embarrassingly enough, there was no immediate response to the telegram from Britain, but eventually word filtered through that a team of British scientists would fly over and assess the situation. Even this concession, which contained no offer of removal, took the combined efforts of Prime Minister Fraser, Defence Minister Killen and Acting Foreign Minister Sinclair, through a meeting with British High Commissioner, Sir Donald Tebbit. A week after the arrival of the British scientists, following a thorough inspection of the site, National Development Minister Newman was of the opinion that the plutonium should stay where it was. At the same time, it was hinted, Britain had indicated she might be prepared to remove the plutonium if absolutely necessary. A Cabinet meeting was held to discuss options, but another week passed without further announcements. Then the South Australian Government began getting restless, and let Mr Fraser know they wanted the waste removed.

Around this period, the news leaked that toxic wastes from the tests had been left lying on the ground for four years after the final test without being treated. This heightened the urgency of getting a decision from the reluctant British on removal, and three weeks after the on-site inspection patience was starting to wear thin. Government officials in Canberra were anxious to deny rumours that Britain had 'snubbed' Australia over the issue, and explained that administrative delays in London were responsible for the hold-up. In the meantime, they assured anyone who wanted to know, cables and telephone calls were flowing thick and fast between the two nations.

Finally, on 16 November 1978, the *Australian* newspaper came right out and said it on their front page. The British Government HAD snubbed Australia, and two specific requests for removal of the waste had evoked no more than a stony silence. Strained relations between the two governments were mentioned, as was the sympathy of British bureaucracy to the Australian request. The flies in the ointment, allegedly, were British politicians, who wanted no part of the waste. Australia had already issued a deadline for a decision, but this had passed nine days earlier, and still no response was forthcoming. And then, on 23 November, a full month after the arrival of the

British scientists, an announcement was made that Britain had finally agreed to pick up her litter and take it home.

Part of the agreement was understood to be that this was definitely the last time Britain would remove waste from her tests from Australian shores. By this stage, Australia would probably have agreed to anything, so anxious was the Government to find a solution to what had become a horribly embarrassing impasse. The actual removal operation itself, of 11 400 kilograms of material, was conducted under a blanket of secrecy in February 1979.

That was the removal saga as viewed by the Australian press and public. Predictably enough, according to a fascinating government document issued in November 1980, everybody had got it all wrong. There had been no discord, no snubbing, the entire affair had been conducted 'in the spirit of the technical co-operation existing between the two countries'. That was the official version as laid down in a paper titled 'Management of Former U.K. Atomic Weapons Test Sites in Australia. Report of 1979 Work Programme'. Whatever its shortcomings, in its description of the events leading up to the removal, the paper contained a wealth of fascinating and surprisingly informal information on the actual operation itself. Everything from the flies to the awful heat of the desert were touched upon in the graphic descriptions of how the waste was removed from its resting place.

In its foreword, the paper touches upon the 'considerable public interest' aroused by Britain's removal of the plutonium, and explains:

> It is intended that the current report should provide a detailed public record of the material removed and of the actual operation which, for security reasons, was undertaken without public announcement.

Fine sentiments. To the best of the authors' knowledge this document was not circulated among the media, surely the first basic step taken by any government wishing to put anything on the 'public record'.

245

Maralinga

Initially the report mentions the removal of half a kilogram of plutonium to Britain, 'dispersed in 1630 kg of salt', an announcement about which was made on 22 March 1979. It also details what was achieved during the programme of radioactive waste management at Maralinga. This announcement was made on 25 March 1980. It left a situation where the sites of all atomic test explosions, and a number of minor tests, had been marked with concrete plinths; the six sites where radiation levels remain above internationally recommended limits for permanent occupancy had been sign-posted thus; burial pits containing potentially hazardous radioactive materials had been capped with concrete, enclosed by high cyclone fencing and covered by warning signs; the removal of residual materials had been prohibited by signs, and a permanent contingent of Australian Federal Police had been assigned to the site. Similar concrete plinths and warning signs were erected at Emu and Monte Bello.

In its background to the detailed account of Britain's removal of the plutonium, the report mentions that Australia ratified the Nuclear Non-Proliferation Treaty (NPT) on 23 January 1973, and concluded the required safeguards agreement with the International Atomic Energy Agency (IAEA) on 10 July 1974. It was because of Australia's obligations in these two directions that it eventually became desirable, if not particularly well-advised, that Britain remove her plutonium. The first step in this direction came when Australia's Foreign Affairs Department reported to the IAEA in Vienna, some time after 1976, that there was recoverable plutonium at Maralinga. By 1978, it had been decided that 'the Government request the United Kingdom to accept responsibility for the plutonium and repatriate it to the United Kingdom'.

On 25 October 1978, a British team from the Atomic Weapons Research Establishment at Aldermaston arrived in Canberra. After opening discussions, the three-man team, Dr Frank Morgan, Mr Noah Pearce and Mr Howard Bristow, visited Maralinga from 28 to 30 October to examine the burial pit and the condition of the six containers. They found no sign of leakage and no health hazard, but despite this, Australia decided to press ahead with her request that Britain remove the material.

All political considerations aside, both Australian and British scientists would probably agree that, in retrospect, the plutonium should have been left in the ground. Given the hazards presented by its removal, compared with those of leaving it where it lay, few men qualified to make the decision would have chosen the former course.

The removal operation itself took from 17 to 28 February 1979, and involved manpower from the Department of National Development, the Australian Atomic Energy Commission, the Atomic Weapons Research Establishment at Aldermaston, the Army, the SA Government's Department of Health and the Commonwealth Police Force. Three Hercules aircraft were required to fly in supplies and equipment, ranging from radiation monitoring equipment to a cement mixer. The report observes: 'At time of arrival the temperature was approximately 35 degrees Celsius, and the party had its first taste of two of the problems which caused considerable difficulty throughout the operation, heat and flies.' Because of the heat work began each day at sunrise, continued until midday, and then resumed in the late afternoon until light was inadequate. Typically enough the sophisticated machinery involved fared much better than its human operators—it was housed in a canvas health physics tent-laboratory complete with air conditioning. Dr J. L. Symonds, chief scientist of the Australian Energy Commission, managed to lose three kilograms in body weight during a little over an hour when involved in a grouting operation in heavy protective clothing in temperatures of over 40 degrees Celsius.

That was well into the operation, but the first step was to excavate the burial pit in which the six mild steel container bins were placed. Inside these bins were inner containers, or pots, holding the plutonium and contaminated materials. The excavation, with a back hoe, took almost five hours on 18 February. When the bins were exposed from above it was not possible to see how badly corroded they were, so it was deemed unsafe to remove them by their handles. Accordingly a special lifting device was improvised and, over the next four days, four more trips were made by the Hercules with further equipment. By the fourth day, the first bin removed was ready for internal exploration. A drill was used to cut through the steel but, to prevent it breaking through unexpectedly and penetrating the pot inside, an inner sleeve of sheet steel had to be inserted and held against the pot. When the pot was finally isolated, the real hazards began. Gaining access to the inside of the pot was likely to result in the release of plutonium contamination, so an area around it was roped off, and only those wearing radiological suits and breathing apparatus were allowed inside. Others remained up-wind from the area.

The report then makes a somewhat alarming revelation:

> The actual dimensions of the conical throat of the pot were not known, and the structure and content of the inside of the pot were not certain.

The question that springs instantly to mind is: 'Why not?' Given the extreme danger of the contents of the pot, and the highly specialized nature of its storage, some form of inventory of the structure of the insides would seem to have been essential. Its absence is still further indication of the haphazard fashion in which far too many vital operations were undertaken during and after the tests.

When the time came for exploration of the interior of the pot, Dr Symonds had to insert his arm through an opening to remove the PVC plug. An inspection immediately afterwards revealed plutonium contamination on Dr Symonds' gloved hand and clothing. The opening had to be sealed up, and it is interesting, that with all the paraphernalia of science at their disposal, the experts chose a commodity used daily by many housewives, thin plastic wrap. Inspection of the inside of the pot was aided by a mirror used to direct sunlight inside. Later, a grouting operation was undertaken to reseal the entrance to the pot. Each pot required between nine and ten buckets of grout for sealing. It was this work that caused Dr Symonds' spectacular weight loss. Oxygen had to be kept on stand-by, and eventually it was decided to place a one-hour limit on the wearing of the radiological suits in the intense heat.

The next stage was to place the pots inside the drums in which the plutonium was to be transported back to Britain. This involved wrapping more cling film around the pots and spraying them with Permax, giving an overall baby blue hue. An ancient generator was 'borrowed' by the Commonwealth Police from the abandoned Maralinga village, brought back to life by the mechanical virtuosity of two Army personnel, and used for flood-lighting for the next stage—concreting. This was done at night because of the heat, but caused concern over security with the bright lights visible for a great distance in the empty desert. The pots were placed inside the drums, sealed in place with liquid concrete, and then topped off with a still drier mix of concrete. High winds blew up during this stage of the operation and an impromptu tent and wind-break had to be constructed.

When it was all over three days later, all contaminated waste was placed in the original burial pit and covered, first by soil and then by layers of wet and dry-mix cement. By 28 February, all equipment and personnel had been taken from the site in aircraft, and the six drums were left under tarpaulins in the custody of the Commonwealth Police, awaiting their removal to the UK a few days later. On 4 April, the IAEA acknowledged with thanks the news that no reportable nuclear material from the tests was left at Maralinga.

The next step was 'rehabilitation programmes' at both Maralinga and Emu, involving the marking of test explosion sites, the fencing of burial pits, the capping with concrete of a number of the burial pits, and the erection of warning signs at test and burial sites. The Ground Zeros of the nine atomic test explosions and two of the minor trial sites were marked by truncated four-sided pyramids. These concrete plinths bore the name and date of the tests and an English language radiation hazard warning. Approximately 900 metres of fencing was erected—1.8 metre high cyclone mesh topped with three strands of barbed wire angled outwards.

After consultation with the Department of Immigration and Ethnic Affairs, the languages chosen for the warning signs were English, Arabic, Greek, Italian, Serbo-Croatian and Spanish. Aboriginal languages were not included after the Department of Aboriginal Affairs had pointed out that Aborigines literate in one of their own languages would almost certainly have also been literate in English. Instead Aboriginal communities were advised of residual radiological hazards.

Among recommendations of the AIRAC for future management of the Maralinga range was that public access to the three enclosed burial grounds be prohibited, and that access to other areas be limited to periods of up to seven days.

The rehabilitation programme for the Monte Bello Islands, where three tests were carried out between 1952 and 1956, did not require such extensive measures. Two onshore test explosion sites were marked with concrete plinths, warning notices were erected and residual structures and debris were removed 'as far as practicable'. The Islands are currently a Prohibited Area under the *Defence (Special Undertakings) Act*, and access is controlled by the Commonwealth Government.

Epilogue

In 1945, when it was realized that Germany was beaten without having produced a nuclear weapon, some of the scientists involved in the Manhattan Project started to worry very deeply about the morality of dropping such a monstrous device on Japan. As we know their pleas and petitions were ignored. Nevertheless, several of them grouped together to form one of the first societies concerned with the social responsibility of science and scientists. They and their successors have continued to produce the outstanding *Bulletin of the Atomic Scientists*. As relevant today as when started, the magazine publishes pithy and thought-provoking articles on topics as diverse as nuclear proliferation and the effects of low-level radiation.

Since 1947, one continuing feature has been the doomsday clock on the front cover. The hands on the clock were originally set at seven minutes to midnight as a symbolic warning of the lateness of the hour as mankind faced (or hid from) the perils of the times. The hands have been moved nine times since then. They went to three minutes to midnight in 1949 when the Soviet Union exploded its first atomic bomb. After the USA and USSR developed hydrogen bombs, the hands were set to two minutes to twelve. Then after the Cold War thaw and the signing of the partial test ban treaty, the hands were eased back to twelve minutes. The Indian nuclear explosion in 1974 advanced the hands three minutes and the increasing world tension during 1980 has made Bernard Feld the current editor of the Bulletin turn the hands forward to four minutes to midnight.

Given the current development in nuclear weaponry and delivery systems, coupled with the threat of more countries developing their own atomic bombs, the world is in as precarious a state as at any time since the Hiroshima bomb was dropped. The nuclear arsenals of the two so-called super-powers, USA and USSR, contain the equivalent of one million—yes one million—times the bomb that destroyed Hiroshima. That is about three tonnes of TNT equivalent for every man, woman and child on the planet tied up in useless, wasteful stockpiles. What a better world it would be if there were three tonnes of food available for everybody!

Such is the irrationality of military planners and their scientific advisers, the USA is at the stage where it can destroy every Russian city, of 150 000 inhabitants or more, *fifty* times over. The Russians in turn have around 2300 delivery vehicles, containing about 7000 warheads with a total delivery capacity of 4500 megatonnes. And both are still producing about three bombs a day.

These weapons are deployed on land, in the air, on and under the sea. They range in size from around 500 tonnes of TNT equivalent, euphemistically entitled tactical weapons, to the massive 20 megatonne strategic devices. They can be fired by field mortars, flown in piloted aeroplanes or hauled by missiles that can fly from one continent to another in the time it takes to play just one quarter of a football match. Some of these missiles can carry ten independent warheads that can be dispatched to ten different targets with an accuracy of a few hundred metres.

However, two major new developments threaten to change the strategic balance. First is the MX system, a new

Intercontinental Ballistic Missile (ICBM) coupled with a complex storage-launch system. What is proposed is a roadway layout about 20 kilometres long and 10 kilometres wide. A transporter-erector-launcher weighing about 450 000 kg would haul its MX rocket to any one of twenty-three different hardened shelter sites on the loop. The Americans would have about 30 minutes warning of a Russian nuclear attack (from detection of the ICBM launch, using spy-in-sky satellites, to the warheads' detonating in the USA). That is sufficient time for the transporter to shift its load from one shelter to another so, to make sure of eliminating just one retaliatory weapon, the Russians would have to attack all twenty-three sites.

Present American thinking is for 200 MXs with 4600 shelters. The cost of the system is estimated to be between $30 000 million and $50 000 million!

The other even more frightening prospect is the cruise missile. This is a modern descendant of the Nazi V-1 rocket of the Second World War. It is a small, jet propelled, pilotless aircraft that flies at subsonic speed (around 800-900 km/hr) with a range of 1000 to 4000 kilometres. It weighs about one tonne and can carry a nuclear warhead of around 200 kilotonnes' yield. It can be launched from the ground by an aircraft or by a submerged submarine. Its key feature is its accuracy which is expected to be considerably better than 30 metres. This gives it a 100 per cent kill probability against even super-hardened missile silos. It is equipped with an on-board computer and observation devices that allow it to compare the terrain over which it flies with a map stored in the computer memory. It can thereby correct any deviations from its prescribed flight path. All made possible by those innocent silicon chips that inflicted *Space Invaders* upon an unsuspecting world. The observation that nuclear weapons and cruise missiles are an unholy alliance of fission and chips would be funny if it was not so frightening. Flying at low altitudes (at most, a few hundred metres) the cruise missiles will be very difficult to detect and intercept unless exceedingly expensive downward-looking radars are deployed. They in turn could be vulnerable to a pre-emptive attack.

Just what the Soviet response to these developments will be is hard to gauge. They have already developed an intermediate range mobile ballistic missile—the SS20 which carries three 250 kilotonne independently targeted warheads. No doubt Soviet planners will be looking to develop more mobile sites to match the MX, especially as advances in anti-submarine warfare (ASW) have made the Soviet nuclear submarine fleet far from invulnerable.

What are being developed are not just counter force or mutually assured destruction (MAD; one of the few totally appropriate acronyms) weapons, but weapons capable of winning a nuclear war. The Stockholm International Peace Research Institute (SIPRI) in its 1979 year book sounded the following sombre warning:

> The situation as a whole demands urgent action. If the USA achieves a first strike capability against Soviet ICBMs, as appears to be one of the objectives of the MX programme [and the cruise missile—author] and if this is coupled with maintenance of the present lead in ASW, there are serious grounds to fear that the concept of mutual assured destruction, with all its faults will be abandoned in favour of a war fighting and war winning strategy.

The Americans, and more particularly their European allies, feel threatened by the overwhelming Russian superiority in conventional forces; the Russians in turn feel menaced by the permanent American lead in sophisticated nuclear weaponry and delivery systems. So the madness goes on—to the tune of $500 thousand million a year, with the two super powers spending half that amount.

It is important to note that cruise missiles are very cheap (at least in the light of the sums just quoted). A production run of 2000 missiles of the type being developed by Boeing would each cost around $750 000 and that is much less than the cost of a modern battle tank. Many 'near nuclear' countries, who have been put off developing atomic bombs because of the

254

prohibitive cost of current effective long-range delivery systems, may now be tempted. The nuclear warheads themselves are pretty cheap. The Indian Government claims it developed its 'device for peaceful purposes', including the preparation of the underground test site, for a cost of around $400 000.

There are a disconcertingly large number of possible nuclear-weapons-producing states, including some in very troubled parts of the world. In a detailed article in the *Scientific American* of July 1980, William Epstein listed the countries he thought were 'near nuclear'. Professor Epstein was, until 1973, Director of the United Nations Disarmament Division and since then has been a special consultant on arms control. So his estimates carry considerable weight.

Epstein considers fifteen countries have the technical capability of exploding a nuclear device within one or two years, if they should decide to do so. They include Argentina, Iraq, Israel, Japan, Pakistan, South Africa, Taiwan and West Germany. A further ten countries would take around two to six years, including Australia, Brazil, South Korea and Yugoslavia. He listed another sixteen countries he thought could develop nuclear weapons in six to ten years, making a total of forty-one potential nuclear states by 1990. That is in addition to the existing six. The late arrivals on the nuclear weapons scene could include Chile, Indonesia, Iran, Libya, Turkey and Venezuela.

Australia's nuclear weapon capability is based on work that has been carried out at the Australian Atomic Energy Research Establishment at Lucas Heights, near Sydney. The commercial upgrading of uranium yellowcake, using highspeed gas centrifuges, has been the main object of the research. However, the technique can be adapted to produce weapons grade uranium-235.

Unlike Australia, several of the countries listed by Epstein, including South Africa, Israel, Pakistan, Argentina and Iraq, are not signatories of the Nuclear Non-Proliferation Treaty. The urgent need for some effective international control of

255

fissile material to prevent the wide spread of nuclear weapons is self-evident.

It can be argued that it was Britain, using Australia, that started nuclear proliferation. After the failure of the Baruch plan, it was inevitable that the USSR would continue to follow the USA in developing their grotesque stockpiles. While there were only two protagonists, there was hope for dialogue, but in this field three rapidly becomes a crowd. If Britain had stayed out of the nuclear weapons field there was a chance, very faint admittedly, that sanity might have prevailed, especially after Stalin's death and the subsequent easing of East-West tensions. With Britain, then France, followed by China and India having gone nuclear, it will be hard, very hard to get the genie back into the bottle.

Since 1945, there have been around 1221 known nuclear explosions, an average rate of nearly one a week. About 653 by the USA, 426 by the USSR, 86 by France, 30 by the UK, 25 by China and one by India. Some 60 per cent of these explosions have taken place since the 1963 Partial Test Ban Treaty. For all their efforts, neither Britain nor France appear to have benefited very much from their nuclear weapons. Britain for instance has had to dig deep into its impoverished treasury to buy American delivery systems. Neither the United Kingdom nor France could themselves threaten the survival of the Soviet Union, but either one could set in motion events that involved the United States to such an extent that the full armoury of deterrence would come into play.

If that happened, Australia would once again get a taste of fallout. There are ten or eleven major American or joint US/Australian bases in this country. Some of them, because of the nature of their functions, would be prime nuclear targets in a pre-emptive strike against the USA.

North-West Cape is the largest and most powerful of the three principal communication stations in the US world-wide submarine communications system. It is also apparently used to monitor Soviet naval communications.

Pine Gap near Alice Springs is the biggest Central Intelligence Agency (CIA) base outside the US. It and Nurrungar, 500 kilometres north of Adelaide, are vital links in the US Space and Missile Systems Organization. Nurrungar is part of the 647 programme designed to provide early warnings of Soviet or Chinese ballistic missile attack.

The controversial Omega station being built in eastern Victoria is part of the only navigational aid that can be used by a fully submerged submarine in mid-ocean. The Tranet Station at Smithfield in South Australia, on the other hand, is part of the Transit Navigational Satellite programme, which is used by US Polaris submarines to get accurate navigational fixes when they are on the surface.

A sonar submarine detection system located on Christmas Island is tied up with Project Flowerless, one of the US Navy's anti-submarine warfare projects.

Just as in the 1950s, when Australia happily played host to Britain's bomb tests, so in the 1970s it would appear that the Government has welcomed the establishment of US bases with little apparent thought as to the strategic significance of what was happening. In his particularly well-researched book, *A Suitable Piece of Real Estate* (Hale and Iremonger 1980), Dr Des Ball, Senior Research Fellow in the Strategic and Defence Studies Centre at the Australian National University, made the following observation:

> In the case of Pine Gap and Nurrungar—two of the most important US installations—three of Australia's past four Prime Ministers have specifically stated that, at the least, they were ignorant of major aspects of the operations of these stations. In December 1978, John Gorton stated: 'I don't even know what Pine Gap is all about. I didn't then (1969). I could have asked but it didn't arise. I didn't ask about it.'
>
> In May 1977, William McMahon stated that, although at the time he was Prime Minister he thought he knew the true functions of Pine Gap and Nurrungar, he was now not so sure: 'I have increasing doubts that the Australian Government knows the entire truth.'
>
> Gough Whitlam has revealed on a number of occasions that there were several critical aspects relating to Pine Gap and

Nurrungar that he was never told about. For example, Mr Whitlam told Parliament on 4 May 1977 that the Australian Government had been unaware that information obtained by these facilities was made available to private American companies such as TRW Systems Incorporated; that the American officer-in-charge of Pine Gap, Richard Stallings, was an employee of the CIA; or that Pine Gap was in fact a CIA operation.

This seems to be an excessive loss of sovereignty to exchange for the doubtful benefits of living under the American nuclear umbrella.

Although the foreign bases may be vulnerable, they are mostly located at some distance from major cities, and Australian cities, because of their relatively low population densities, are as well able as any to survive a nuclear attack. Following a one megatonne ground burst, the most serious effects are within about 8 kilometres of Ground Zero. There would be fatal ionizing radiation injuries up to about 3 kilometres, fatal blast injuries up to 4 kilometres and fatal flash burns up to 8 kilometres.

In a city of 2 500 000, with an explosion timed for midday, when the city centre's population is highest, there would be about 200 000 people killed, about 200 000 severely injured, and about 150 000 moderately injured from the initial effects. The long-term effects from fallout depend on the prevailing winds and the quantity of activation products produced. A westerly wind would blow the fallout over the densely populated eastern suburbs if Melbourne were hit. The same winds would blow the fallout mostly out to sea if a bomb was dropped on Sydney. Northerlies would have different effects.

Areas beneath the fallout cloud would need to be evacuated and this poses a great problem for emergency planners. How much time and effort is put into preparing for an unlikely event? Australian capital cities with the possible exception of Canberra and Darwin, if it becomes a B52 bomber base, would be very near the bottom of anybody's strategic target list.

But let us not lose sight of the horror of nuclear war. The sufferings of the veterans of Maralinga are as nothing compared with what could happen. In a speech to the 1979 Pugwash Conference, Lord Zuckerman, one of the UK Government's most senior scientific advisers said:

> My first point is that one real danger of the possibility of nuclear war is that we have ceased to understand what we are talking about. How can one imagine the reality: the possible elimination, not only of say half the population of the Northern Hemisphere, but also the elimination of the better part of the cultural history of our globe?

As Earl Mountbatten put it in his last speech in May 1979, a few months before his senseless murder:

> The world stands on the brink of the final abyss. Let us resolve to take all possible practical steps to ensure that we do not, through our own folly, go over the edge.

If the retelling of the history of nuclear warfare, and the setting out of the follies that took place in the Australian desert nearly thirty years ago awaken in just a few readers a sense of just how near mankind is to going over the edge our purpose will have been well served.

STOP PRESS

On 28 May 1981, Pat Creevey, Information Officer for the ANVA, received a letter from Senator John L. Carrick, then Minister for National Development and Energy. That letter promised much of what Creevey and his ANVA colleague, Harold Crosbie, had spent the previous year fighting to achieve.

Senator Carrick's letter promised full co-operation from the Federal Health, Defence, Aboriginal Affairs and Social Security Departments in investigating the tests and their aftermath. It also promised that no time limitations would be imposed on the submission of claims for possible radiation-induced damages arising from the tests. Information on safety procedures in force for all the tests was being sought from UK authorities and, more specifically, exposure records of Australian personnel were being requested from the same sources. The letter promised that non-government employees and RAAF personnel at airbases providing support for the tests would also come under scrutiny.

Although Senator Carrick wrote, 'It would be premature to anticipate the ultimate outcome of the investigations currently in progress,' to Creevey and Crosbie his letter represented a major breakthrough. By the time this book is published, it is hoped that the Federal Government will be well on its way towards atoning for at least some of the tragedies and injustices resulting from the tests.

January 1982 saw the hands on the clock (Epilogue p. 251) moved forward to two minutes to midnight. This was in recognition of the fact that the risk of a holocaust is as great as at any time since the Second World War.

APPENDIX

Units of Radioactivity and Radiation

THE HISTORICAL UNITS

To measure *radioactivity*, that is the number of atoms undergoing radioactive decay, we determine how many atoms decay per unit time, usually taken as the second. One gram of radium was taken as the base and it was found that 37 000 000 000 radium atoms undergo radioactive decay every second. This quantity, appropriately enough, was called one curie (abbreviated to Ci).

Thus 1 curie = 37 000 000 000 disintegrations per second, usually written $1Ci = 3.7 \times 10^{10}$ dps. This is a rather large unit, so fractions of it are used:

1 millicurie   = 37 000 000 disintegrations per second

  i.e. 1mCi   = 3.7×10^7 dps

1 microcurie   = 37 000 disintegrations per second (1 millionth)

  i.e. 1μCi   = 3.7×10^4 dps

1 nanocurie   = 37 disintegrations per second (1 thousand millionth)

  i.e. 1nCi   = 37 dps

The smallest subunit used is the picocurie (one million millionth) which is equal to two disintegrations per *minute*.

i.e. 1pCi   = 2.2 dpm

(This picocurie, sometimes called the micro-microcurie, although very small is important when measurements of fallout in food and water have to be made.)

The measurement of *radiation* is rather more complicated. The most important property of the sort of radiation we are concerned about is that it can cause ionization. To understand this process, we need to go back to our picture of the atom as a miniature solar system, with the positively charged nucleus occupying the position of the sun and the negatively charged electrons tracing their elliptical paths like miniscule planets.

The process of ionization is the splitting of one or more of the orbiting electrons from the atom. The separated electrons are called *negative ions*; the nucleus now carrying one or more positive charges (depending on the number of electrons removed from orbit) is called a *positive ion*. Those radiations that can cause the process are called, naturally enough, ionizing radiation. What happens is a transfer of energy from the incident radiation to the electron, giving it the strength to escape from its orbit—rather as if a giant asteroid had hit Mars and sent it whizzing into deepest space.

Ions can be captured. If the ionization process takes place inside a gas-filled chamber, and a voltage is applied across the chamber, the electrons being negatively charged will be attracted to the positive plate (anode). The current collected can be fed into a sensitive meter and some estimate made of the amount of ionizing radiation passing through the chamber. This is one of the ways such radiation can be detected and measured.

But the health physicist or radiologist is concerned with what the ionization is doing in human cells, another unit is needed to measure how much energy has been deposited in tissue (the amount of ionization depends on the amount of energy deposited). Unfortunately, the story doesn't end there.

Some radiations are more effective at producing biological damage than are others. For instance, for the same amount of energy deposited, alpha particles will be about ten times more damaging than X- or gamma rays. Some neutrons will be about two or three times more damaging. This is because the actual damage produced is dependent not only on the energy deposited but also on the rate of the deposition. So alpha particles, being large and relatively slow moving, transfer their energy to cells they are passing through much more rapidly than do gamma rays. The term used is Linear Energy Transfer Rate (LET). So to measure radiation we need three units to measure three different concepts:

1. ionization in air—called the unit of exposure;
2. energy deposition in tissue—called the unit of absorbed dose;
3. differing biological effects of different sorts of radiation—called the unit of dose equivalent.

The *exposure dose* is measured in roentgens. It was originally defined as that amount of radiation which produced in one cubic centimetre of air one electrostatic unit of charge (ionization)

i.e. one roentgen = 1 esu/cc

As the esu fell into disfavour, it was replaced by the coulomb, and one roentgen became equivalent to 0.000258 coulombs of charge per kilogram of air

i.e. 1 roentgen = 2.58×10^{-4} C/kg

The *absorbed dose* is measured in rads. The rad is equal to 100 ergs of energy deposited on one gram of tissue. The rad can relate to anything, cabbages or kings. It was chosen because in *most* cases one roentgen in air is just about equivalent to one rad in tissue.

i.e. 1 rad = 100 ergs/g

The *dose equivalent* is measured in rems. The rem is equal to the number of rads multiplied by the appropriate modifying factor. In radiation protection work this is called the quality factor (QF) and it ranges from 1 (for X and gamma radiation) up to 20 (for some high energy particles).

Thus rem = rad × QF

The quality factors to be used for a particular type of radiation are recommended by the body responsible for all these definitions, the International Commission on Radiological Units (ICRU).

The roentgen, the rad and the rem are relatively large units and in protection work the subunit of one thousandth is used, i.e. millirem, millirad, etc.

SI UNITS

The historical units have been replaced by SI units as follows:

The curie has been replaced by the becquerel (Bq). The becquerel (named after the discoverer of radioactivity) is one disintegration per second.

So 1 curie = 37 giga becquerel (giga = one thousand million i.e. 10^9)

The roentgen has been replaced by the coulomb/kg (no special name).

1 roentgen = 2.58 × 10^{-4} C/kg

The rad has been replaced by the gray (Gy). The gray (named after one of the inventors of a radiation measuring device, the Bragg-Gray cavity chamber) is defined as one joule (of energy) deposited per kilogram.

1 rad = 0.01 Gy

The rem has been replaced by the sievert (Sv). The sievert (named after Rolf M. Sievert, one of the first people to suggest some limits on radiation exposure) is defined as gray × QF.

1 rem = 0.01 Sv

INDEX

265

AUSTRALIAN NUCLEAR VETERANS' ASSOCIATION

DECEASED NUCLEAR VETERANS— MARALINGA

Name	Cause of death	Age at death	Date of death	Service
A. G. S. Alexander	Cancer	49	15.10.67	Comm. Police
D. J. Anicic	Cancer	53	24.6.76	Civilian
E. Audley	Cancer	—	1964	RAAF
T. E. Barrett	Metastasis, left kidney	62	15.8.80	Meteorology
J. A. Barry	Cancer	50	10.7.66	Civilian
J. F. Batey	Cancer	—	—	Civilian
— Blewitt	Cancer	—	1960	—
E. Boulton	Cancer	—	—	RAAF
— Boyd	Cancer	—	—	—
M. K. Bradford	Cancer	57	29.12.72	RAAF
S. Brazier	Cancer	—	—	RAAF
F. J. Brown	Cancer	48	3.7.71	Civilian
K. Busby	Cancer	48	15.2.71	RAAF
T. D. Clarke	Cancer	37	27.10.79	Civilian
J. B. Cook	Cancer	—	1960	—
W. Cope	Leukaemia	—	1960	RAN
R. Crimmins	Cancer	—	1979	RAAF
J. Curruthers	Leukaemia	—	1980	—
J. Dallow	Cancer	48	6.11.78	Civilian
P. V. Davis	Cancer	38	—	Army
O. Donnelly	Cancer	—	1959	—
J. Dooley	Cancer	—	—	RAAF
F. S. Eaclen	Cancer	48	1.5.81	RAAF
H. R. Ennis	Cancer	—	—	Comm. Police
B. J. Farrelly	Cancer	—	1971	Civilian
A. Finney	Cancer	—	1978	Civilian
P. C. Finucane	Leukaemia	25	18.5.61	RAF/RAAF
H. M. Flinn	Cancer	57	13.5.71	Civilian
G. A. C. Ford	Cancer	57	29.10.78	Civilian
D. G. Fountain	Cancer	51	2.3.65	Civilian
P. Giles	Cancer	—	1964	Civilian
T. Gillan	Leukaemia	31	—	—

Maralinga

Name	Cause of death	Age at death	Date of death	Service
R. S. Greys	Cancer	—	—	—
E. Hagen	Cancer	54	1972	Army
E. Hall	Cancer	71	2.7.78	Civilian
L. R. Harley	Cancer	—	1977	Civilian
W. C. Harvey	Cancer	—	1970	—
R. Hawse	Cancer	—	—	RAAF
G. Hayes	Cancer	—	1976	—
M. A. Hendley	Cancer	—	1977	Civilian
P. W. Hills	Cancer	—	1977	Civilian
K. J. Holden	Leukaemia	—	1968	Civilian
J. H. Howard	Cancer /Heart	67	19.8.77	RAAF
W. Hume	Cancer /Liver	64	21.1.63	Civilian
J. Ireson	Cancer	—	1968	Comm. Police
J. E. Jackson	Lung /Heart	58	31.7.66	RAAF
W. Jones	Cancer	39	1966	Army
F. L. Knight	Cancer	60	—	—
G. B. Komoll	Cancer	—	—	Civilian
C. Lee	Cancer	—	1979	Civilian
K. Leponated	Cancer	—	1972	RAAF
S. A. Lester	Cancer	65	10.8.65	Comm. Police
W. J. Lewis	Cancer	64	7.7.79	Civilian
W. Lloyd	Cancer	—	1979	RAAF
F. F. Lokan	Cancer	—	1972	—
J. McDonald	Cancer	—	1971	—
— McKewin	Cancer	—	—	RAAF
A. Marsh	Cancer	61	24.8.75	Civilian
J. E. May	Brain Tumour	—	1971	Civilian
H. G. Miller	Cancer	40	27.3.75	Civilian
K. Miscon	Cancer	—	1960	RAAF
B. F. Moore	Cancer	52	−.1.76	Civilian
J. A. Morone	Ventricular Fibrillation /Heart	56 ·	29.1.79	RAN
W. G. Munt	Cancer	56	28.10.79	RAAF
C. Newman	Cancer	—	—	Army
R. W. Nobes	Cancer	—	1973	RAN

Name	Cause of death	Age at death	Date of death	Service
R. B. Odgers	Cancer	67	8.1.75	Civilian
G. Oliver	Cancer	62	30.4.72	Comm. Police
— Onions	Cancer	—	—	RAAF
J. Ord	Cancer	60	18.3.81	Army
J. Pettitt	Cancer	55	24.4.80	Army
N. A. Phelps	Brain Tumour	—	1971	—
R. Phillips	Cancer	—	—	RAAF
J. E. Pickering	Cancer	59	1975	Civilian
N. W. Pirie	Cancer	55	8.10.62	Civilian
J. M. Ratcliffe	Cancer	—	—	Civilian
T. A. Roberts	Cancer	—	1975	—
L. F. Robinson	Cancer	48	13.1.81	RAAF
W. F. Rogers	Cancer	—	1975	Civilian
M. M. Roszko	Cancer	—	—	Civilian
G. E. Rotherham	Cancer	62	19.1.71	Comm. Police
G. Russi	Cancer	70	1969	Civilian
P. Savage	Cancer	—	1964	Army
— Sawyer	Cancer	—	1966	RAAF
H. L. C. Sharpe	—	—	-.7.67	Army
P. J. Simpson	Cancer	—	—	RAAF
E. Skuse	Cancer	—	1966	Civilian
H. Stauber	Cancer /Heart	46	24.12.72	Civilian
L. J. Stephens	Cancer	—	1980	RAN
C. Stodart	Cancer	—	1959	Civilian
A. Sutherland	Cancer	42	19.6.69	Army
R. Swanston	Cancer	—	—	Civilian
V. Sweeney	Cancer	54	14.1.81	Civilian
C. Taplin	Cancer	—	1954	RAAF
— Taylor	Cancer	—	—	RAAF
M. Thiele	Cancer	58	14.8.66	Civilian
J. V. Thompson	Cancer	—	1975	Civilian
W. Thornton	Cancer	54	12.8.75	Civilian
E. Till	Cancer	57	11.1.80	Civilian
J. B. Treleaven	Cancer	56	18.7.68	Civilian
S. Trottman	Brain Tumour	—	1980	Comm. Police
G. Tuck	Cancer	34	9.4.55	RAAF
— Turpin	Cancer	—	1960	Army

Maralinga

Name	Cause of death	Age at death	Date of death	Service
H. V. Van Der Straaten	Heart	65	22.11.79	RAAF
R. C. Wallace	Cancer	57	2.12.75	Civilian
M. L. Ward	Cancer	49	16.8.81	RAAF
V. W. Waters	Cancer	54	1977	—
— Watson	Cancer	—	1973	—
J. White	Cancer	—	—	Comm. Police
A. J. Wiggin	Leukaemia	63	21.1.74	Army
T. R. Wilson	Cancer	—	1975	Army
R. Wotherspoon	Kidney failure	56	22.11.72	Civilian
L. Wutke	Cancer	—	1960	Civilian
H. E. Whyte	Cancer	40	7.3.77	Army